MznLnx

Missing Links Exam Preps

Exam Prep for

Introduction to Hydrogeology

Deming, 1st Edition

The MznLnx Exam Prep is your link from the texbook and lecture to your exams.
The MznLnx Exam Preps are unauthorized and comprehensive reviews of your textbooks.

All material provided by MznLnx and Rico Publications (c) 2010
Textbook publishers and textbook authors do not particpate in or contribute to these reviews.

MznLnx

Rico
Publications

Exam Prep for Introduction to Hydrogeology
1st Edition
Deming

Publisher: Raymond Houge
Assistant Editor: Michael Rouger
Text and Cover Designer: Lisa Buckner
Marketing Manager: Sara Swagger
Project Manager, Editorial Production: Jerry Emerson
Art Director: Vernon Lowerui

Product Manager: Dave Mason
Editorial Assitant: Rachel Guzmanji
Pedagogy: Debra Long
Cover Image: Jim Reed/Getty Images
Text and Cover Printer: City Printing, Inc.
Compositor: Media Mix, Inc.

(c) 2010 Rico Publications
ALL RIGHTS RESERVED. No part of this work
covered by the copyright may be reproduced or
used in any form or by an means--graphic, electronic,
or mechanical, including photocopying, recording,
taping, Web distribution, information storage, and
retrieval systems, or in any other manner--without the
written permission of the publisher.

Printed in the United States
ISBN:

For more information about our products, contact us at:

Dave.Mason@RicoPublications.com

For permission to use material from this text or

product, submit a request online to:

Dave.Mason@RicoPublications.com

Contents

CHAPTER 1
FLUIDS IN THE CRUST: THE SCIENCE OF HYDROGEOLOGY 1

CHAPTER 2
DARCY`S LAW AND HYDRAULIC HEAD 20

CHAPTER 3
PROPERTIES OF POROUS MEDIA 28

CHAPTER 4
PROPERTIES OF GEOLOGIC FLUIDS 39

CHAPTER 5
TRANSIENT FLOW 55

CHAPTER 6
NEAR SURFACE FLOW 61

CHAPTER 7
DRIVING FORCES AND MECHANISMS OF FLUID FLOW 77

CHAPTER 8
ABNORMAL FLUID PRESSURES 91

CHAPTER 9
ENVIRONMENTAL HYDROGEOLOGY 99

CHAPTER 10
PETROLEUM MIGRATION 132

CHAPTER 11
HEAT TRANSPORT 142

CHAPTER 12
EARTHQUAKES, STRESS, AND FLUIDS 154

CHAPTER 13
FLUIDS IN THE OCEANIC CRUST 166

CHAPTER 14
FLUIDS AND ORE DEPOSITS 185

ANSWER KEY 201

TO THE STUDENT

COMPREHENSIVE

The *MznLnx* Exam Prep series is designed to help you pass your exams. Editors at MznLnx review your textbooks and then prepare these practice exams to help you master the textbook material. Unlike study guides, workbooks, and practice tests provided by the texbook publisher and textbook authors, *MznLnx* gives you **all** of the material in each chapter in exam form, not just samples, so you can be sure to nail your exam.

MECHANICAL

The MznLnx Exam Prep series creates exams that will help you learn the subject matter as well as test you on your understanding. Each question is designed to help you master the concept. Just working through the exams, you gain an understanding of the subject--its a simple mechanical process that produces success.

INTEGRATED STUDY GUIDE AND REVIEW

MznLnx is not just a set of exams designed to test you, its also a comprehensive review of the subject content. Each exam question is also a review of the concept, making sure that you will get the answer correct without having to go to other sources of material. You learn as you go! Its the easiest way to pass an exam.

HUMOR

Studying can be tedious and dry. MznLnx's instructional design includes moderate humor within the exam questions on occassion, to break the tedium and revitalize the brain

Chapter 1. FLUIDS IN THE CRUST: THE SCIENCE OF HYDROGEOLOGY 1

1. _____ refers to things having to do with the land or with the planet Earth.
   a. Terrestrial0
   b. Thing
   c. Undefined
   d. Undefined

2. _____ is the part of hydrology that deals with the distribution and movement of groundwater in the soil and rocks of the Earth's crust.
   a. Thing
   b. Hydrogeology0
   c. Undefined
   d. Undefined

3. _____ is the study of the movement, distribution, and quality of water throughout the Earth, and thus addresses both the hydrologic cycle and water resources.
   a. Hydrology0
   b. Thing
   c. Undefined
   d. Undefined

4. In geology, a _____ is the outermost layer of a planet, part of its lithosphere. They are generally composed of a less dense material than its deeper layers. Earths' is composed mainly of basalt and granite. It is cooler and more rigid than the deeper layers of the mantle and core.
   a. Thing
   b. Crust0
   c. Undefined
   d. Undefined

5. _____ is the branch of Earth Sciences that studies the Earth's oceans and seas. It covers a wide range of topics, including marine organisms and ecosystem dynamics; ocean currents, waves, and geophysical fluid dynamics; plate tectonics and the geology of the sea floor; and fluxes of various chemical substances and physical properties within the ocean and across its boundaries.
   a. Oceanography0
   b. Thing
   c. Undefined
   d. Undefined

6. A _____ is one of several large landmasses on Earth. They are generally identified by convention rather than any strict criteria, but seven areas are commonly reckoned as continents – they are: Asia, Africa, North America, South America, Antarctica, Europe, and Australia.
   a. Continent0
   b. Thing
   c. Undefined
   d. Undefined

7. An _____ is a layer of gases that may surround a material body of sufficient mass. The gases are attracted by the gravity of the body, and are retained for a longer duration if gravity is high and the _____'s temperature is low. Some planets consist mainly of various gases, and thus have very deep atmospheres.
   a. Atmosphere0
   b. Place
   c. Undefined
   d. Undefined

8. In physical geography, a _____ is an environment "at the interface between truly terrestrial ecosystems and aquatic systems making them inherently different from each other yet highly dependent on both". In essence, they are ecotones.
   a. Wetland0
   b. Place
   c. Undefined
   d. Undefined

Chapter 1. FLUIDS IN THE CRUST: THE SCIENCE OF HYDROGEOLOGY

9. _____, or channel runoff, is the flow of water in streams, rivers, and other channels, and is a major element of the water cycle. It is one component of the runoff of water from the land to waterbodies, the other component being surface runoff. Water flowing in channels comes from surface runoff from adjacent hillslopes, from groundwater flow out of the ground, and from water discharged from pipes.
  a. Streamflow0
  b. Thing
  c. Undefined
  d. Undefined

10. _____ is displacement of solids by the agents of ocean currents, wind, water, or ice by downward or down-slope movement in response to gravity or by living organisms.
  a. Thing
  b. Erosion0
  c. Undefined
  d. Undefined

11. _____ is the process by which molecules in a liquid state become a gas.
  a. Evaporation0
  b. Thing
  c. Undefined
  d. Undefined

12. A _____ is a body of water or other liquid of considerable size contained on a body of land. A vast majority are fresh water, and lie in the Northern Hemisphere at higher latitudes. Most have a natural outflow in the form of a river or stream, but some do not, and lose water solely by evaporation and/or underground seepage.
  a. Thing
  b. Lake0
  c. Undefined
  d. Undefined

13. A _____ is a body of water with a current, confined within a bed and banks. Streams are important as conduits in the water cycle, instruments in aquifer recharge, and corridors for fish and wildlife migration.
  a. Stream0
  b. Thing
  c. Undefined
  d. Undefined

14. An _____ is a volume of rock containing components or minerals in a mode of occurrence that renders it valuable for mining.
  a. Ore0
  b. Thing
  c. Undefined
  d. Undefined

15. _____ is a naturally occurring liquid found in formations in the Earth consisting of a complex mixture of hydrocarbons of various lengths.
  a. Thing
  b. Petroleum0
  c. Undefined
  d. Undefined

16. _____ is water located beneath the ground surface in soil pore spaces and in the fractures of geologic formations. _____ is recharged from, and eventually flows to, the surface naturally; natural discharge often occurs at springs and seeps, streams and can often form oases or wetlands.
  a. Thing
  b. Groundwater0
  c. Undefined
  d. Undefined

17. _____ is a measure of the void spaces in a material, and is measured as a fraction, between 0–1, or as a percentage between 0–100%.

Chapter 1. FLUIDS IN THE CRUST: THE SCIENCE OF HYDROGEOLOGY

   a. Porosity0
   b. Thing
   c. Undefined
   d. Undefined

18. _____ is rock that is of a certain particle size range. In geology, _____ is any loose rock that is at least two millimeters in its largest dimension and no more than 75 millimeters.
   a. Gravel0
   b. Thing
   c. Undefined
   d. Undefined

19. _____ is soil or rock derived granular material of a specific grain size. _____ may occur as a soil or alternatively as suspended sediment in a water column of any surface water body. It may also exist as deposition soil at the bottom of a water body.
   a. Thing
   b. Silt0
   c. Undefined
   d. Undefined

20. _____ is any particulate matter that can be transported by fluid flow and which eventually is deposited as a layer of solid particles on the bed or bottom of a body of water or other liquid.
   a. Thing
   b. Sediment0
   c. Undefined
   d. Undefined

21. In the earth sciences, _____ is a measure of the ability of a material to transmit fluids. It is of great importance in determining the flow characteristics of hydrocarbons in oil and gas reservoirs, and of groundwater in aquifers.
   a. Thing
   b. Permeability0
   c. Undefined
   d. Undefined

22. _____ is the work done by a force when the relative positions of objects are changed within a physical system. In other words, it is the work done when an object is moved from one point to another. Conceptually, _____ can be thought of as the energy of an object as a result of the work done to bring it to that position from a reference point.
   a. Potential energy0
   b. Thing
   c. Undefined
   d. Undefined

23. _____ is the production of food, feed, fiber, fuel and other goods by the systematic raizing of plants and animals.
   a. Thing
   b. Agriculture0
   c. Undefined
   d. Undefined

24. _____ is a highly sought-after precious metal which, for many centuries, has been used as money, a store of value and in jewelery. The metal occurs as nuggets or grains in rocks, underground "veins" and in alluvial deposits. It is one of the coinage metals. Itis dense, soft, shiny and the most malleable and ductile of the known metals.
   a. Thing
   b. Gold0
   c. Undefined
   d. Undefined

25. _____ is a chemical element in the periodic table that has the symbol Zn and atomic number 30. In some historical and sculptural contexts, it is known as spelter.
   a. Zinc0
   b. Thing
   c. Undefined
   d. Undefined

4 *Chapter 1. FLUIDS IN THE CRUST: THE SCIENCE OF HYDROGEOLOGY*

26. An _____ is the result from the sudden release of stored energy in the Earth's crust that creates seismic waves. At the Earth's surface, earthquakes may manifest themselves by a shaking or displacement of the ground. An _____ is caused by tectonic plates getting stuck and putting a strain on the ground. The strain becomes so great that rocks give way by breaking and sliding along fault planes.
   a. Thing
   b. Earthquake0
   c. Undefined
   d. Undefined

27. In geology and oceanography, _____ is any chemical, physical, or biological change undergone by a sediment after its initial deposition and during and after its lithification, exclusive of surface alteration, weathering and metamorphism. These changes happen at relatively low temperatures and pressures and result in changes to the rock's original mineralogy and texture
   a. Thing
   b. Diagenesis0
   c. Undefined
   d. Undefined

28. A _____ column is a column of rizing air in the lower altitudes of the Earth's atmosphere. Thermals are created by the uneven heating of the Earth's surface from solar radiation, and are an example of convection. The Sun warms the ground, which in turn warms the air directly above it.
   a. Thermal0
   b. Thing
   c. Undefined
   d. Undefined

29. A _____ is a landform that extends above the surrounding terrain in a limited area. A _____ is generally steeper than a hill, but there is no universally accepted standard definition for the height of a _____ or a hill although a _____ usually has an identifiable summit.
   a. Mountain0
   b. Place
   c. Undefined
   d. Undefined

30. _____ is a sedimentary rock composed largely of the mineral calcite. _____ often contains variable amounts of silica in the form of chert or flint, as well as varying amounts of clay, silt and sand as disseminations, nodules, or layers within the rock. The primary source of the calcite in _____ is most commonly marine organisms. These organisms secrete shells that settle out of the water column and are deposited on ocean floors as pelagic ooze or alternatively is conglomerated in a coral reef.
   a. Thing
   b. Limestone0
   c. Undefined
   d. Undefined

31. _____ in meteorology are large scale patterns in the atmospheric pressure field that are nearly stationary, effectively "blocking" or redirecting migratory cyclones. These _____ can remain in place for several days or even weeks, causing the areas affected by them to have the same kind of weather for an extended period of time.
   a. Blocks0
   b. Thing
   c. Undefined
   d. Undefined

32. _____ contains low concentrations of dissolved salts and other total dissolved solids. It is an important renewable resource, necessary for the survival of most terrestrial organisms, and required by humans for drinking and agriculture, among many other uses.
   a. Thing
   b. Fresh water0
   c. Undefined
   d. Undefined

Chapter 1. FLUIDS IN THE CRUST: THE SCIENCE OF HYDROGEOLOGY

33. _____ was a Greek philosopher, a student of Plato and teacher of Alexander the Great. He wrote on diverse subjects, including physics, metaphysics, poetry, biology and zoology, logic, rhetoric, politics, government, and ethics.
   a. Person
   b. Aristotle0
   c. Undefined
   d. Undefined

34. _____ is the change in matter of a substance to a denser phase, such as a gas to a liquid. _____ commonly occurs when a vapor is cooled to a liquid, but can also occur if a vapor is compressed into a liquid, or undergoes a combination of cooling and compression.
   a. Thing
   b. Condensation0
   c. Undefined
   d. Undefined

35. _____, in everyday life, is most familiar as the agency that endows objects with weight. _____ is responsible for keeping the Earth and the other planets in their orbits around the Sun; for the formation of tides; and for various other phenomena that we observe. _____ is also the reason for the very existence of the Earth, the Sun, and most macroscopic objects in the universe; without it, matter would not have coalesced into these large masses, and life, as we know it, would not exist.
   a. Thing
   b. Gravitation0
   c. Undefined
   d. Undefined

36. _____ is the study of Earth's surface features or those of other planets, moons, and asteroids
   a. Topography0
   b. Thing
   c. Undefined
   d. Undefined

37. _____, palaeontology or palæontology is the study of prehistoric life forms on Earth through the examination of plant and animal fossils. This includes the study of body fossils, tracks, burrows, cast-off parts, fossilised faeces, palynomorphs and chemical residues. See also paleoanthropology.
   a. Thing
   b. Paleontology0
   c. Undefined
   d. Undefined

38. _____ is any product of the condensation of atmospheric water vapor that is deposited on the earth's surface. It occurs when the atmosphere becomes saturated with water vapour and the water condenses and falls out of solution. Air becomes saturated via two processes, cooling and adding moisture.
   a. Precipitation0
   b. Thing
   c. Undefined
   d. Undefined

39. _____ is the process by which water on the ground surface enters the soil.
   a. Thing
   b. Infiltration0
   c. Undefined
   d. Undefined

40. The Earth's water is always in movement, and the _____, describes the continuous movement of water on, above, and below the surface of the Earth. Since the _____ is truly a "cycle," there is no beginning or end. Water can change states among liquid, vapor, and ice at various places in the _____, with these processes happening in the blink of an eye and over millions of years. Although the balance of water on Earth remains fairly constant over time, individual water molecules can come and go in a hurry.

Chapter 1. FLUIDS IN THE CRUST: THE SCIENCE OF HYDROGEOLOGY

a. Thing
b. Hydrologic cycle0
c. Undefined
d. Undefined

41. In physics, _____ is defined as the rate of change of displacement or the rate of displacement. Simply put, it is distance per units of time.
a. Velocity0
b. Thing
c. Undefined
d. Undefined

42. An _____ is an underground layer of water-bearing permeable rock or unconsolidated materials from which groundwater can be usefully extracted using a water well.
a. Aquifer0
b. Thing
c. Undefined
d. Undefined

43. An _____ occurs in recharging aquifers, this happens because the water table at its recharge zone is at a higher elevation than the head of the well.
a. Thing
b. Artesian well0
c. Undefined
d. Undefined

44. The _____ are the broad expanse of prairie and steppe which lie east of the Rocky Mountains in the United States and Canada.
a. Great Plains0
b. Place
c. Undefined
d. Undefined

45. _____ is the science and study of the solid matter that constitute the Earth. Encompassing such things as rocks, soil, and gemstones, _____ studies the composition, structure, physical properties, history, and the processes that shape Earth's components.
a. Geology0
b. Thing
c. Undefined
d. Undefined

46. An _____ is a long period of time with different technical and colloquial meanings, and usages in language. It begins with some beginning event known as an epoch, epochal date, epochal event or epochal moment.
a. Era0
b. Thing
c. Undefined
d. Undefined

47. _____ is the artificial application of water to the soil usually for assisting in growing crops. In crop production it is mainly used to replace missing rainfall in periods of drought, but also to protect plants against frost.
a. Thing
b. Irrigation0
c. Undefined
d. Undefined

48. _____ is a sedimentary rock composed mainly of sand-size mineral or rock grains. Most _____ is composed of quartz and/or feldspar because these are the most common minerals in the Earth's crust. Like sand, _____ may be any color, but the most common colors are tan, brown, yellow, red, gray and white.
a. Sandstone0
b. Thing
c. Undefined
d. Undefined

49. _____ refers to directed, regular, or systematic movement of a group of objects, organisms, or people.

Chapter 1. FLUIDS IN THE CRUST: THE SCIENCE OF HYDROGEOLOGY

a. Thing
c. Undefined

b. Migration0
d. Undefined

50. _____ is a field of study within geology concerned generally with the structures within the crust of the Earth, or other planets, and particularly with the forces and movements that have operated in a region to create these structures.

a. Thing
c. Undefined

b. Tectonics0
d. Undefined

51. _____ is a theory of geology that has been developed to explain the observed evidence for large scale motions of the Earth's lithosphere. The theory encompassed and superseded the older theory of continental drift.

a. Thing
c. Undefined

b. Plate tectonics0
d. Undefined

52. _____ rock is one of the three main rock groups. Rock formed from these covers 75% of the Earth's land area, and includes common types such as chalk, limestone, dolomite, sandstone, and shale.

a. Thing
c. Undefined

b. Sedimentary0
d. Undefined

53. A _____ is a naturally occurring substance formed through geological processes that has a characteristic chemical composition, a highly ordered atomic structure and specific physical properties. A rock, by comparison, is an aggregate of minerals and need not have a specific chemical composition. Minerals range in composition from pure elements and simple salts to very complex silicates with thousands of known forms.

a. Thing
c. Undefined

b. Mineral0
d. Undefined

54. The _____ is the layer of granitic, sedimentary, and metamorphic rocks which form the continents and the areas of shallow seabed close to their shores, known as continental shelves. It is less dense than the material of the Earth's mantle and thus "floats" on top of it. _____ is also less dense than oceanic crust, though it is considerably thicker. About 40% of the Earth's surface is now underlain by _____.

a. Continental crust0
c. Undefined

b. Thing
d. Undefined

55. A _____ is a solid in which the constituent atoms, molecules, or ions are packed in a regularly ordered, repeating pattern extending in all three spatial dimensions. Most metals encountered in everyday life are polycrystals. Crystals are often symmetrically intergrown to form _____ twins.

a. Thing
c. Undefined

b. Crystal0
d. Undefined

56. Water collecting on the ground or in a stream, river, lake, or wetland is called _____; as opposed to groundwater. _____ is naturally replenished by precipitation and naturally lost through discharge to the oceans, evaporation, and sub-surface seepage into the groundwater. _____ is the largest source of fresh water.

a. Thing
c. Undefined

b. Surface water0
d. Undefined

Chapter 1. FLUIDS IN THE CRUST: THE SCIENCE OF HYDROGEOLOGY

57. _____ is a general term for a variety of phenomena resulting from the presence and flow of charge. This includes many well-known physical phenomena such as lightning, electromagnetic fields and electric currents, and is put to use in industrial applications such as electronics and electric power.
- a. Electricity0
- b. Thing
- c. Undefined
- d. Undefined

58. The _____ is an area extending over 100 miles from the central regions of the U.S. state of Montana to southern Alberta, Canada. The majority of the _____ lies in Waterton Lakes National Park in Alberta, and Glacier National Park, Lewis and Clark National Forest as well as on private lands and the Blackfeet Indian Reservation, all of which are in Montana.
- a. Place
- b. Rocky Mountain front0
- c. Undefined
- d. Undefined

59. The _____ are a small, isolated mountain range rizing from the Great Plains of North America in western South Dakota and extending into Wyoming, USA. Set off from the main body of the Rocky Mountains, the region is somewhat of a geological anomaly—accurately described as an "island of trees in a sea of grass.
- a. Black Hills0
- b. Place
- c. Undefined
- d. Undefined

60. _____ is concerned with earth materials that can be utilized for economic and/or industrial purposes. These materials include precious and base metals, nonmetallic minerals, construction-grade stone, petroleum minerals, coal, and water. The term commonly refers to metallic mineral deposits and mineral resources. The techniques employed by other earth science disciplines might all be used to understand, describe, and exploit an ore deposit.
- a. Thing
- b. Economic geology0
- c. Undefined
- d. Undefined

61. _____ is a branch of physics which studies the properties of elastic materials. A material is said to be elastic if it deforms under stress but then returns to its original shape when the stress is removed.
- a. Thing
- b. Elasticity0
- c. Undefined
- d. Undefined

62. An _____ is any piece of land that is completely surrounded by water, above high tide. There are two main types of islands: continental islands and oceanic islands. There are also artificial islands. A grouping of geographically and/or geologically related islands is called an archipelago.
- a. Thing
- b. Island0
- c. Undefined
- d. Undefined

63. The _____ is a nonprofit organization dedicated to the advancement of the geosciences. The society was founded in New York in 1888 by James Hall, James D. Dana, and Alexander Winchell, and has been headquartered at 3300 Penrose Place, Boulder, Colorado since 1968. As of 2007, the society has over 21,000 members in more than 85 countries. The stated mission is "to advance the geosciences, to enhance the professional growth of its members, and to promote the geosciences in the service of humankind".
- a. Person
- b. Geological Society of America0
- c. Undefined
- d. Undefined

Chapter 1. FLUIDS IN THE CRUST: THE SCIENCE OF HYDROGEOLOGY

64. _____ was a leading US geomorphologist. A famous US hydrologist, he suggested that a new philosophy of water management is needed, one based on geologic, geographic, and climatic factors as well as traditional economic, social, and political factors.
   a. Person
   b. Luna Leopold0
   c. Undefined
   d. Undefined

65. _____ can be defined as the solid state recrystallisation of pre-existing rocks due to changes in heat and/or pressure and/or introduction of fluids. There will be mineralogical, chemical and crystallographic changes. _____ produced with increasing pressure and temperature conditions is known as prograde _____. Conversely, decreasing temperatures and pressure characterize retrograde _____.
   a. Metamorphism0
   b. Thing
   c. Undefined
   d. Undefined

66. _____ in the most general terms refers to the movement of currents within fluids. _____ is one of the major modes of Heat and mass transfer. In fluids, convective heat and mass transfer take place through both diffusion and by advection, in which matter or heat is transported by the larger-scale motion of currents in the fluid.
   a. Convection0
   b. Thing
   c. Undefined
   d. Undefined

67. Faults are planar rock fractures, which show evidence of relative movement. Large faults within the Earth's crust are the result of shear motion and active _____ zones are the causal locations of most earthquakes. Earthquakes are caused by energy release during rapid slippage along faults. The largest examples are at tectonic plate boundaries but many faults occur far from active plate boundaries. Since faults do not usually consist of a single, clean fracture, the term _____ zone is used when referring to the zone of complex deformation that is associated with the _____ plane.
   a. Fault0
   b. Thing
   c. Undefined
   d. Undefined

68. Most often, a _____ refers to an artificial lake, used to store water for various uses. Reservoirs are created first by building a sturdy dam, usually out of cement, earth, rock, or a mixture. Once the dam is completed, a stream is allowed to flow behind it and eventually fill it to capacity.
   a. Thing
   b. Reservoir0
   c. Undefined
   d. Undefined

69. _____ is the reduction in amplitude and intensity of a signal.
   a. Thing
   b. Attenuation0
   c. Undefined
   d. Undefined

70. _____ or specific conductivity is a measure of a material's ability to conduct an electric current. When an electrical potential difference is placed across a conductor, its movable charges flow, giving rise to an electric current.
   a. Thing
   b. Electrical conductivity0
   c. Undefined
   d. Undefined

71. The _____ is used by geologists and other scientists to describe the timing and relationships between events that have occurred during the history of Earth.

Chapter 1. FLUIDS IN THE CRUST: THE SCIENCE OF HYDROGEOLOGY

a. Thing
b. Geological time scale0
c. Undefined
d. Undefined

72. _____ is the part of Earth's lithosphere that surfaces in the ocean basins. _____ is primarily composed of mafic rocks, or sima. It is thinner than continental crust, or sial, generally less than 10 kilometers thick, however it is more dense, having a mean density of about 3.3 grams per cubic centimeter.
a. Oceanic crust0
b. Thing
c. Undefined
d. Undefined

73. _____ is an intrusive igneous rock similar to granite, but contains more plagioclase than potassium feldspar. It usually contains abundant biotite mica and hornblende, giving it a darker appearance than true granite.
a. Granodiorite0
b. Thing
c. Undefined
d. Undefined

74. _____ is a dark, coarse-grained, intrusive igneous rock chemically equivalent to basalt. It is a plutonic rock, formed when molten magma is trapped beneath the Earth's surface and cools into a crystalline mass.
a. Thing
b. Gabbro0
c. Undefined
d. Undefined

75. _____ is a small island located in the middle of San Francisco Bay in California, United States. It served as a lighthouse, then a military fortification, then a military prison followed by a federal prison until 1963, when it became a national recreation area.
a. Alcatraz Island0
b. Place
c. Undefined
d. Undefined

76. _____ is a common gray to black extrusive volcanic rock. It is usually fine-grained due to rapid cooling of lava on the Earth's surface. It may be porphyritic containing larger crystals in a fine matrix, or vesicular, or frothy scoria.
a. Basalt0
b. Thing
c. Undefined
d. Undefined

77. _____ is water from a sea or ocean. On average, _____ in the world's oceans has a salinity of ~3.5%, or 35 parts per thousand. This means that every 1 kg of _____ has approximately 35 grams of dissolved salts.
a. Seawater0
b. Thing
c. Undefined
d. Undefined

78. The _____ is the portion of Earth between the land surface and the phreatic zone or zone of saturation.
a. Vadose Zone0
b. Thing
c. Undefined
d. Undefined

79. _____ is the average and variations of weather over long periods of time. _____ zones can be defined using parameters such as temperature and rainfall.
a. Thing
b. Climate0
c. Undefined
d. Undefined

Chapter 1. FLUIDS IN THE CRUST: THE SCIENCE OF HYDROGEOLOGY

80. The _____ provides the only reliable source of water through much of inland Australia. The basin is the largest and deepest artesian basin in the world. The basin is 3000 metres deep in places and is estimated to contain 64,900 cubic kilometres of groundwater.
- a. Thing
- b. Great Artesian Basin0
- c. Undefined
- d. Undefined

81. _____ is formed from ocean water that freezes. Because the oceans consist of saltwater, this occurs at about -1.8 °C.
- a. Sea ice0
- b. Thing
- c. Undefined
- d. Undefined

82. An _____ is a dome-shaped ice mass that covers less than 50,000 km² of land area. Masses of ice covering more than 50,000 km² are termed an ice sheet.
- a. Thing
- b. Ice cap0
- c. Undefined
- d. Undefined

83. A _____ is a large, slow moving river of ice, formed from compacted layers of snow, that slowly deforms and flows in response to gravity. _____ ice is the largest reservoir of fresh water on Earth, and second only to oceans as the largest reservoir of total water. Glaciers cover vast areas of polar regions but are restricted to the highest mountains in the tropics.
- a. Glacier0
- b. Thing
- c. Undefined
- d. Undefined

84. A _____ is a wetland that features temporary or permanent inundation of large areas of land by shallow bodies of water, generally with a substantial number of hummocks, or dry-land protrusions, and covered by aquatic vegetation, or vegetation that tolerates periodical inundation.
- a. Thing
- b. Swamp0
- c. Undefined
- d. Undefined

85. _____ is a broadly useful concept that expresses how fast something moves through a system in equilibrium. It is the average time a substance spends within a specified region of space, such as a reservoir.
- a. Residence time0
- b. Thing
- c. Undefined
- d. Undefined

86. In chemistry, a _____ is defined as a sufficiently stable electrically neutral group of at least two atoms in a definite arrangement held together by strong chemical bonds.
- a. Molecule0
- b. Thing
- c. Undefined
- d. Undefined

87. _____ concerns the movement and filtering of fluids through porous materials. During the last three decades, _____ theory, an extensive mathematical model of _____, has brought new understanding and techniques to a broad range of topics in physics and materials science.
- a. Thing
- b. Percolation0
- c. Undefined
- d. Undefined

Chapter 1. FLUIDS IN THE CRUST: THE SCIENCE OF HYDROGEOLOGY

88. The _____ on the geologic timescale had been intended to cover the world's recent period of repeated glaciations. The _____ follows the Pliocene and is followed by the Holocene. The _____ is the third epoch of the Neogene period or 6th epoch of the Cenozoic era. The end of the _____ corresponds with the end of the Paleolithic age used in archaeology. The _____ is divided into the Early _____, Middle _____ and Late _____, and numerous faunal stages.
   a. Pleistocene0
   b. Thing
   c. Undefined
   d. Undefined

89. An _____ is a period of long-term reduction in the temperature of Earth's climate, resulting in an expansion of the continental ice sheets, polar ice sheets and mountain glaciers.
   a. Ice Age0
   b. Thing
   c. Undefined
   d. Undefined

90. An _____ is a mass of glacier ice that covers surrounding terrain and is greater than 19,305 mile². The only current ice sheets are in Antarctica and Greenland. Ice sheets are bigger than ice shelves or glaciers. Masses of ice covering less than 50,000 km² are termed an ice cap. An ice cap will typically feed a series of glaciers around its periphery. Although the surface is cold, the base of an _____ is generally warmer. This process produces fast-flowing channels in the _____.
   a. Thing
   b. Ice sheet0
   c. Undefined
   d. Undefined

91. Mean _____ is the average height of the sea, with reference to a suitable reference surface.
   a. Thing
   b. Sea level0
   c. Undefined
   d. Undefined

92. _____ is one of the four seasons of temperate zones. Almost all English-language calendars, going by astronomy, state that _____ begins on the _____ solstice, and ends on the spring equinox. Calculated more by the weather, it begins and ends earlier and is the season with the shortest days and the lowest temperatures.
   a. Thing
   b. Winter0
   c. Undefined
   d. Undefined

93. In geology, engineering, and surveying, _____ is the motion of a surface as it shifts downward relative to a datum such as sea-level. The opposite of _____ is uplift, which results in an increase in elevation. In meteorology, _____ refers to the downward movement of air.
   a. Subsidence0
   b. Thing
   c. Undefined
   d. Undefined

94. _____ is an increase in sea level. Multiple complex factors may influence such changes.
   a. Sea level rise0
   b. Thing
   c. Undefined
   d. Undefined

95. The _____ is the current eon in the geologic timescale, and the one during which abundant animal life has existed. It covers roughly 545 million years and goes back to the time when diverse hard-shelled animals first appeared.
   a. Phanerozoic0
   b. Thing
   c. Undefined
   d. Undefined

Chapter 1. FLUIDS IN THE CRUST: THE SCIENCE OF HYDROGEOLOGY

96. _____ are large geologic basins that are below sea level. Geologically, there are other undersea geomorphological features such as the continental shelves, the deep ocean trenches, and the undersea mountain rangeswhich are not considered to be part of the _____.
   a. Ocean basins0
   b. Thing
   c. Undefined
   d. Undefined

97. The _____ consists of the Sun and the other celestial objects gravitationally bound to it: the eight planets, their 165 known moons, three currently identified dwarf planets and their four known moons, and billions of small bodies.
   a. Solar system0
   b. Thing
   c. Undefined
   d. Undefined

98. A _____, as defined by the International Astronomical Union, is a celestial body orbiting a star or stellar remnant that is massive enough to be rounded by its own gravity, not massive enough to cause thermonuclear fusion in its core, and has cleared its neighboring region of planetesimals.
   a. Thing
   b. Planet0
   c. Undefined
   d. Undefined

99. _____ is the gas phase of water. _____ is one state of the water cycle within the hydrosphere. _____ can be produced from the evaporation of liquid water or from the sublimation of ice. Under normal atmospheric conditions, _____ is continuously evaporating and condensing.
   a. Thing
   b. Water vapor0
   c. Undefined
   d. Undefined

100. _____ is the gas phase component of a another state of matter which does not completely fill its container. It is distinguished from the pure gas phase by the presence of the same substance in another state of matter. Hence when a liquid has completely evaporated, it is said that the system has been completely transformed to the gas phase.
   a. Vapor0
   b. Thing
   c. Undefined
   d. Undefined

101. A _____ is a building where plants are cultivated.
   a. Greenhouse0
   b. Thing
   c. Undefined
   d. Undefined

102. The _____, discovered by Joseph Fourier in 1829 and first investigated quantitatively by Svante Arrhenius in 1896, is the process in which the emission of infrared radiation by the atmosphere warms a planet's surface.
   a. Thing
   b. Greenhouse effect0
   c. Undefined
   d. Undefined

103. An _____ is any more or less continuous, directed movement of ocean water that flows in one of the Earth's oceans.Ocean Currents are rivers of hot or cold water within the ocean. The currents are generated from the forces acting upon the water like the earth's rotation, the wind, the temperature and salinity differences and the gravitation of the moon. The depth contours, the shoreline and other currents influence the current's direction and strength.
   a. Thing
   b. Ocean current0
   c. Undefined
   d. Undefined

14 *Chapter 1. FLUIDS IN THE CRUST: THE SCIENCE OF HYDROGEOLOGY*

104. Ocean _____ are any more or less continuous, directed movement of ocean water that flows in one of the Earth's oceans.They are rivers of hot or cold water within the ocean. They are generated from the forces acting upon the water like the earth's rotation, the wind, the temperature and salinity differences and the gravitation of the moon.
- a. Thing
- b. Currents0
- c. Undefined
- d. Undefined

105. The _____ is a powerful, warm, and swift Atlantic ocean current that originates in the Gulf of Mexico, exits through the Strait of Florida, and follows the eastern coastlines of the United States and Newfoundland before crossing the Atlantic Ocean. It then splits in two, with the northern stream crossing to northern Europe and the southern stream recirculating off West Africa. The _____ influences the climate of the east coast of North America from Florida to Newfoundland, and the west coast of Europe.
- a. Thing
- b. Gulf stream0
- c. Undefined
- d. Undefined

106. The _____ is the second-largest of the world's oceanic divisions; with a total area of about 106.4 million square kilometres , it covers approximately one-fifth of the Earth's surface. The _____ occupies an elongated, S-shaped basin extending longitudinally between the Americas to the west, and Eurasia and Africa to the east.
- a. Atlantic Ocean0
- b. Place
- c. Undefined
- d. Undefined

107. The _____ is defined as the part of the land adjoining or near the ocean. A coastline is properly a line on a map indicating the disposition of a _____, but the word is often used to refer to the _____ itself. The adjective coastal describes something as being on, near to, or associated with a _____.
- a. Coast0
- b. Place
- c. Undefined
- d. Undefined

108. The _____ is the largest of the Earth's oceanic divisions. It extends from the Arctic in the north to the Antarctic in the south, bounded by Asia and Australia on the west and the Americas on the east. At 169.2 million square kilometres in area, this largest division of the World Ocean – and, in turn, the hydrosphere – covers about 46% of the Earth's water surface and about 32% of its total surface area, making it larger than all of the Earth's land area combined.
- a. Place
- b. Pacific Ocean0
- c. Undefined
- d. Undefined

109. _____ in the broad sense is the total spectrum of the electromagnetic radiation given off by the Sun. On Earth, it is filtered through the atmosphere, and the solar radiation is obvious as daylight when the Sun is above the horizon.
- a. Sunlight0
- b. Thing
- c. Undefined
- d. Undefined

110. _____ as used in physics, is energy in the form of waves or moving subatomic particles.
- a. Thing
- b. Radiation0
- c. Undefined
- d. Undefined

111. _____ is electromagnetic radiation of a wavelength longer than that of visible light, but shorter than that of radio waves. The name means "below red", red being the color of visible light with the longest wavelength. _____ has wavelengths between about 750 nm and 1 mm, spanning three orders of magnitude.

Chapter 1. FLUIDS IN THE CRUST: THE SCIENCE OF HYDROGEOLOGY 15

    a. Infrared0
    c. Undefined
    b. Thing
    d. Undefined

112. _____ is a chemical element. An abundant nonmetallic, tetravalent element, _____ has several allotropic forms. This element is the basis of the chemistry of all known life.
    a. Thing
    c. Undefined
    b. Carbon0
    d. Undefined

113. _____ is a chemical compound, normally in a gaseous state, and is composed of one carbon and two oxygen atoms. It is often referred to by its formula CO_2. It is present in the Earth's atmosphere at a concentration of approximately .000383 by volume and is an important greenhouse gas due to its ability to absorb many infrared wavelengths of sunlight, and due to the length of time it stays in the atmosphere.
    a. Thing
    c. Undefined
    b. Carbon dioxide0
    d. Undefined

114. _____ is a measure of solar radiation energy incident on a surface. It is the amount of solar energy received on a given area; and may be expressed in W/m^2 or over time measured in kilowatt-hours per square meter.
    a. Thing
    c. Undefined
    b. Insolation0
    d. Undefined

115. _____ is radiant energy emitted by the sun from a nuclear fusion reaction that creates electromagnetic energy. The spectrum of _____ is close to that of a black body with a temperature of about 5800 K. About half of the radiation is in the visible short-wave part of the electromagnetic spectrum. The other half is mostly in the near-infrared part, with some in the ultraviolet part of the spectrum.
    a. Thing
    c. Undefined
    b. Solar radiation0
    d. Undefined

116. _____ are the SI unit of energy.
    a. Joules0
    c. Undefined
    b. Thing
    d. Undefined

117. _____ gives the location of a place on Earth north or south of the equator. Lines of _____ are the horizontal lines shown running east-to-west on maps. Technically, _____ is an angular measurement in degrees ranging from 0° at the Equator to 90° at the poles.
    a. Thing
    c. Undefined
    b. Latitude0
    d. Undefined

118. _____ is a term used to describe the flow of water, from rain, snowmelt, or other sources, over the land surface, and is a major component of the water cycle.
    a. Thing
    c. Undefined
    b. Surface runoff0
    d. Undefined

119. _____ is the complete set of chemical reactions that occur in living cells. These processes are the basis of life, allowing cells to grow and reproduce, maintain their structures, and respond to their environments.

Chapter 1. FLUIDS IN THE CRUST: THE SCIENCE OF HYDROGEOLOGY

a. Thing
b. Metabolism0
c. Undefined
d. Undefined

120. A _____ is a section of a river of relatively steep gradient causing an increase in water flow and turbulence. A _____ is a hydrological feature between a run and a cascade. It is characterized by the river becoming shallower and having some rocks exposed above the flow surface.
a. Thing
b. Rapid0
c. Undefined
d. Undefined

121. _____ is the reprocessing of materials into new products. It prevents useful material resources being wasted, reduces the consumption of raw materials and reduces energy usage, and hence greenhouse gas emissions, compared to virgin production.
a. Thing
b. Recycling0
c. Undefined
d. Undefined

122. _____ is the physical, chemical and biological characteristics of water, characterized through the methods of hydrometry.
a. Thing
b. Water quality0
c. Undefined
d. Undefined

123. _____ is electricity produced by hydropower. _____ now supplies about 715,000 MWe or 19% of world electricity. It is also the world's leading form of renewable energy, accounting for over 63% of the total in 2005.
a. Hydroelectricity0
b. Thing
c. Undefined
d. Undefined

124. _____ is the extraction of valuable minerals or other geological materials from the earth, usually from an ore body, vein, or seam. Any material that cannot be grown from agricultural processes, or created artificially in a laboratory or factory, is usually extracted from the earth by this method.
a. Mining0
b. Thing
c. Undefined
d. Undefined

125. A natural resource qualifies as a _____ if it is replenished by natural processes at a rate comparable to its rate of consumption by humans or other users. Resources such as solar radiation, tides, and winds are perpetual resources that are in no danger of being used in excess of their long-term availability.
a. Thing
b. Renewable resource0
c. Undefined
d. Undefined

126. The _____ is a vast yet shallow underground water table aquifer located beneath the Great Plains in the United States.
a. Ogallala Aquifer0
b. Thing
c. Undefined
d. Undefined

127. The _____ are a subregion of the Great Plains in the central United States, located in eastern Colorado, western Kansas, western Nebraska, central and eastern Montana, eastern New Mexico, western Oklahoma, northwestern Texas, and southeastern Wyoming. In some definitions of the subregion, parts of western South Dakota and North Dakota are included. From east to west, the _____ rise in elevation from around 750 m to over 1800 m.

Chapter 1. FLUIDS IN THE CRUST: THE SCIENCE OF HYDROGEOLOGY 17

a. Place
b. High Plains0
c. Undefined
d. Undefined

128. The _____ are a broad mountain range in western North America. The _____ stretch more than 4,800 kilometers from northernmost British Columbia, in Canada, to New Mexico, in the United States.
 a. Rocky Mountains0
 b. Place
 c. Undefined
 d. Undefined

129. A _____ is an extended period of months or years when a region notes a deficiency in its water supply. Generally, this occurs when a region receives consistently below average precipitation.
 a. Thing
 b. Drought0
 c. Undefined
 d. Undefined

130. _____ refers to an area of land of low topographic relief that historically supported grasses and herbs, with few trees, and having generally a mesic climate.
 a. Prairie0
 b. Place
 c. Undefined
 d. Undefined

131. A _____ is a type of open-pit mine from which rock or minerals are extracted. They are generally used for extracting building materials, such as dimension stone. They are usually shallower than other types of open-pit mines.
 a. Quarry0
 b. Thing
 c. Undefined
 d. Undefined

132. Fossils are the mineralized or otherwise preserved remains or traces of animals, plants, and other organisms. The totality of fossils, both discovered and undiscovered, and their placement in fossiliferous rock formations and sedimentary layers is known as the _____ record.
 a. Thing
 b. Fossil0
 c. Undefined
 d. Undefined

133. An _____ is an electro-static phenomenon, characterized by a bright glow and caused by the collision of charged particles in the magnetosphere with atoms in the Earth's upper atmosphere.
 a. Thing
 b. Aurora0
 c. Undefined
 d. Undefined

134. In science, the term _____ refers to a rational approach to the study of the universe, which is understood as obeying rules or laws of natural origin.
 a. Natural science0
 b. Thing
 c. Undefined
 d. Undefined

135. The _____ is a scientific agency of the United States government. The scientists of the USGS study the landscape of the United States, its natural resources, and the natural hazards that threaten it.
 a. Person
 b. U.S. Geological Survey0
 c. Undefined
 d. Undefined

18   *Chapter 1. FLUIDS IN THE CRUST: THE SCIENCE OF HYDROGEOLOGY*

136. _____ is a body of techniques for investigating phenomena and acquiring new knowledge, as well as for correcting and integrating previous knowledge. It is based on gathering observable, empirical and measurable evidence subject to specific principles of reasoning,
- a. Scientific method0
- b. Thing
- c. Undefined
- d. Undefined

137. _____ is the discipline concerned with the questions of how one should live ; what sorts of things exist and what are their essential natures ; what counts as genuine knowledge; and what are the correct principles of reasoning.
- a. Philosophy0
- b. Thing
- c. Undefined
- d. Undefined

138. _____ is a general term that refers to deformation of the Earth's crust.
- a. Thing
- b. Diastrophism0
- c. Undefined
- d. Undefined

139. _____ is the process of building mountains, and may be studied as a tectonic structural event, as a geographical event and a chronological event, in that orogenic events cause distinctive structural phenomena and related tectonic activity, affect certain regions of rocks and crust and happen within a time frame.
- a. Thing
- b. Orogeny0
- c. Undefined
- d. Undefined

140. _____ is the process in which an unstable atomic nucleus loses energy by emitting radiation in the form of particles or electromagnetic waves.
- a. Thing
- b. Radioactive decay0
- c. Undefined
- d. Undefined

141. _____, 1st Viscount St Alban was an English philosopher, statesman, and essayist, but is best known as a philosophical advocate and defender of the scientific revolution. Indeed, his dedication brought him into a rare historical group of scientists who were killed by their own experiments.
- a. Person
- b. Francis Bacon0
- c. Undefined
- d. Undefined

142. _____ is the fifth planet from the Sun and the largest planet within the solar system. It is two and a half times as massive as all of the other planets in our solar system combined. _____, along with Saturn, Uranus and Neptune, is classified as a gas giant.
- a. Jupiter0
- b. Place
- c. Undefined
- d. Undefined

143. The _____ is Earth's only natural satellite. It makes a complete orbit around the Earth every 27.3 days, and the periodic variations in the geometry of the Earth–_____–Sun system are responsible for the lunar phases that repeat every 29.5 days.
- a. Moon0
- b. Thing
- c. Undefined
- d. Undefined

Chapter 1. FLUIDS IN THE CRUST: THE SCIENCE OF HYDROGEOLOGY

144. _____ was an Italian physicist, mathematician, astronomer, and philosopher closely associated with the scientific revolution. His achievements include the first systematic studies of uniformly accelerated motion, improvements to the telescope, a variety of astronomical observations, and support for Copernicanism.
   a. Galileo Galilei0
   b. Person
   c. Undefined
   d. Undefined

145. A _____ is an instrument designed for the observation of remote objects. The term usually refers to optical telescopes, but there are telescopes for most of the spectrum of electromagnetic radiation and for other signal types.
   a. Thing
   b. Telescope0
   c. Undefined
   d. Undefined

146. The _____ is defined as the summation of all particles and energy that exist and the space-time in which all events occur.
   a. Place
   b. Universe0
   c. Undefined
   d. Undefined

147. _____ is the substance of which physical objects are composed. _____ can be solid, liquid, plasma or gas. It constitutes the observable universe.
   a. Thing
   b. Matter0
   c. Undefined
   d. Undefined

148. _____ is a soft white lustrous transition metal, it has the highest electrical and thermal conductivity for a metal.
   a. Thing
   b. Silver0
   c. Undefined
   d. Undefined

149. The term _____ is used to categorize countries with developed economies in which the tertiary and quaternary sectors of industry dominate. This level of economic development usually translates into a high income per capita and a high Human Development Index.
   a. Thing
   b. Developed country0
   c. Undefined
   d. Undefined

150. A _____ is a biological agent that causes disease or illness to its host.
   a. Thing
   b. Pathogen0
   c. Undefined
   d. Undefined

Chapter 2. DARCY`S LAW AND HYDRAULIC HEAD

1. In geology, a _____ is the outermost layer of a planet, part of its lithosphere. They are generally composed of a less dense material than its deeper layers. Earths' is composed mainly of basalt and granite. It is cooler and more rigid than the deeper layers of the mantle and core.
   - a. Thing
   - b. Crust0
   - c. Undefined
   - d. Undefined

2. _____ is the work done by a force when the relative positions of objects are changed within a physical system. In other words, it is the work done when an object is moved from one point to another. Conceptually, _____ can be thought of as the energy of an object as a result of the work done to bring it to that position from a reference point.
   - a. Thing
   - b. Potential energy0
   - c. Undefined
   - d. Undefined

3. _____, symbolically represented as K, is a property of vascular plants, soil or rock, that describes the ease with which water can move through pore spaces or fractures
   - a. Thing
   - b. Hydraulic Conductivity0
   - c. Undefined
   - d. Undefined

4. In physics, _____ is defined as the rate of change of displacement or the rate of displacement. Simply put, it is distance per units of time.
   - a. Thing
   - b. Velocity0
   - c. Undefined
   - d. Undefined

5. _____ is the part of hydrology that deals with the distribution and movement of groundwater in the soil and rocks of the Earth's crust.
   - a. Thing
   - b. Hydrogeology0
   - c. Undefined
   - d. Undefined

6. The _____ is a physical quantity that describes in which direction and at what rate the pressure changes the most rapidly around a particular location. The _____ is a dimensional quantity expressed in units of pressure per unit length.
   - a. Thing
   - b. Pressure gradient0
   - c. Undefined
   - d. Undefined

7. _____, in everyday life, is most familiar as the agency that endows objects with weight. _____ is responsible for keeping the Earth and the other planets in their orbits around the Sun; for the formation of tides; and for various other phenomena that we observe. _____ is also the reason for the very existence of the Earth, the Sun, and most macroscopic objects in the universe; without it, matter would not have coalesced into these large masses, and life, as we know it, would not exist.
   - a. Thing
   - b. Gravitation0
   - c. Undefined
   - d. Undefined

8. In physics, _____ is the upward force on an object produced by the surrounding fluid in which it is fully or partially immersed, due to the pressure difference of the fluid between the top and bottom of the object. The net upward _____ force is equal to the magnitude of the weight of fluid displaced by the body.
   - a. Thing
   - b. Buoyancy0
   - c. Undefined
   - d. Undefined

Chapter 2. DARCY`S LAW AND HYDRAULIC HEAD   21

9. _____ is the saltiness or dissolved salt content of a body of water. In oceanography, it has been traditional to express halinity not as percent, but as parts per thousand, which is approximately grams of salt per liter of solution.
   a. Thing
   b. Salinity0
   c. Undefined
   d. Undefined

10. A _____ is formed when a thick bed of evaporite minerals found at depth intrudes vertically into surrounding rock strata, forming a diapir.
    a. Thing
    b. Salt dome0
    c. Undefined
    d. Undefined

11. In geology, a _____ is a deformational feature consisting of symmetrically-dipping anticlines; their general outline on a geologic map is circular or oval.
    a. Thing
    b. Dome0
    c. Undefined
    d. Undefined

12. In geology, _____ refers to heat sources within the planet. The planet's internal heat was originally generated during its accretion, due to gravitational binding energy, and since then additional heat has continued to be generated by the radioactive decay of elements such as uranium, thorium, and potassium.
    a. Geothermal0
    b. Thing
    c. Undefined
    d. Undefined

13. In the earth sciences, _____ is a measure of the ability of a material to transmit fluids. It is of great importance in determining the flow characteristics of hydrocarbons in oil and gas reservoirs, and of groundwater in aquifers.
    a. Thing
    b. Permeability0
    c. Undefined
    d. Undefined

14. _____ are where one sedimetary deposit ends and another one begins. The rock is prone to breakage at these points because of the weakness between the layers.
    a. Bedding planes0
    b. Thing
    c. Undefined
    d. Undefined

15. _____ rock is one of the three main rock groups. Rock formed from these covers 75% of the Earth's land area, and includes common types such as chalk, limestone, dolomite, sandstone, and shale.
    a. Sedimentary0
    b. Thing
    c. Undefined
    d. Undefined

16. _____ is one of the three main rock groups. _____ covers 75% of the Earth's land area. Four basic processes are involved in the formation of a clastic _____: weathering caused mainly by friction of waves, transportation where the sediment is carried along by a current, deposition and compaction where the sediment is squashed together to form a rock of this kind.
    a. Thing
    b. Sedimentary rock0
    c. Undefined
    d. Undefined

17. _____ is a small island located in the middle of San Francisco Bay in California, United States. It served as a lighthouse, then a military fortification, then a military prison followed by a federal prison until 1963, when it became a national recreation area.

Chapter 2. DARCY`S LAW AND HYDRAULIC HEAD

    a. Place
    b. Alcatraz Island0
    c. Undefined
    d. Undefined

18. A _____ is a body of water with a current, confined within a bed and banks. Streams are important as conduits in the water cycle, instruments in aquifer recharge, and corridors for fish and wildlife migration.
    a. Stream0
    b. Thing
    c. Undefined
    d. Undefined

19. _____ is the natural or artificial removal of surface and sub-surface water from a given area. Many agricultural soils need _____ to improve production or to manage water supplies.
    a. Drainage0
    b. Thing
    c. Undefined
    d. Undefined

20. In chemistry, a _____ is defined as a sufficiently stable electrically neutral group of at least two atoms in a definite arrangement held together by strong chemical bonds.
    a. Molecule0
    b. Thing
    c. Undefined
    d. Undefined

21. _____ is a measure of the void spaces in a material, and is measured as a fraction, between 0–1, or as a percentage between 0–100%.
    a. Thing
    b. Porosity0
    c. Undefined
    d. Undefined

22. _____ is water located beneath the ground surface in soil pore spaces and in the fractures of geologic formations. _____ is recharged from, and eventually flows to, the surface naturally; natural discharge often occurs at springs and seeps, streams and can often form oases or wetlands.
    a. Groundwater0
    b. Thing
    c. Undefined
    d. Undefined

23. _____ are habitats characterized by open, low growing woody vegetation, found on mainly infertile acidic soils. In the latter respect they are similar to moorland, but they differ in terms of climate, it is generally warmer and drier than moorland, and vegetation.
    a. Thing
    b. Heaths0
    c. Undefined
    d. Undefined

24. _____ is the third or vertical dimension of land surface. When _____ is described underwater, the term bathymetry is used.
    a. Terrain0
    b. Thing
    c. Undefined
    d. Undefined

25. _____ deals with soil as a natural resource on the surface of the earth including soil formation, classification and mapping; physical, chemical, biological, and fertility properties of soils per se; and these properties in relation to the use and management of soils.
    a. Soil science0
    b. Thing
    c. Undefined
    d. Undefined

Chapter 2. DARCY`S LAW AND HYDRAULIC HEAD

26. A _____ is the amount of force required to accelerate a body with a mass of one kilogram at a rate of one meter per second squared.
   a. Thing
   b. Newton0
   c. Undefined
   d. Undefined

27. _____ is a layer of gases surrounding the planet Earth and retained by the Earth's gravity. This mixture of gases is commonly known as air.
   a. Thing
   b. Earths atmosphere0
   c. Undefined
   d. Undefined

28. _____ is the pressure at any point in the Earth's atmosphere.
   a. Thing
   b. Atmospheric pressure0
   c. Undefined
   d. Undefined

29. In physics, the _____ states that the total amount of energy in an isolated system remains constant, although it may change forms, e.g. friction turns kinetic energy into thermal energy. In thermodynamics, the first law of thermodynamics is a statement of the _____ for thermodynamic systems, and is the more encompassing version of the _____.
   a. Conservation of energy0
   b. Thing
   c. Undefined
   d. Undefined

30. The _____ of an object is the extra energy which it possesses due to its motion. It is defined as the work needed to accelerate a body of a given mass from rest to its current velocity. Term or phrase NOT in the knowledge-core.
   a. Kinetic energy0
   b. Thing
   c. Undefined
   d. Undefined

31. _____ is the branch of Earth Sciences that studies the Earth's oceans and seas. It covers a wide range of topics, including marine organisms and ecosystem dynamics; ocean currents, waves, and geophysical fluid dynamics; plate tectonics and the geology of the sea floor; and fluxes of various chemical substances and physical properties within the ocean and across its boundaries.
   a. Oceanography0
   b. Thing
   c. Undefined
   d. Undefined

32. An _____ is an underground layer of water-bearing permeable rock or unconsolidated materials from which groundwater can be usefully extracted using a water well.
   a. Thing
   b. Aquifer0
   c. Undefined
   d. Undefined

33. Mean _____ is the average height of the sea, with reference to a suitable reference surface.
   a. Thing
   b. Sea level0
   c. Undefined
   d. Undefined

34. _____ is a general term for a variety of phenomena resulting from the presence and flow of charge. This includes many well-known physical phenomena such as lightning, electromagnetic fields and electric currents, and is put to use in industrial applications such as electronics and electric power.

Chapter 2. DARCY`S LAW AND HYDRAULIC HEAD

    a. Thing   b. Electricity0
    c. Undefined   d. Undefined

35. The _____ all have abundant watery juice, furrowed scaly bark which is heavily charged with salicylic acid, soft, pliant, tough wood, slender branches and large fibrous often stoloniferious roots. These roots are remarkable for their toughness, size, and tenacity of life.
    a. Thing   b. Willows0
    c. Undefined   d. Undefined

36. _____ is the most commonly used technique within the science of archaeology. It is the exposure, processing and recording of archaeological remains.
    a. Excavation0   b. Thing
    c. Undefined   d. Undefined

37. A _____ is a landform that extends above the surrounding terrain in a limited area. A _____ is generally steeper than a hill, but there is no universally accepted standard definition for the height of a _____ or a hill although a _____ usually has an identifiable summit.
    a. Place   b. Mountain0
    c. Undefined   d. Undefined

38. _____ is the extraction of valuable minerals or other geological materials from the earth, usually from an ore body, vein, or seam. Any material that cannot be grown from agricultural processes, or created artificially in a laboratory or factory, is usually extracted from the earth by this method.
    a. Thing   b. Mining0
    c. Undefined   d. Undefined

39. A _____ in geology is an intrusive igneous rock body that crystallized from a magma below the surface of the Earth. Plutons include batholiths, dikes, sills, laccoliths, lopoliths, and other igneous bodies. In practice, "_____" usually refers to a distinctive mass of igneous rock, typically kilometers in dimension, without a tabular shape like those of dikes and sills.
    a. Pluton0   b. Thing
    c. Undefined   d. Undefined

40. _____ is the production of food, feed, fiber, fuel and other goods by the systematic raizing of plants and animals.
    a. Agriculture0   b. Thing
    c. Undefined   d. Undefined

41. _____ is the science and study of the solid matter that constitute the Earth. Encompassing such things as rocks, soil, and gemstones, _____ studies the composition, structure, physical properties, history, and the processes that shape Earth's components.
    a. Thing   b. Geology0
    c. Undefined   d. Undefined

42. The _____ is a scientific agency of the United States government. The scientists of the USGS study the landscape of the United States, its natural resources, and the natural hazards that threaten it.

Chapter 2. DARCY`S LAW AND HYDRAULIC HEAD

a. U.S. Geological Survey0
b. Person
c. Undefined
d. Undefined

43. _____ is the substance of which physical objects are composed. _____ can be solid, liquid, plasma or gas. It constitutes the observable universe.
a. Matter0
b. Thing
c. Undefined
d. Undefined

44. A _____ is a naturally occurring substance formed through geological processes that has a characteristic chemical composition, a highly ordered atomic structure and specific physical properties. A rock, by comparison, is an aggregate of minerals and need not have a specific chemical composition. Minerals range in composition from pure elements and simple salts to very complex silicates with thousands of known forms.
a. Mineral0
b. Thing
c. Undefined
d. Undefined

45. _____ is the native consolidated rock underlying the Earth's surface. Above the _____ is usually an area of broken and weathered unconsolidated rock in the basal subsoil.
a. Bedrock0
b. Thing
c. Undefined
d. Undefined

46. _____ is any particulate matter that can be transported by fluid flow and which eventually is deposited as a layer of solid particles on the bed or bottom of a body of water or other liquid.
a. Thing
b. Sediment0
c. Undefined
d. Undefined

47. A _____ is a wet place where a liquid, usually groundwater, has oozed from the ground to the surface. They are usually not flowing, with the liquid sourced only from underground. The term may also refer to the movement of liquid hydrocarbons to the surface through fractures and fissures in the rock and between geological layers. It may be a significant source of pollution.
a. Seep0
b. Thing
c. Undefined
d. Undefined

48. A _____ is a wetland that features temporary or permanent inundation of large areas of land by shallow bodies of water, generally with a substantial number of hummocks, or dry-land protrusions, and covered by aquatic vegetation, or vegetation that tolerates periodical inundation.
a. Swamp0
b. Thing
c. Undefined
d. Undefined

49. A _____ is a body of water or other liquid of considerable size contained on a body of land. A vast majority are fresh water, and lie in the Northern Hemisphere at higher latitudes. Most have a natural outflow in the form of a river or stream, but some do not, and lose water solely by evaporation and/or underground seepage.
a. Lake0
b. Thing
c. Undefined
d. Undefined

50. An _____ is a volume of rock containing components or minerals in a mode of occurrence that renders it valuable for mining.

26 Chapter 2. DARCY`S LAW AND HYDRAULIC HEAD

   a. Thing
   b. Ore0
   c. Undefined
   d. Undefined

51. _____ in meteorology are large scale patterns in the atmospheric pressure field that are nearly stationary, effectively "blocking" or redirecting migratory cyclones. These _____ can remain in place for several days or even weeks, causing the areas affected by them to have the same kind of weather for an extended period of time.
   a. Thing
   b. Blocks0
   c. Undefined
   d. Undefined

52. In physics, a _____ is a solenoidal vector field in the space surrounding moving electric charges and magnetic dipoles, such as those in electric currents and magnets.
   a. Magnetic field0
   b. Thing
   c. Undefined
   d. Undefined

53. _____ is one of the phenomena by which materials exert attractive or repulsive forces on other materials. Some well known materials that exhibit easily detectable magnetic properties are nickel, iron, some steels, and the mineral magnetite; however, all materials are influenced to greater or lesser degree by the presence of a magnetic field.
   a. Magnetism0
   b. Thing
   c. Undefined
   d. Undefined

54. _____ is the physics of the electromagnetic field: a field which exerts a force on particles that possess the property of electric charge, and is in turn affected by the presence and motion of those particles. The magnetic field is produced by the motion of electric charges, i.e. electric current.
   a. Electromagnetism0
   b. Thing
   c. Undefined
   d. Undefined

55. _____ refers to the diameter of individual grains of sediment, or the lithified particles in clastic rocks. The term may also be applied to other granular materials. This is different from the crystallite size, which is the size of a single crystal inside the particles or grains.
   a. Particle size0
   b. Thing
   c. Undefined
   d. Undefined

56. _____ is a flow regime characterized by chaotic, stochastic property changes. This includes low momentum diffusion, high momentum convection, and rapid variation of pressure and velocity in space and time.
   a. Turbulent flow0
   b. Thing
   c. Undefined
   d. Undefined

57. _____, occurs when a fluid flows in parallel layers, with no disruption between the layers. In fluid dynamics, _____ is a flow regime characterized by high momentum diffusion, low momentum convection, and pressure and velocity independence from time.
   a. Laminar flow0
   b. Thing
   c. Undefined
   d. Undefined

58. _____ is a stress state where the stress is parallel or tangential to a face of the material, as opposed to normal stress when the stress is perpendicular to the face. The variable used to denote _____ is τ.

a. Shear stress0
b. Thing
c. Undefined
d. Undefined

Chapter 3. PROPERTIES OF POROUS MEDIA

1. _____ is any particulate matter that can be transported by fluid flow and which eventually is deposited as a layer of solid particles on the bed or bottom of a body of water or other liquid.
   - a. Thing
   - b. Sediment0
   - c. Undefined
   - d. Undefined

2. _____ is the process of a material being more closely packed together.
   - a. Compaction0
   - b. Thing
   - c. Undefined
   - d. Undefined

3. _____ is a measure of the void spaces in a material, and is measured as a fraction, between 0–1, or as a percentage between 0–100%.
   - a. Thing
   - b. Porosity0
   - c. Undefined
   - d. Undefined

4. _____ is the process of deposition of dissolved mineral components in the interstices of sediments. It is an important factor in the consolidation of coarse-grained clastic sedimentary rocks such as sandstones, conglomerates, or breccias during diagenesis or lithification. Cementing materials may include silica, carbonates, iron oxides, or clay minerals.
   - a. Cementation0
   - b. Thing
   - c. Undefined
   - d. Undefined

5. A _____ is a solid in which the constituent atoms, molecules, or ions are packed in a regularly ordered, repeating pattern extending in all three spatial dimensions. Most metals encountered in everyday life are polycrystals. Crystals are often symmetrically intergrown to form _____ twins.
   - a. Thing
   - b. Crystal0
   - c. Undefined
   - d. Undefined

6. _____ is rock that is of a certain particle size range. In geology, _____ is any loose rock that is at least two millimeters in its largest dimension and no more than 75 millimeters.
   - a. Thing
   - b. Gravel0
   - c. Undefined
   - d. Undefined

7. _____ is soil or rock derived granular material of a specific grain size. _____ may occur as a soil or alternatively as suspended sediment in a water column of any surface water body. It may also exist as deposition soil at the bottom of a water body.
   - a. Thing
   - b. Silt0
   - c. Undefined
   - d. Undefined

8. _____ refers to the diameter of individual grains of sediment, or the lithified particles in clastic rocks. The term may also be applied to other granular materials. This is different from the crystallite size, which is the size of a single crystal inside the particles or grains.
   - a. Particle size0
   - b. Thing
   - c. Undefined
   - d. Undefined

9. _____ is any product of the condensation of atmospheric water vapor that is deposited on the earth's surface. It occurs when the atmosphere becomes saturated with water vapour and the water condenses and falls out of solution. Air becomes saturated via two processes, cooling and adding moisture.

Chapter 3. PROPERTIES OF POROUS MEDIA

a. Thing	b. Precipitation0
c. Undefined	d. Undefined

10. _____ is a term used to describe a group of hydrous aluminium phyllosilicate minerals, that are typically less than 2 micrometres in diameter. _____ consists of a variety of phyllosilicate minerals rich in silicon and aluminium oxides and hydroxides which include variable amounts of structural water. Clays are generally formed by the chemical weathering of silicate-bearing rocks by carbonic acid but some are formed by hydrothermal activity.

a. Clay0	b. Thing
c. Undefined	d. Undefined

11. An _____ is a term for any perforation through the Earth's surface designed to find and release both petroleum oil and gas hydrocarbons.

a. Thing	b. Oil well0
c. Undefined	d. Undefined

12. _____ is a fine-grained sedimentary rock whose original constituents were clays or muds. It is characterized by thin laminae breaking with an irregular curving fracture, often splintery and usually parallel to the often-indistinguishable bedding plane.

a. Thing	b. Shale0
c. Undefined	d. Undefined

13. The _____ is an epoch of the Carboniferous period lasting from roughly 325 Ma to 299 Ma. As with most other geologic periods, the rock beds that define the period are well identified, but the exact date of the start and end are uncertain by a few million years.

a. Thing	b. Pennsylvanian0
c. Undefined	d. Undefined

14. _____ is a sedimentary rock composed mainly of sand-size mineral or rock grains. Most _____ is composed of quartz and/or feldspar because these are the most common minerals in the Earth's crust. Like sand, _____ may be any color, but the most common colors are tan, brown, yellow, red, gray and white.

a. Thing	b. Sandstone0
c. Undefined	d. Undefined

15. _____ is the second most common mineral in the Earth's continental crust. It is made up of a lattice of silica tetrahedra. _____ belongs to the rhombohedral crystal system. In nature _____ crystals are often twinned, distorted, or so intergrown with adjacent crystals of _____ or other minerals as to only show part of this shape, or to lack obvious crystal faces altogether and appear massive.

a. Quartz0	b. Thing
c. Undefined	d. Undefined

16. The _____ is a major division of the geologic timescale that extends from the end of the Devonian period to the beginning of the Permian period. As with most older geologic periods, the rock beds that define the period's start and end are well identified, but the exact dates are uncertain. The first third of the _____ is called the Mississippian epoch, and the remainder is called the Pennsylvanian.

Chapter 3. PROPERTIES OF POROUS MEDIA

  a. Carboniferous0
  b. Thing
  c. Undefined
  d. Undefined

17. _____ is the part of hydrology that deals with the distribution and movement of groundwater in the soil and rocks of the Earth's crust.
  a. Thing
  b. Hydrogeology0
  c. Undefined
  d. Undefined

18. The _____ is the last period of the Palaeozoic Era. As the _____ opened, the Earth was still in the grip of an ice age, so the polar regions were covered with deep layers of ice. During the _____, all the Earth's major land masses except portions of East Asia were collected into a single supercontinent known as Pangaea. The _____ ended with the most extensive extinction event recorded in paleontology: the _____-Triassic extinction event.
  a. Thing
  b. Permian0
  c. Undefined
  d. Undefined

19. In geology, _____ refers to heat sources within the planet. The planet's internal heat was originally generated during its accretion, due to gravitational binding energy, and since then additional heat has continued to be generated by the radioactive decay of elements such as uranium, thorium, and potassium.
  a. Thing
  b. Geothermal0
  c. Undefined
  d. Undefined

20. The _____ is the rate of increase in temperature per unit depth in the Earth. It varies with location and is typically measured by determining the bottom open-hole temperature after the drilling of a borehole.
  a. Thing
  b. Geothermal gradient0
  c. Undefined
  d. Undefined

21. A _____ is a process that results in the interconversion of chemical substances. The substance or substances initially involved in a _____ are called reactants. Chemical reactions are characterized by a chemical change, and they yield one or more products which are, in general, different from the reactants.
  a. Chemical reaction0
  b. Thing
  c. Undefined
  d. Undefined

22. In geology, _____ is soil at or below the freezing point of water for two or more years. Ice is not always present, as may be in the case of nonporous bedrock, but it frequently occurs and it may be in amounts exceeding the potential hydraulic saturation of the ground material. Most _____ is located in high latitudes, but alpine _____ exists at high altitudes.
  a. Permafrost0
  b. Thing
  c. Undefined
  d. Undefined

23. In the earth sciences, _____ is a measure of the ability of a material to transmit fluids. It is of great importance in determining the flow characteristics of hydrocarbons in oil and gas reservoirs, and of groundwater in aquifers.
  a. Permeability0
  b. Thing
  c. Undefined
  d. Undefined

24. _____ is the part of Earth's lithosphere that surfaces in the ocean basins. _____ is primarily composed of mafic rocks, or sima. It is thinner than continental crust, or sial, generally less than 10 kilometers thick, however it is more dense, having a mean density of about 3.3 grams per cubic centimeter.

Chapter 3. PROPERTIES OF POROUS MEDIA

a. Oceanic crust0
b. Thing
c. Undefined
d. Undefined

25. The _____ is the layer of granitic, sedimentary, and metamorphic rocks which form the continents and the areas of shallow seabed close to their shores, known as continental shelves. It is less dense than the material of the Earth's mantle and thus "floats" on top of it. _____ is also less dense than oceanic crust, though it is considerably thicker. About 40% of the Earth's surface is now underlain by _____.
a. Thing
b. Continental crust0
c. Undefined
d. Undefined

26. Faults are planar rock fractures, which show evidence of relative movement. Large faults within the Earth's crust are the result of shear motion and active _____ zones are the causal locations of most earthquakes. Earthquakes are caused by energy release during rapid slippage along faults. The largest examples are at tectonic plate boundaries but many faults occur far from active plate boundaries. Since faults do not usually consist of a single, clean fracture, the term _____ zone is used when referring to the zone of complex deformation that is associated with the _____ plane.
a. Thing
b. Fault0
c. Undefined
d. Undefined

27. _____ is a sedimentary rock composed largely of the mineral calcite. _____ often contains variable amounts of silica in the form of chert or flint, as well as varying amounts of clay, silt and sand as disseminations, nodules, or layers within the rock. The primary source of the calcite in _____ is most commonly marine organisms. These organisms secrete shells that settle out of the water column and are deposited on ocean floors as pelagic ooze or alternatively is conglomerated in a coral reef.
a. Thing
b. Limestone0
c. Undefined
d. Undefined

28. In geology, a _____ is the outermost layer of a planet, part of its lithosphere. They are generally composed of a less dense material than its deeper layers. Earths' is composed mainly of basalt and granite. It is cooler and more rigid than the deeper layers of the mantle and core.
a. Crust0
b. Thing
c. Undefined
d. Undefined

29. An _____ is an underground layer of water-bearing permeable rock or unconsolidated materials from which groundwater can be usefully extracted using a water well.
a. Thing
b. Aquifer0
c. Undefined
d. Undefined

30. An _____ is a zone within the earth that restricts the flow of groundwater from one aquifer to another.
a. Aquitard0
b. Thing
c. Undefined
d. Undefined

31. A _____ is any aspect of an object or substance that can be measured or perceived without changing its identity. Physical properties can be intensive or extensive. An intensive property does not depend on the size or amount of matter in the object, while an extensive property does.

Chapter 3. PROPERTIES OF POROUS MEDIA

a. Thing
b. Physical property0
c. Undefined
d. Undefined

32. _____ is the theory that Earth has been affected by sudden, short-lived, violent events that were sometimes worldwide in scope. The dominant paradigm of geology has been uniformitarianism, but recently a more inclusive and integrated view of geologic events has developed resulting in a gradual change in the scientific consensus, reflecting acceptance of some catastrophic events.
a. Thing
b. Catastrophism0
c. Undefined
d. Undefined

33. A _____, is a site for the disposal of waste materials by burial and is the oldest form of waste treatment.
a. Thing
b. Landfill0
c. Undefined
d. Undefined

34. _____, symbolically represented as K, is a property of vascular plants, soil or rock, that describes the ease with which water can move through pore spaces or fractures
a. Thing
b. Hydraulic Conductivity0
c. Undefined
d. Undefined

35. _____ is the third or vertical dimension of land surface. When _____ is described underwater, the term bathymetry is used.
a. Terrain0
b. Thing
c. Undefined
d. Undefined

36. An _____ is the result from the sudden release of stored energy in the Earth's crust that creates seismic waves. At the Earth's surface, earthquakes may manifest themselves by a shaking or displacement of the ground. An _____ is caused by tectonic plates getting stuck and putting a strain on the ground. The strain becomes so great that rocks give way by breaking and sliding along fault planes.
a. Thing
b. Earthquake0
c. Undefined
d. Undefined

37. _____ is the oxide of silicon, chemical formula SiO_2, and is known for its hardness as early as the 16th century. It is a principle component in most types of glass and substances such as concrete.
a. Thing
b. Silica0
c. Undefined
d. Undefined

38. A _____ is a naturally occurring substance formed through geological processes that has a characteristic chemical composition, a highly ordered atomic structure and specific physical properties. A rock, by comparison, is an aggregate of minerals and need not have a specific chemical composition. Minerals range in composition from pure elements and simple salts to very complex silicates with thousands of known forms.
a. Thing
b. Mineral0
c. Undefined
d. Undefined

39. _____ rock is one of the three main rock groups. Rock formed from these covers 75% of the Earth's land area, and includes common types such as chalk, limestone, dolomite, sandstone, and shale.

Chapter 3. PROPERTIES OF POROUS MEDIA 33

    a. Sedimentary0   b. Thing
    c. Undefined   d. Undefined

40. _____ is one of the three main rock groups. _____ covers 75% of the Earth's land area. Four basic processes are involved in the formation of a clastic _____: weathering caused mainly by friction of waves, transportation where the sediment is carried along by a current, deposition and compaction where the sediment is squashed together to form a rock of this kind.
    a. Sedimentary rock0   b. Thing
    c. Undefined   d. Undefined

41. The term _____ is used to refer to any geographical feature exhibiting subsidence and consequent infilling by sedimentation. As the sediments are buried, they are subjected to increasing pressure and begin the process of lithification.
    a. Thing   b. Sedimentary basin0
    c. Undefined   d. Undefined

42. _____ is a field of geology which focuses on the study of rocks and the conditions by which they form. There are three branches of _____, corresponding to the three types of rocks: igneous, metamorphic, and sedimentary. _____ utilizes the classical fields of mineralogy, petrography, optical mineralogy, and chemical analyses to describe the composition and texture of rocks.
    a. Petrology0   b. Thing
    c. Undefined   d. Undefined

43. A _____ should ideally be a distinctive rock that forms under certain conditions of sedimentation, reflecting a particular process or environment.
    a. Facies0   b. Thing
    c. Undefined   d. Undefined

44. _____ is a small island located in the middle of San Francisco Bay in California, United States. It served as a lighthouse, then a military fortification, then a military prison followed by a federal prison until 1963, when it became a national recreation area.
    a. Place   b. Alcatraz Island0
    c. Undefined   d. Undefined

45. A _____ is a tidal phenomenon in which the leading edge of the incoming tide forms a wave of water that travel up a river or narrow bay against the direction of the current. As such, it is a true tidal wave.
    a. Thing   b. Bore0
    c. Undefined   d. Undefined

46. _____ is a naturally occurring liquid found in formations in the Earth consisting of a complex mixture of hydrocarbons of various lengths.
    a. Petroleum0   b. Thing
    c. Undefined   d. Undefined

47. _____ is the condition of a system in which competing influences are balanced.

a. Equilibrium0 b. Thing
c. Undefined d. Undefined

48. In physics, _____ is defined as the rate of change of displacement or the rate of displacement. Simply put, it is distance per units of time.
 a. Thing b. Velocity0
 c. Undefined d. Undefined

49. _____ is water located beneath the ground surface in soil pore spaces and in the fractures of geologic formations. _____ is recharged from, and eventually flows to, the surface naturally; natural discharge often occurs at springs and seeps, streams and can often form oases or wetlands.
 a. Thing b. Groundwater0
 c. Undefined d. Undefined

50. _____ is the process by which water on the ground surface enters the soil.
 a. Thing b. Infiltration0
 c. Undefined d. Undefined

51. The _____ is defined as the part of the land adjoining or near the ocean. A coastline is properly a line on a map indicating the disposition of a _____, but the word is often used to refer to the _____ itself. The adjective coastal describes something as being on, near to, or associated with a _____.
 a. Place b. Coast0
 c. Undefined d. Undefined

52. The _____ provides the only reliable source of water through much of inland Australia. The basin is the largest and deepest artesian basin in the world. The basin is 3000 metres deep in places and is estimated to contain 64,900 cubic kilometres of groundwater.
 a. Thing b. Great Artesian Basin0
 c. Undefined d. Undefined

53. _____ is a measure of the resistance of a fluid to deform under shear stress. It is commonly perceived as "thickness", or resistance to flow. _____ describes a fluid's internal resistance to flow and may be thought of as a measure of fluid friction.
 a. Thing b. Viscosity0
 c. Undefined d. Undefined

54. _____ is a common and widely occurring type of intrusive, felsic, igneous rock. Granites are usually medium to coarsely crystalline, occasionally with some individual crystals larger than the groundmass forming a rock known as porphyry. Granites can be pink to dark gray or even black, depending on their chemistry and mineralogy.
 a. Thing b. Granite0
 c. Undefined d. Undefined

Chapter 3. PROPERTIES OF POROUS MEDIA

55. _____ is the process of breaking down rocks, soils and their minerals through direct contact with the atmosphere. _____ occurs without movement. Two main classifications of _____ processes exist. Mechanical or physical _____ involves the breakdown of rocks and soils through direct contact with atmospheric conditions. The second classification, chemical _____, involves the direct effect of atmospheric chemicals in the breakdown of rocks, soils and minerals.
   a. Thing
   b. Weathering0
   c. Undefined
   d. Undefined

56. _____ is the result of the transformation of a pre-existing rock type, the protolith, in a process called metamorphism, which means "change in form". The protolith is subjected to heat and extreme pressure causing profound physical and/or chemical change. The protolith may be sedimentary rock, igneous rock or another older rock.
   a. Thing
   b. Metamorphic rock0
   c. Undefined
   d. Undefined

57. Metamorphic rock is the result of the transformation of a pre-existing rock type, the protolith, in a process called metamorphism. The protolith is subjected to heat and extreme pressure causing profound physical and/or chemical change. _____ make up a large part of the Earth's crust. They are formed deep beneath the Earth's surface by great stresses from rocks above and high pressures and temperatures.
   a. Metamorphic rocks0
   b. Thing
   c. Undefined
   d. Undefined

58. _____ can be defined as the solid state recrystallisation of pre-existing rocks due to changes in heat and/or pressure and/or introduction of fluids. There will be mineralogical, chemical and crystallographic changes. _____ produced with increasing pressure and temperature conditions is known as prograde _____. Conversely, decreasing temperatures and pressure characterize retrograde _____.
   a. Metamorphism0
   b. Thing
   c. Undefined
   d. Undefined

59. An _____ is a volume of rock containing components or minerals in a mode of occurrence that renders it valuable for mining.
   a. Ore0
   b. Thing
   c. Undefined
   d. Undefined

60. _____ is the science and study of the solid matter that constitute the Earth. Encompassing such things as rocks, soil, and gemstones, _____ studies the composition, structure, physical properties, history, and the processes that shape Earth's components.
   a. Thing
   b. Geology0
   c. Undefined
   d. Undefined

61. _____ is the application of the geologic sciences to engineering practice for the purpose of assuring that the geologic factors affecting the location, design, construction, operation and maintenance of engineering works are recognized and adequately provided for.
   a. Thing
   b. Engineering geology0
   c. Undefined
   d. Undefined

36 *Chapter 3. PROPERTIES OF POROUS MEDIA*

62. In geology the term _____ refers to the system of forces that tend to decrease the volume of or shorten rocks. Compressive strength refers to the maximum compressive stress that can be applied to a material before failure occurs.
   a. Compression0
   b. Thing
   c. Undefined
   d. Undefined

63. _____ is a term used in geology to denote the pressure imposed on a stratigraphic layer by the weight of overlying layers of material.
   a. Event
   b. Lithostatic pressure0
   c. Undefined
   d. Undefined

64. In physics, _____ is the upward force on an object produced by the surrounding fluid in which it is fully or partially immersed, due to the pressure difference of the fluid between the top and bottom of the object. The net upward _____ force is equal to the magnitude of the weight of fluid displaced by the body.
   a. Buoyancy0
   b. Thing
   c. Undefined
   d. Undefined

65. _____, in everyday life, is most familiar as the agency that endows objects with weight. _____ is responsible for keeping the Earth and the other planets in their orbits around the Sun; for the formation of tides; and for various other phenomena that we observe. _____ is also the reason for the very existence of the Earth, the Sun, and most macroscopic objects in the universe; without it, matter would not have coalesced into these large masses, and life, as we know it, would not exist.
   a. Gravitation0
   b. Thing
   c. Undefined
   d. Undefined

66. A _____ is a natural depression or hole in the surface topography caused by the removal of soil or bedrock, often both, by water. They may vary in size from less than a meter to several hundred meters both in diameter and depth, and vary in form from soil-lined bowls to bedrock-edged chasms.
   a. Thing
   b. Sinkhole0
   c. Undefined
   d. Undefined

67. _____ of Syracuse was an ancient Greek mathematician, physicist and engineer. Although little is known about his life, he is regarded as one of the most important scientists in classical antiquity. In addition to making important discoveries in the field of mathematics and geometry, he is credited with producing machines that were well ahead of their time.
   a. Archimedes0
   b. Person
   c. Undefined
   d. Undefined

68. _____ is a highly sought-after precious metal which, for many centuries, has been used as money, a store of value and in jewelery. The metal occurs as nuggets or grains in rocks, underground "veins" and in alluvial deposits. It is one of the coinage metals. Itis dense, soft, shiny and the most malleable and ductile of the known metals.
   a. Gold0
   b. Thing
   c. Undefined
   d. Undefined

69. _____ is a soft white lustrous transition metal, it has the highest electrical and thermal conductivity for a metal.

Chapter 3. PROPERTIES OF POROUS MEDIA

a. Silver0
b. Thing
c. Undefined
d. Undefined

70. An _____ is any piece of land that is completely surrounded by water, above high tide. There are two main types of islands: continental islands and oceanic islands. There are also artificial islands. A grouping of geographically and/or geologically related islands is called an archipelago.

a. Island0
b. Thing
c. Undefined
d. Undefined

71. _____ is a chemical element metal. It is a lustrous, silvery soft metal. It and nickel are notable for being the final elements produced by stellar nucleosynthesis, and thus are the heaviest elements which do not require a supernova or similarly cataclysmic event for formation.

a. Iron0
b. Thing
c. Undefined
d. Undefined

72. _____ in the broad sense is the total spectrum of the electromagnetic radiation given off by the Sun. On Earth, it is filtered through the atmosphere, and the solar radiation is obvious as daylight when the Sun is above the horizon.

a. Sunlight0
b. Thing
c. Undefined
d. Undefined

73. _____ rocks form when molten rock, magma, cools and solidifies, with or without crystallization, either below the surface as intrusive, plutonic rocks or on the surface as extrusive, volcanic, rocks.

a. Igneous0
b. Thing
c. Undefined
d. Undefined

74. The _____ is used by geologists and other scientists to describe the timing and relationships between events that have occurred during the history of Earth.

a. Thing
b. Geological time scale0
c. Undefined
d. Undefined

75. The _____ are a small, isolated mountain range rizing from the Great Plains of North America in western South Dakota and extending into Wyoming, USA. Set off from the main body of the Rocky Mountains, the region is somewhat of a geological anomaly—accurately described as an "island of trees in a sea of grass.

a. Black Hills0
b. Place
c. Undefined
d. Undefined

76. A _____ is a section of land devoted to the production and management of food, either produce or livestock. It is the basic unit in agricultural production.

a. Thing
b. Farm0
c. Undefined
d. Undefined

77. Fossils are the mineralized or otherwise preserved remains or traces of animals, plants, and other organisms. The totality of fossils, both discovered and undiscovered, and their placement in fossiliferous rock formations and sedimentary layers is known as the _____ record.

Chapter 3. PROPERTIES OF POROUS MEDIA

a. Thing
b. Fossil0
c. Undefined
d. Undefined

78. In geology, _____ are rock s with a grain size of usually no less than 256 mm diameter.
a. Boulders0
b. Thing
c. Undefined
d. Undefined

79. A _____ is a section of a river of relatively steep gradient causing an increase in water flow and turbulence. A _____ is a hydrological feature between a run and a cascade. It is characterized by the river becoming shallower and having some rocks exposed above the flow surface.
a. Thing
b. Rapid0
c. Undefined
d. Undefined

80. _____ is the study of the movement, distribution, and quality of water throughout the Earth, and thus addresses both the hydrologic cycle and water resources.
a. Hydrology0
b. Thing
c. Undefined
d. Undefined

81. An _____ is a long period of time with different technical and colloquial meanings, and usages in language. It begins with some beginning event known as an epoch, epochal date, epochal event or epochal moment.
a. Era0
b. Thing
c. Undefined
d. Undefined

82. The _____ is a nonprofit organization dedicated to the advancement of the geosciences. The society was founded in New York in 1888 by James Hall, James D. Dana, and Alexander Winchell, and has been headquartered at 3300 Penrose Place, Boulder, Colorado since 1968. As of 2007, the society has over 21,000 members in more than 85 countries. The stated mission is "to advance the geosciences, to enhance the professional growth of its members, and to promote the geosciences in the service of humankind".
a. Geological Society of America0
b. Person
c. Undefined
d. Undefined

Chapter 4. PROPERTIES OF GEOLOGIC FLUIDS

1. _____ is a field of study within geology concerned generally with the structures within the crust of the Earth, or other planets, and particularly with the forces and movements that have operated in a region to create these structures.
   a. Thing
   b. Tectonics0
   c. Undefined
   d. Undefined

2. A _____ column is a column of rizing air in the lower altitudes of the Earth's atmosphere. Thermals are created by the uneven heating of the Earth's surface from solar radiation, and are an example of convection. The Sun warms the ground, which in turn warms the air directly above it.
   a. Thing
   b. Thermal0
   c. Undefined
   d. Undefined

3. _____ is water saturated or nearly saturated with salt and is a common fluid used in the transport of heat from place to place. It is used because the addition of salt to water lowers the freezing temperature of the solution and a relatively great efficiency in the transport can be obtained for the low cost of the material.
   a. Thing
   b. Brine0
   c. Undefined
   d. Undefined

4. In geology, a _____ is the outermost layer of a planet, part of its lithosphere. They are generally composed of a less dense material than its deeper layers. Earths' is composed mainly of basalt and granite. It is cooler and more rigid than the deeper layers of the mantle and core.
   a. Thing
   b. Crust0
   c. Undefined
   d. Undefined

5. An _____ is an atom or group of atoms which have lost or gained one or more electrons, making them negatively or positively charged.
   a. Thing
   b. Ion0
   c. Undefined
   d. Undefined

6. In chemistry, a _____ is defined as a sufficiently stable electrically neutral group of at least two atoms in a definite arrangement held together by strong chemical bonds.
   a. Thing
   b. Molecule0
   c. Undefined
   d. Undefined

7. _____ : a _____ is an ion with a positive charge. It is the inverse anion.
   a. Cation0
   b. Thing
   c. Undefined
   d. Undefined

8. An _____ is a negetive ion.
   a. Thing
   b. Anion0
   c. Undefined
   d. Undefined

9. _____ is the saltiness or dissolved salt content of a body of water. In oceanography, it has been traditional to express halinity not as percent, but as parts per thousand, which is approximately grams of salt per liter of solution.
   a. Thing
   b. Salinity0
   c. Undefined
   d. Undefined

Chapter 4. PROPERTIES OF GEOLOGIC FLUIDS

10. _____ is the part of Earth's lithosphere that surfaces in the ocean basins. _____ is primarily composed of mafic rocks, or sima. It is thinner than continental crust, or sial, generally less than 10 kilometers thick, however it is more dense, having a mean density of about 3.3 grams per cubic centimeter.
    a. Oceanic crust0
    b. Thing
    c. Undefined
    d. Undefined

11. _____ is a naturally occurring liquid found in formations in the Earth consisting of a complex mixture of hydrocarbons of various lengths.
    a. Thing
    b. Petroleum0
    c. Undefined
    d. Undefined

12. _____ usually refers to the thick foundation of ancient, and oldest metamorphic and igneous rock that forms the crust of continents, often in the form of granite. _____ is contrasted to overlying sedimentary rocks which are laid down on top of the basement rocks after the continent was formed, such as sandstone and limestone.
    a. Basement rock0
    b. Thing
    c. Undefined
    d. Undefined

13. _____ rock is one of the three main rock groups. Rock formed from these covers 75% of the Earth's land area, and includes common types such as chalk, limestone, dolomite, sandstone, and shale.
    a. Sedimentary0
    b. Thing
    c. Undefined
    d. Undefined

14. The term _____ is used to refer to any geographical feature exhibiting subsidence and consequent infilling by sedimentation. As the sediments are buried, they are subjected to increasing pressure and begin the process of lithification.
    a. Thing
    b. Sedimentary basin0
    c. Undefined
    d. Undefined

15. The _____ is a large shield covered by a thin layer of soil that forms the nucleus of the North American craton. It has a deep, common, joined bedrock region in eastern and central Canada and stretches North from the Great Lakes to the Arctic Ocean, covering half the country.
    a. Thing
    b. Canadian Shield0
    c. Undefined
    d. Undefined

16. _____ is the process by which molecules in a liquid state become a gas.
    a. Evaporation0
    b. Thing
    c. Undefined
    d. Undefined

17. _____ refers to water-soluble, mineral sediments that result from the evaporation of bodies of surficial water.
    a. Evaporite0
    b. Thing
    c. Undefined
    d. Undefined

18. _____ is water from a sea or ocean. On average, _____ in the world's oceans has a salinity of ~3.5%, or 35 parts per thousand. This means that every 1 kg of _____ has approximately 35 grams of dissolved salts.
    a. Seawater0
    b. Thing
    c. Undefined
    d. Undefined

Chapter 4. PROPERTIES OF GEOLOGIC FLUIDS

19. _____ is any particulate matter that can be transported by fluid flow and which eventually is deposited as a layer of solid particles on the bed or bottom of a body of water or other liquid.
    a. Sediment0
    b. Thing
    c. Undefined
    d. Undefined

20. The _____ is a geologic basin centered on the lower peninsula of the US state of Michigan. The feature is represented by a nearly circular pattern of geologic sedimentary strata in the area with a nearly uniform structural dip toward the center of the peninsula.
    a. Michigan Basin0
    b. Place
    c. Undefined
    d. Undefined

21. A _____ is a tidal phenomenon in which the leading edge of the incoming tide forms a wave of water that travel up a river or narrow bay against the direction of the current. As such, it is a true tidal wave.
    a. Thing
    b. Bore0
    c. Undefined
    d. Undefined

22. In inorganic chemistry, a _____ is a salt of sulfuric acid
    a. Sulfate0
    b. Thing
    c. Undefined
    d. Undefined

23. _____ contains low concentrations of dissolved salts and other total dissolved solids. It is an important renewable resource, necessary for the survival of most terrestrial organisms, and required by humans for drinking and agriculture, among many other uses.
    a. Thing
    b. Fresh water0
    c. Undefined
    d. Undefined

24. The _____ is defined as the part of the land adjoining or near the ocean. A coastline is properly a line on a map indicating the disposition of a _____, but the word is often used to refer to the _____ itself. The adjective coastal describes something as being on, near to, or associated with a _____.
    a. Coast0
    b. Place
    c. Undefined
    d. Undefined

25. The _____ region of the United States comprises the coasts of states which border the Gulf of Mexico. The states of Texas, Louisiana, Mississippi, Alabama, and Florida are known as the Gulf States. All Gulf States are located in the Southern region of the United States.
    a. Gulf Coast0
    b. Place
    c. Undefined
    d. Undefined

26. _____ is the part of hydrology that deals with the distribution and movement of groundwater in the soil and rocks of the Earth's crust.
    a. Thing
    b. Hydrogeology0
    c. Undefined
    d. Undefined

27. A _____ is a body of water or other liquid of considerable size contained on a body of land. A vast majority are fresh water, and lie in the Northern Hemisphere at higher latitudes. Most have a natural outflow in the form of a river or stream, but some do not, and lose water solely by evaporation and/or underground seepage.

Chapter 4. PROPERTIES OF GEOLOGIC FLUIDS

    a. Thing   b. Lake0
    c. Undefined   d. Undefined

28. _____ is an ecological concept referring to the relative representation of a species in a particular ecosystem. It is usually measured as the mean number of individuals found per sample.
    a. Thing   b. Abundance0
    c. Undefined   d. Undefined

29. _____ is the mineral form of sodium chloride. _____ forms isometric crystals. It commonly occurs with other evaporite deposit minerals such as several of the sulfates, halides and borates. _____ occurs in vast lakes of sedimentary evaporite minerals that result from the drying up of enclosed beds, playas, and seas.
    a. Halite0   b. Thing
    c. Undefined   d. Undefined

30. In geology, a _____ is a deformational feature consisting of symmetrically-dipping anticlines; their general outline on a geologic map is circular or oval.
    a. Dome0   b. Thing
    c. Undefined   d. Undefined

31. _____ is a term used to describe a group of hydrous aluminium phyllosilicate minerals, that are typically less than 2 micrometres in diameter. _____ consists of a variety of phyllosilicate minerals rich in silicon and aluminium oxides and hydroxides which include variable amounts of structural water. Clays are generally formed by the chemical weathering of silicate-bearing rocks by carbonic acid but some are formed by hydrothermal activity.
    a. Thing   b. Clay0
    c. Undefined   d. Undefined

32. A _____ is a naturally occurring substance formed through geological processes that has a characteristic chemical composition, a highly ordered atomic structure and specific physical properties. A rock, by comparison, is an aggregate of minerals and need not have a specific chemical composition. Minerals range in composition from pure elements and simple salts to very complex silicates with thousands of known forms.
    a. Mineral0   b. Thing
    c. Undefined   d. Undefined

33. _____ are hydrous aluminium phyllosilicates, sometimes with variable amounts of iron, magnesium, alkali metals, alkaline earths and other cations. Clays have structures similar to the micas and therefore form flat hexagonal sheets. _____ are common weathering products and low temperature hydrothermal alteration products.
    a. Clay minerals0   b. Thing
    c. Undefined   d. Undefined

34. _____ is a fine-grained sedimentary rock whose original constituents were clays or muds. It is characterized by thin laminae breaking with an irregular curving fracture, often splintery and usually parallel to the often-indistinguishable bedding plane.
    a. Shale0   b. Thing
    c. Undefined   d. Undefined

Chapter 4. PROPERTIES OF GEOLOGIC FLUIDS

35. _____ is a measure of the void spaces in a material, and is measured as a fraction, between 0–1, or as a percentage between 0–100%.
   a. Thing
   b. Porosity0
   c. Undefined
   d. Undefined

36. _____ is the science and study of the solid matter that constitute the Earth. Encompassing such things as rocks, soil, and gemstones, _____ studies the composition, structure, physical properties, history, and the processes that shape Earth's components.
   a. Thing
   b. Geology0
   c. Undefined
   d. Undefined

37. A _____ is an area of flat, low-lying land adjacent to a seacoast and separated from the interior by other features.
   a. Coastal plain0
   b. Thing
   c. Undefined
   d. Undefined

38. An _____ occurs in recharging aquifers, this happens because the water table at its recharge zone is at a higher elevation than the head of the well.
   a. Artesian well0
   b. Thing
   c. Undefined
   d. Undefined

39. The _____ is the flat stretch of land that borders the Atlantic Ocean. It is approximately 2,200 miles long, stretching from Newark, through the southeast United States and through Mexico, ending with the Yucatán Peninsula.
   a. Atlantic Coastal Plain0
   b. Place
   c. Undefined
   d. Undefined

40. A _____ is one of the major divisions of the year, generally based on yearly periodic changes in weather. They are recognized as: spring, summer, autumn, and winter.
   a. Season0
   b. Thing
   c. Undefined
   d. Undefined

41. The _____ are the broad expanse of prairie and steppe which lie east of the Rocky Mountains in the United States and Canada.
   a. Place
   b. Great Plains0
   c. Undefined
   d. Undefined

42. The _____ is a nonprofit organization dedicated to the advancement of the geosciences. The society was founded in New York in 1888 by James Hall, James D. Dana, and Alexander Winchell, and has been headquartered at 3300 Penrose Place, Boulder, Colorado since 1968. As of 2007, the society has over 21,000 members in more than 85 countries. The stated mission is "to advance the geosciences, to enhance the professional growth of its members, and to promote the geosciences in the service of humankind".
   a. Person
   b. Geological Society of America0
   c. Undefined
   d. Undefined

43. In geology and astronomy, the term _____ is used to denote types of rock that consist predominantly of _____ minerals. Such rocks include a wide range of igneous, metamorphic and sedimentary types. Most of the Earth's mantle and crust are made up of _____ rocks. The same is true of the Moon and the other rocky planets.

Chapter 4. PROPERTIES OF GEOLOGIC FLUIDS

a. Thing
b. Silicate0
c. Undefined
d. Undefined

44. A _____ is a process that results in the interconversion of chemical substances. The substance or substances initially involved in a _____ are called reactants. Chemical reactions are characterized by a chemical change, and they yield one or more products which are, in general, different from the reactants.
   a. Chemical reaction0
   b. Thing
   c. Undefined
   d. Undefined

45. _____ is one of the four seasons of temperate zones. Almost all English-language calendars, going by astronomy, state that _____ begins on the _____ solstice, and ends on the spring equinox. Calculated more by the weather, it begins and ends earlier and is the season with the shortest days and the lowest temperatures.
   a. Winter0
   b. Thing
   c. Undefined
   d. Undefined

46. _____ is water located beneath the ground surface in soil pore spaces and in the fractures of geologic formations. _____ is recharged from, and eventually flows to, the surface naturally; natural discharge often occurs at springs and seeps, streams and can often form oases or wetlands.
   a. Groundwater0
   b. Thing
   c. Undefined
   d. Undefined

47. An _____ is an underground layer of water-bearing permeable rock or unconsolidated materials from which groundwater can be usefully extracted using a water well.
   a. Thing
   b. Aquifer0
   c. Undefined
   d. Undefined

48. _____ is a highly sought-after precious metal which, for many centuries, has been used as money, a store of value and in jewelery. The metal occurs as nuggets or grains in rocks, underground "veins" and in alluvial deposits. It is one of the coinage metals. Itis dense, soft, shiny and the most malleable and ductile of the known metals.
   a. Thing
   b. Gold0
   c. Undefined
   d. Undefined

49. _____ is the extraction of valuable minerals or other geological materials from the earth, usually from an ore body, vein, or seam. Any material that cannot be grown from agricultural processes, or created artificially in a laboratory or factory, is usually extracted from the earth by this method.
   a. Mining0
   b. Thing
   c. Undefined
   d. Undefined

50. _____ are any of the several different forms of an element each having different atomic mass. _____ of an element have nuclei with the same number of protons but different numbers of neutrons.
   a. Isotopes0
   b. Thing
   c. Undefined
   d. Undefined

51. In physics, the _____ is a subatomic particle with no net electric charge.

Chapter 4. PROPERTIES OF GEOLOGIC FLUIDS

a. Neutron0
b. Thing
c. Undefined
d. Undefined

52. In physics, the _____ is a subatomic particle with an electric charge of one positive fundamental unit a diameter of about 1.5×10^{-15} m, and a mass of 938.27231(28) MeV/c2 (1.6726×10^{-27} kg), 1.007 276 466 88(13) u or about 1836 times the mass of an electron.

a. Proton0
b. Thing
c. Undefined
d. Undefined

53. An _____ is a type of atom that is defined by its atomic number; that is, by the number of protons in its nucleus.

a. Thing
b. Element0
c. Undefined
d. Undefined

54. The _____ is the mass of an atom at rest, most often expressed in unified _____ units.[

a. Thing
b. Atomic mass0
c. Undefined
d. Undefined

55. A _____ is an optical instrument used to measure properties of light over a specific portion of the electromagnetic spectrum. The variable measured is most often the light's intensity but could also, for instance, be the polarization state.

a. Spectrometer0
b. Thing
c. Undefined
d. Undefined

56. Mass spectrometry or informally is an analytical technique used to measure the mass-to-charge ratio of ions. It is most generally used to find the composition of a physical sample by generating a mass spectrum representing the masses of sample components. The mass spectrum is measured by a _____.

a. Mass spectrometer0
b. Thing
c. Undefined
d. Undefined

57. In physics, a _____ is a solenoidal vector field in the space surrounding moving electric charges and magnetic dipoles, such as those in electric currents and magnets.

a. Magnetic field0
b. Thing
c. Undefined
d. Undefined

58. A _____ is a body of water with a current, confined within a bed and banks. Streams are important as conduits in the water cycle, instruments in aquifer recharge, and corridors for fish and wildlife migration.

a. Thing
b. Stream0
c. Undefined
d. Undefined

59. _____ is one of the phenomena by which materials exert attractive or repulsive forces on other materials. Some well known materials that exhibit easily detectable magnetic properties are nickel, iron, some steels, and the mineral magnetite; however, all materials are influenced to greater or lesser degree by the presence of a magnetic field.

a. Magnetism0
b. Thing
c. Undefined
d. Undefined

60. _____ is approximately a magnetic dipole, with one pole near the north pole and the other near the geographic south pole.

Chapter 4. PROPERTIES OF GEOLOGIC FLUIDS

    a. Earths magnetic field0
    b. Thing
    c. Undefined
    d. Undefined

61. _____ are the fundamental building blocks of chemistry, and are conserved in chemical reactions.
    a. Atoms0
    b. Thing
    c. Undefined
    d. Undefined

62. The _____ is a fundamental subatomic particle that carries a negative electric charge.
    a. Electron0
    b. Thing
    c. Undefined
    d. Undefined

63. This _____ exerts a force on other electrically charged objects. The concept of _____ was introduced by Michael Faraday. The _____ is a vector with SI units of newtons per coulomb or, equivalently, volts per meter. The direction of the field at a point is defined by the direction of the electric force exerted on a positive test charge placed at that point.
    a. Thing
    b. Electric field0
    c. Undefined
    d. Undefined

64. _____ is the process in which an unstable atomic nucleus loses energy by emitting radiation in the form of particles or electromagnetic waves.
    a. Radioactive decay0
    b. Thing
    c. Undefined
    d. Undefined

65. _____ is a chemical element represented by the symbol H and an atomic number of 1. At standard temperature and pressure it is a colorless, odorless, nonmetallic, tasteless, highly flammable diatomic gas . With an atomic mass of 1.00794 g/mol, _____ is the lightest element. _____ is the most abundant of the chemical elements, constituting roughly 75% of the universe's elemental mass.
    a. Thing
    b. Hydrogen0
    c. Undefined
    d. Undefined

66. _____ is the process of heating a solid substance to a point where it turns into a liquid. An object that has melted is molten.
    a. Melting0
    b. Thing
    c. Undefined
    d. Undefined

67. _____ is the change in matter of a substance to a denser phase, such as a gas to a liquid. _____ commonly occurs when a vapor is cooled to a liquid, but can also occur if a vapor is compressed into a liquid, or undergoes a combination of cooling and compression.
    a. Condensation0
    b. Thing
    c. Undefined
    d. Undefined

68. The _____ is an inlet of the Indian Ocean between Africa and Asia. The connection to the ocean is in the south through the Bab el Mandeb sound and the Gulf of Aden. In the north are the Sinai Peninsula, the Gulf of Aqaba and the Gulf of Suez. The _____ is a Global 200 ecoregion.

Chapter 4. PROPERTIES OF GEOLOGIC FLUIDS 47

a. Red Sea0
b. Place
c. Undefined
d. Undefined

69. _____ is the gas phase of water. _____ is one state of the water cycle within the hydrosphere. _____ can be produced from the evaporation of liquid water or from the sublimation of ice. Under normal atmospheric conditions, _____ is continuously evaporating and condensing.
   a. Water vapor0
   b. Thing
   c. Undefined
   d. Undefined

70. _____ is the gas phase component of a another state of matter which does not completely fill its container. It is distinguished from the pure gas phase by the presence of the same substance in another state of matter. Hence when a liquid has completely evaporated, it is said that the system has been completely transformed to the gas phase.
   a. Vapor0
   b. Thing
   c. Undefined
   d. Undefined

71. The _____ is an imaginary line on the Earth's surface equidistant from the North Pole and South Pole. It thus divides the Earth into a Northern Hemisphere and a Southern Hemisphere.
   a. Thing
   b. Equator0
   c. Undefined
   d. Undefined

72. _____ is a layer of gases surrounding the planet Earth and retained by the Earth's gravity. This mixture of gases is commonly known as air.
   a. Earths atmosphere0
   b. Thing
   c. Undefined
   d. Undefined

73. In organic chemistry, a _____ is a salt of carbonic acid.
   a. Thing
   b. Carbonate0
   c. Undefined
   d. Undefined

74. _____ is any product of the condensation of atmospheric water vapor that is deposited on the earth's surface. It occurs when the atmosphere becomes saturated with water vapour and the water condenses and falls out of solution. Air becomes saturated via two processes, cooling and adding moisture.
   a. Thing
   b. Precipitation0
   c. Undefined
   d. Undefined

75. An _____ is a period of long-term reduction in the temperature of Earth's climate, resulting in an expansion of the continental ice sheets, polar ice sheets and mountain glaciers .
   a. Thing
   b. Ice Age0
   c. Undefined
   d. Undefined

76. An _____ is a geological interval of warmer global average temperature that separates glacials, or ice ages. The current Holocene _____ has persisted since the Pleistocene, about 11,400 years ago.
   a. Interglacial0
   b. Thing
   c. Undefined
   d. Undefined

48 *Chapter 4. PROPERTIES OF GEOLOGIC FLUIDS*

77. _____ gives the location of a place on Earth north or south of the equator. Lines of _____ are the horizontal lines shown running east-to-west on maps. Technically, _____ is an angular measurement in degrees ranging from 0° at the Equator to 90° at the poles.
- a. Latitude0
- b. Thing
- c. Undefined
- d. Undefined

78. An _____ is a mass of glacier ice that covers surrounding terrain and is greater than 19,305 mile². The only current ice sheets are in Antarctica and Greenland. Ice sheets are bigger than ice shelves or glaciers. Masses of ice covering less than 50,000 km² are termed an ice cap. An ice cap will typically feed a series of glaciers around its periphery. Although the surface is cold, the base of an _____ is generally warmer. This process produces fast-flowing channels in the _____.
- a. Thing
- b. Ice sheet0
- c. Undefined
- d. Undefined

79. _____ is a chemical element. An abundant nonmetallic, tetravalent element, _____ has several allotropic forms. This element is the basis of the chemistry of all known life.
- a. Thing
- b. Carbon0
- c. Undefined
- d. Undefined

80. _____ is a chemical element which has the symbol N and atomic number 7. Elemental _____ is a colorless, odourless, tasteless and mostly inert diatomic gas at standard conditions, constituting 78.1% by volume of Earth's atmosphere.
- a. Nitrogen0
- b. Thing
- c. Undefined
- d. Undefined

81. _____ is the condition of a system in which competing influences are balanced.
- a. Thing
- b. Equilibrium0
- c. Undefined
- d. Undefined

82. A _____ occurs when two reversible processes occur at the same rate.
- a. Thing
- b. Dynamic Equilibrium0
- c. Undefined
- d. Undefined

83. An _____ is a layer of gases that may surround a material body of sufficient mass. The gases are attracted by the gravity of the body, and are retained for a longer duration if gravity is high and the _____'s temperature is low. Some planets consist mainly of various gases, and thus have very deep atmospheres.
- a. Place
- b. Atmosphere0
- c. Undefined
- d. Undefined

84. _____ is a chemical compound, normally in a gaseous state, and is composed of one carbon and two oxygen atoms. It is often referred to by its formula CO_2. It is present in the Earth's atmosphere at a concentration of approximately .000383 by volume and is an important greenhouse gas due to its ability to absorb many infrared wavelengths of sunlight, and due to the length of time it stays in the atmosphere.
- a. Carbon dioxide0
- b. Thing
- c. Undefined
- d. Undefined

Chapter 4. PROPERTIES OF GEOLOGIC FLUIDS

85. Water collecting on the ground or in a stream, river, lake, or wetland is called _____; as opposed to groundwater. _____ is naturally replenished by precipitation and naturally lost through discharge to the oceans, evaporation, and sub-surface seepage into the groundwater. _____ is the largest source of fresh water.
    a. Thing
    b. Surface water0
    c. Undefined
    d. Undefined

86. An _____ is a chemical compound containing an oxygen atom and other elements. Most of the earth's crust consists of them. They result when elements are oxidized by air.
    a. Thing
    b. Oxide0
    c. Undefined
    d. Undefined

87. The Earth's water is always in movement, and the _____, describes the continuous movement of water on, above, and below the surface of the Earth. Since the _____ is truly a "cycle," there is no beginning or end. Water can change states among liquid, vapor, and ice at various places in the _____, with these processes happening in the blink of an eye and over millions of years. Although the balance of water on Earth remains fairly constant over time, individual water molecules can come and go in a hurry.
    a. Hydrologic cycle0
    b. Thing
    c. Undefined
    d. Undefined

88. A _____ is a section of a river of relatively steep gradient causing an increase in water flow and turbulence. A _____ is a hydrological feature between a run and a cascade. It is characterized by the river becoming shallower and having some rocks exposed above the flow surface.
    a. Rapid0
    b. Thing
    c. Undefined
    d. Undefined

89. In nuclear physics, a _____, also known as a daughter product, daughter isotope or daughter nuclide, is a nuclide resulting from the radioactive decay of a parent isotope or precursor nuclide. The daughter product may be stable or it may decay to form a daughter product of its own. The daughter of a daughter product is sometimes called a granddaughter product.
    a. Thing
    b. Decay product0
    c. Undefined
    d. Undefined

90. _____ refers to directed, regular, or systematic movement of a group of objects, organisms, or people.
    a. Thing
    b. Migration0
    c. Undefined
    d. Undefined

91. _____ is the process by which water on the ground surface enters the soil.
    a. Infiltration0
    b. Thing
    c. Undefined
    d. Undefined

92. _____ is approximately 70% more dense than lead and is weakly radioactive. It occurs naturally in low concentrations in soil, rock and water.
    a. Uranium0
    b. Thing
    c. Undefined
    d. Undefined

Chapter 4. PROPERTIES OF GEOLOGIC FLUIDS

93. In geology, _____ refers to heat sources within the planet. The planet's internal heat was originally generated during its accretion, due to gravitational binding energy, and since then additional heat has continued to be generated by the radioactive decay of elements such as uranium, thorium, and potassium.
    a. Geothermal0
    b. Thing
    c. Undefined
    d. Undefined

94. The _____ provides the only reliable source of water through much of inland Australia. The basin is the largest and deepest artesian basin in the world. The basin is 3000 metres deep in places and is estimated to contain 64,900 cubic kilometres of groundwater.
    a. Great Artesian Basin0
    b. Thing
    c. Undefined
    d. Undefined

95. _____ refers to things having to do with the land or with the planet Earth.
    a. Terrestrial0
    b. Thing
    c. Undefined
    d. Undefined

96. _____ is a process by which sediment is added to a tectonic plate. When two tectonic plates collide, one of the plates may slide under the other. This process is called subduction. The plate which is being subducted, is floating on the asthenosphere and is pushed up and against the other plate, which will often be scraped by the subducted plate.
    a. Accretion0
    b. Thing
    c. Undefined
    d. Undefined

97. Earth's _____ is a ~2,900 km thick rocky shell comprizing approximately 70% of Earth's volume. It is predominantly solid and overlies the Earth's iron-rich core, which occupies about 30% of Earth's volume. Past episodes of melting and volcanism at the shallower levels of the _____ have produced a very thin crust of crystallized melt products near the surface, upon which we live.
    a. Thing
    b. Mantle0
    c. Undefined
    d. Undefined

98. A _____ is a natural object originating in outer space that survives an impact with the Earth's surface without being destroyed. While in space it is called a meteoroid. When it enters the atmosphere, air resistance causes the body to heat up and emit light, thus forming a fireball.
    a. Thing
    b. Meteorite0
    c. Undefined
    d. Undefined

99. In the earth sciences, _____ is a measure of the ability of a material to transmit fluids. It is of great importance in determining the flow characteristics of hydrocarbons in oil and gas reservoirs, and of groundwater in aquifers.
    a. Permeability0
    b. Thing
    c. Undefined
    d. Undefined

100. _____ is the geological process whereby material is added to a landform. This is the process by which wind and water create a sediment deposit, through the laying down of granular material that has been eroded and transported from another geographical location.
    a. Thing
    b. Deposition0
    c. Undefined
    d. Undefined

Chapter 4. PROPERTIES OF GEOLOGIC FLUIDS

101. The _____ is used by geologists and other scientists to describe the timing and relationships between events that have occurred during the history of Earth.
   a. Thing
   b. Geological time scale0
   c. Undefined
   d. Undefined

102. The _____ is chemically divided into layers. The Earth has an outer silicate solid crust, a highly viscous mantle, a liquid outer core that is much less viscous than the mantle, and a solid inner core. Many of the rocks now making up the Earth's crust formed less than 100 million ago.
   a. Earth's interior0
   b. Thing
   c. Undefined
   d. Undefined

103. _____ is a theory of geology that has been developed to explain the observed evidence for large scale motions of the Earth's lithosphere. The theory encompassed and superseded the older theory of continental drift.
   a. Plate tectonics0
   b. Thing
   c. Undefined
   d. Undefined

104. In geology, a _____ zone is an area on Earth where two tectonic plates meet and move towards one another, with one sliding underneath the other and moving down into the mantle, at rates typically measured in centimeters per year. An oceanic plate ordinarily slides underneath a continental plate; this often creates an orogenic zone with many volcanoes and earthquakes.
   a. Thing
   b. Subduction0
   c. Undefined
   d. Undefined

105. _____ is one of the three main rock groups. _____ covers 75% of the Earth's land area. Four basic processes are involved in the formation of a clastic _____: weathering caused mainly by friction of waves, transportation where the sediment is carried along by a current, deposition and compaction where the sediment is squashed together to form a rock of this kind.
   a. Sedimentary rock0
   b. Thing
   c. Undefined
   d. Undefined

106. The carbonate mineral _____ is a chemical or biochemical calcium carbonate and is one of the most widely distributed minerals on the Earth's surface. It is a common constituent of sedimentary rocks, limestone in particular. It is also the primary mineral in metamorphic marble
   a. Thing
   b. Calcite0
   c. Undefined
   d. Undefined

107. In geology, engineering, and surveying, _____ is the motion of a surface as it shifts downward relative to a datum such as sea-level. The opposite of _____ is uplift, which results in an increase in elevation. In meteorology, _____ refers to the downward movement of air.
   a. Subsidence0
   b. Thing
   c. Undefined
   d. Undefined

108. In geology, a _____ is a depression with predominant extent in one direction. The terms U-shaped and V-shaped are descriptive terms of geography to characterize the form of valleys. Most valleys belong to one of these two main types or a mixture of them, at least with respect of the cross section of the slopes or hillsides.

Chapter 4. PROPERTIES OF GEOLOGIC FLUIDS

a. Valley0
b. Thing
c. Undefined
d. Undefined

109. _____ is a fossil fuel formed in swamp ecosystems where plant remains were saved by water and mud from oxidization and biodegradation. It is a sedimentary rock, but the harder forms, such as anthracite _____, can be regarded as metamorphic rocks because of later exposure to elevated temperature and pressure. It is composed primarily of carbon along with assorted other elements, including sulfur.
 a. Thing
 b. Coal0
 c. Undefined
 d. Undefined

110. The _____ is the ninth largest body of water in the world. It is an ocean basin largely surrounded by the North American continent and the island of Cuba. It is bounded on the northeast, north and northwest by the Gulf Coast of the United States, on the southwest and south by Mexico, and on the southeast by Cuba.
 a. Place
 b. Gulf of Mexico0
 c. Undefined
 d. Undefined

111. A _____ is any aspect of an object or substance that can be measured or perceived without changing its identity. Physical properties can be intensive or extensive. An intensive property does not depend on the size or amount of matter in the object, while an extensive property does.
 a. Physical property0
 b. Thing
 c. Undefined
 d. Undefined

112. The _____ of a substance is the maximum temperature at which a liquid can remain a liquid.
 a. Boiling point0
 b. Thing
 c. Undefined
 d. Undefined

113. A _____ is any substance at a temperature and pressure above its thermodynamic critical point. It has the unique ability to diffuse through solids like a gas, and dissolve materials like a liquid. Additionally, it can readily change in density upon minor changes in temperature or pressure.
 a. Thing
 b. Supercritical fluid0
 c. Undefined
 d. Undefined

114. _____ is an essentially physical process that has meanings in chemistry, metallurgy and geology. In geology, solid-state _____ is a metamorphic process that occurs under situations of intense temperature and pressure where grains, atoms or molecules of a rock or mineral are packed closer together, creating a new crystal structure.
 a. Recrystallization0
 b. Thing
 c. Undefined
 d. Undefined

115. _____ is a measure of the resistance of a fluid to deform under shear stress. It is commonly perceived as "thickness", or resistance to flow. _____ describes a fluid's internal resistance to flow and may be thought of as a measure of fluid friction.
 a. Thing
 b. Viscosity0
 c. Undefined
 d. Undefined

Chapter 4. PROPERTIES OF GEOLOGIC FLUIDS

116. In physics, _____ is the upward force on an object produced by the surrounding fluid in which it is fully or partially immersed, due to the pressure difference of the fluid between the top and bottom of the object. The net upward _____ force is equal to the magnitude of the weight of fluid displaced by the body.
    a. Buoyancy0
    b. Thing
    c. Undefined
    d. Undefined

117. An _____ is a volume of rock containing components or minerals in a mode of occurrence that renders it valuable for mining.
    a. Thing
    b. Ore0
    c. Undefined
    d. Undefined

118. The _____ is the rate of increase in temperature per unit depth in the Earth. It varies with location and is typically measured by determining the bottom open-hole temperature after the drilling of a borehole.
    a. Geothermal gradient0
    b. Thing
    c. Undefined
    d. Undefined

119. _____ is the average and variations of weather over long periods of time. _____ zones can be defined using parameters such as temperature and rainfall.
    a. Climate0
    b. Thing
    c. Undefined
    d. Undefined

120. The _____ is the layer of granitic, sedimentary, and metamorphic rocks which form the continents and the areas of shallow seabed close to their shores, known as continental shelves. It is less dense than the material of the Earth's mantle and thus "floats" on top of it. _____ is also less dense than oceanic crust, though it is considerably thicker. About 40% of the Earth's surface is now underlain by _____.
    a. Thing
    b. Continental crust0
    c. Undefined
    d. Undefined

121. _____ is a stress state where the stress is parallel or tangential to a face of the material, as opposed to normal stress when the stress is perpendicular to the face. The variable used to denote _____ is τ.
    a. Thing
    b. Shear stress0
    c. Undefined
    d. Undefined

122. _____ is an effect within the surface layer of a liquid that causes that layer to behave as an elastic sheet. This effect allows insects to walk on water. It allows small metal objects such as needles, razor blades, or foil fragments to float on the surface of water, and causes capillary action.
    a. Surface tension0
    b. Thing
    c. Undefined
    d. Undefined

123. _____ is a reaction force applied by a stretched string, rope or a similar object on the objects which stretch it. The direction of the force of it is parallel to the string, towards the string.
    a. Tension0
    b. Thing
    c. Undefined
    d. Undefined

124. _____ is a chemical element in the periodic table that has the symbol Hg and atomic number 80. A heavy, silvery transition metal, _____ is one of five elements that are liquid at or near room temperature and pressure.

a. Thing
b. Mercury0
c. Undefined
d. Undefined

125. _____ is the study of the movement, distribution, and quality of water throughout the Earth, and thus addresses both the hydrologic cycle and water resources.

a. Thing
b. Hydrology0
c. Undefined
d. Undefined

Chapter 5. TRANSIENT FLOW

1. _____ is the net action of matter, particles or molecules, heat, momentum, or light whose end is to minimize a concentration gradient.
   a. Diffusion0
   b. Thing
   c. Undefined
   d. Undefined

2. The law of _____, also known as law of mass/matter conservation, states that the mass of a closed system of substances will remain constant, regardless of the processes acting inside the system. An equivalent statement is that matter cannot be created nor destroyed, although it may change form.
   a. Conservation of mass0
   b. Thing
   c. Undefined
   d. Undefined

3. _____ is a measure of the void spaces in a material, and is measured as a fraction, between 0–1, or as a percentage between 0–100%.
   a. Porosity0
   b. Thing
   c. Undefined
   d. Undefined

4. In physics, _____ is defined as the rate of change of displacement or the rate of displacement. Simply put, it is distance per units of time.
   a. Velocity0
   b. Thing
   c. Undefined
   d. Undefined

5. _____ is the part of hydrology that deals with the distribution and movement of groundwater in the soil and rocks of the Earth's crust.
   a. Thing
   b. Hydrogeology0
   c. Undefined
   d. Undefined

6. An _____ is any piece of land that is completely surrounded by water, above high tide. There are two main types of islands: continental islands and oceanic islands. There are also artificial islands. A grouping of geographically and/or geologically related islands is called an archipelago.
   a. Island0
   b. Thing
   c. Undefined
   d. Undefined

7. _____, in everyday life, is most familiar as the agency that endows objects with weight. _____ is responsible for keeping the Earth and the other planets in their orbits around the Sun; for the formation of tides; and for various other phenomena that we observe. _____ is also the reason for the very existence of the Earth, the Sun, and most macroscopic objects in the universe; without it, matter would not have coalesced into these large masses, and life, as we know it, would not exist.
   a. Gravitation0
   b. Thing
   c. Undefined
   d. Undefined

8. A _____ is any aspect of an object or substance that can be measured or perceived without changing its identity. Physical properties can be intensive or extensive. An intensive property does not depend on the size or amount of matter in the object, while an extensive property does.
   a. Physical property0
   b. Thing
   c. Undefined
   d. Undefined

Chapter 5. TRANSIENT FLOW

9. _____, symbolically represented as K, is a property of vascular plants, soil or rock, that describes the ease with which water can move through pore spaces or fractures
   a. Hydraulic Conductivity0
   b. Thing
   c. Undefined
   d. Undefined

10. _____ is a part of mathematics concerned with questions of size, shape, and relative position of figures and with properties of space. _____ is one of the oldest sciences. Initially a body of practical knowledge concerning lengths, areas, and volumes, in the third century B.C. _____ was put into an axiomatic form by Euclid, whose treatment set a standard for many centuries to follow.
    a. Thing
    b. Geometry0
    c. Undefined
    d. Undefined

11. _____ is water located beneath the ground surface in soil pore spaces and in the fractures of geologic formations. _____ is recharged from, and eventually flows to, the surface naturally; natural discharge often occurs at springs and seeps, streams and can often form oases or wetlands.
    a. Groundwater0
    b. Thing
    c. Undefined
    d. Undefined

12. An _____ is an underground layer of water-bearing permeable rock or unconsolidated materials from which groundwater can be usefully extracted using a water well.
    a. Thing
    b. Aquifer0
    c. Undefined
    d. Undefined

13. An _____ occurs in recharging aquifers, this happens because the water table at its recharge zone is at a higher elevation than the head of the well.
    a. Thing
    b. Artesian well0
    c. Undefined
    d. Undefined

14. _____ is a branch of physics which studies the properties of elastic materials. A material is said to be elastic if it deforms under stress but then returns to its original shape when the stress is removed.
    a. Thing
    b. Elasticity0
    c. Undefined
    d. Undefined

15. _____ is a small island located in the middle of San Francisco Bay in California, United States. It served as a lighthouse, then a military fortification, then a military prison followed by a federal prison until 1963, when it became a national recreation area.
    a. Place
    b. Alcatraz Island0
    c. Undefined
    d. Undefined

16. _____ is the study of the movement, distribution, and quality of water throughout the Earth, and thus addresses both the hydrologic cycle and water resources.
    a. Hydrology0
    b. Thing
    c. Undefined
    d. Undefined

Chapter 5. TRANSIENT FLOW

17. _____ is the extraction of valuable minerals or other geological materials from the earth, usually from an ore body, vein, or seam. Any material that cannot be grown from agricultural processes, or created artificially in a laboratory or factory, is usually extracted from the earth by this method.
- a. Thing
- b. Mining0
- c. Undefined
- d. Undefined

18. _____ is an all-embracing term for the sciences related to the planet Earth. It is arguably a special case in planetary science, being the only known life-bearing planet. There are both reductionist and holistic approaches to _____. The major historic disciplines use physics, geology, geography, mathematics, chemistry, and biology to build a quantitative understanding of the principal areas or spheres of the Earth system.
- a. Thing
- b. Earth science0
- c. Undefined
- d. Undefined

19. _____ is the science and study of the solid matter that constitute the Earth. Encompassing such things as rocks, soil, and gemstones, _____ studies the composition, structure, physical properties, history, and the processes that shape Earth's components.
- a. Geology0
- b. Thing
- c. Undefined
- d. Undefined

20. The _____ is a nonprofit organization dedicated to the advancement of the geosciences. The society was founded in New York in 1888 by James Hall, James D. Dana, and Alexander Winchell, and has been headquartered at 3300 Penrose Place, Boulder, Colorado since 1968. As of 2007, the society has over 21,000 members in more than 85 countries. The stated mission is "to advance the geosciences, to enhance the professional growth of its members, and to promote the geosciences in the service of humankind".
- a. Geological Society of America0
- b. Person
- c. Undefined
- d. Undefined

21. A _____ is a barrier across flowing water that obstructs, directs or slows down the flow, often creating a reservoir, lake or impoundment.
- a. Dam0
- b. Thing
- c. Undefined
- d. Undefined

22. In the earth sciences, _____ is a measure of the ability of a material to transmit fluids. It is of great importance in determining the flow characteristics of hydrocarbons in oil and gas reservoirs, and of groundwater in aquifers.
- a. Thing
- b. Permeability0
- c. Undefined
- d. Undefined

23. _____ is any particulate matter that can be transported by fluid flow and which eventually is deposited as a layer of solid particles on the bed or bottom of a body of water or other liquid.
- a. Sediment0
- b. Thing
- c. Undefined
- d. Undefined

24. _____ rock is one of the three main rock groups. Rock formed from these covers 75% of the Earth's land area, and includes common types such as chalk, limestone, dolomite, sandstone, and shale.

Chapter 5. TRANSIENT FLOW

    a. Sedimentary0
    b. Thing
    c. Undefined
    d. Undefined

25. _____ is one of the three main rock groups. _____ covers 75% of the Earth's land area. Four basic processes are involved in the formation of a clastic _____: weathering caused mainly by friction of waves, transportation where the sediment is carried along by a current, deposition and compaction where the sediment is squashed together to form a rock of this kind.
    a. Sedimentary rock0
    b. Thing
    c. Undefined
    d. Undefined

26. _____ is the change in direction of a wave due to a change in its speed. This is most commonly seen when a wave passes from one medium to another.
    a. Refraction0
    b. Thing
    c. Undefined
    d. Undefined

27. An _____ is a zone within the earth that restricts the flow of groundwater from one aquifer to another.
    a. Thing
    b. Aquitard0
    c. Undefined
    d. Undefined

28. _____ is a fine-grained sedimentary rock whose original constituents were clays or muds. It is characterized by thin laminae breaking with an irregular curving fracture, often splintery and usually parallel to the often-indistinguishable bedding plane.
    a. Thing
    b. Shale0
    c. Undefined
    d. Undefined

29. _____ is a sedimentary rock composed mainly of sand-size mineral or rock grains. Most _____ is composed of quartz and/or feldspar because these are the most common minerals in the Earth's crust. Like sand, _____ may be any color, but the most common colors are tan, brown, yellow, red, gray and white.
    a. Sandstone0
    b. Thing
    c. Undefined
    d. Undefined

30. A _____ is a point along a standing wave where the wave has minimal amplitude. This has implications in several fields. For instance, in a guitar string, the ends of the string are nodes. By changing the position of one of these nodes through frets, the guitarist changes the effective length of the vibrating string and thereby the note played.
    a. Node0
    b. Thing
    c. Undefined
    d. Undefined

31. _____ is one of the four seasons of temperate zones. Almost all English-language calendars, going by astronomy, state that _____ begins on the _____ solstice, and ends on the spring equinox. Calculated more by the weather, it begins and ends earlier and is the season with the shortest days and the lowest temperatures.
    a. Winter0
    b. Thing
    c. Undefined
    d. Undefined

32. A _____ is a section of a river of relatively steep gradient causing an increase in water flow and turbulence. A _____ is a hydrological feature between a run and a cascade. It is characterized by the river becoming shallower and having some rocks exposed above the flow surface.

Chapter 5. TRANSIENT FLOW

    a. Rapid0
    c. Undefined
    b. Thing
    d. Undefined

33. _____ is a term used to describe the flow of water, from rain, snowmelt, or other sources, over the land surface, and is a major component of the water cycle.
    a. Surface runoff0
    c. Undefined
    b. Thing
    d. Undefined

34. A _____ is a body of water with a current, confined within a bed and banks. Streams are important as conduits in the water cycle, instruments in aquifer recharge, and corridors for fish and wildlife migration.
    a. Thing
    c. Undefined
    b. Stream0
    d. Undefined

35. _____ is the artificial application of water to the soil usually for assisting in growing crops. In crop production it is mainly used to replace missing rainfall in periods of drought, but also to protect plants against frost.
    a. Irrigation0
    c. Undefined
    b. Thing
    d. Undefined

36. A _____ is an area of highland, usually consisting of relatively flat rural area.
    a. Plateau0
    c. Undefined
    b. Place
    d. Undefined

37. An _____ plain is a relatively flat and gently sloping landform found at the base of a range of hills or mountains, formed by the deposition of _____ soil over a long period of time by one or more rivers coming from the mountains.
    a. Alluvial0
    c. Undefined
    b. Thing
    d. Undefined

38. An alluvial fan is a fan-shaped deposit formed where a fast flowing stream flattens, slows, and spreads typically at the exit of a canyon onto a flatter plain. A convergence of neighboring _____ into a single apron of deposits against a slope is called a bajada, or compound alluvial fan.
    a. Alluvial fans0
    c. Undefined
    b. Thing
    d. Undefined

39. _____ is soil or rock derived granular material of a specific grain size. _____ may occur as a soil or alternatively as suspended sediment in a water column of any surface water body. It may also exist as deposition soil at the bottom of a water body.
    a. Silt0
    c. Undefined
    b. Thing
    d. Undefined

40. _____ refers to the diameter of individual grains of sediment, or the lithified particles in clastic rocks. The term may also be applied to other granular materials. This is different from the crystallite size, which is the size of a single crystal inside the particles or grains.
    a. Thing
    c. Undefined
    b. Particle size0
    d. Undefined

Chapter 5. TRANSIENT FLOW

41. In geography _____ are isolated areas of vegetation in a desert, typically surrounding a spring or similar water source. The location of _____ has been of critical importance for trade and transportation routes in desert areas.
   a. Thing
   b. Oases0
   c. Undefined
   d. Undefined

42. A _____ is a wet place where a liquid, usually groundwater, has oozed from the ground to the surface. They are usually not flowing, with the liquid sourced only from underground. The term may also refer to the movement of liquid hydrocarbons to the surface through fractures and fissures in the rock and between geological layers. It may be a significant source of pollution.
   a. Thing
   b. Seep0
   c. Undefined
   d. Undefined

43. _____ is the most commonly used technique within the science of archaeology. It is the exposure, processing and recording of archaeological remains.
   a. Excavation0
   b. Thing
   c. Undefined
   d. Undefined

44. _____ in the broad sense is the total spectrum of the electromagnetic radiation given off by the Sun. On Earth, it is filtered through the atmosphere, and the solar radiation is obvious as daylight when the Sun is above the horizon.
   a. Thing
   b. Sunlight0
   c. Undefined
   d. Undefined

45. _____ is the substance of which physical objects are composed. _____ can be solid, liquid, plasma or gas. It constitutes the observable universe.
   a. Matter0
   b. Thing
   c. Undefined
   d. Undefined

46. _____ is a sedimentary rock composed largely of the mineral calcite. _____ often contains variable amounts of silica in the form of chert or flint, as well as varying amounts of clay, silt and sand as disseminations, nodules, or layers within the rock. The primary source of the calcite in _____ is most commonly marine organisms. These organisms secrete shells that settle out of the water column and are deposited on ocean floors as pelagic ooze or alternatively is conglomerated in a coral reef.
   a. Thing
   b. Limestone0
   c. Undefined
   d. Undefined

Chapter 6. NEAR SURFACE FLOW

1. The _____ is the portion of Earth between the land surface and the phreatic zone or zone of saturation.
   a. Vadose Zone0
   b. Thing
   c. Undefined
   d. Undefined

2. _____ is a layer of gases surrounding the planet Earth and retained by the Earth's gravity. This mixture of gases is commonly known as air.
   a. Thing
   b. Earths atmosphere0
   c. Undefined
   d. Undefined

3. _____ is the pressure at any point in the Earth's atmosphere.
   a. Thing
   b. Atmospheric pressure0
   c. Undefined
   d. Undefined

4. The term _____, taken literally, refers to movement that goes on forever. This is possible in the current theoretical understanding of physics as in Newton's First Law of Motion. However, _____ usually refers to a device or system that stores and/or outputs more energy than is put into it.
   a. Thing
   b. Perpetual motion0
   c. Undefined
   d. Undefined

5. _____, in everyday life, is most familiar as the agency that endows objects with weight. _____ is responsible for keeping the Earth and the other planets in their orbits around the Sun; for the formation of tides; and for various other phenomena that we observe. _____ is also the reason for the very existence of the Earth, the Sun, and most macroscopic objects in the universe; without it, matter would not have coalesced into these large masses, and life, as we know it, would not exist.
   a. Thing
   b. Gravitation0
   c. Undefined
   d. Undefined

6. In chemistry, a _____ is defined as a sufficiently stable electrically neutral group of at least two atoms in a definite arrangement held together by strong chemical bonds.
   a. Molecule0
   b. Thing
   c. Undefined
   d. Undefined

7. _____, symbolically represented as K, is a property of vascular plants, soil or rock, that describes the ease with which water can move through pore spaces or fractures
   a. Hydraulic Conductivity0
   b. Thing
   c. Undefined
   d. Undefined

8. _____ is the part of hydrology that deals with the distribution and movement of groundwater in the soil and rocks of the Earth's crust.
   a. Hydrogeology0
   b. Thing
   c. Undefined
   d. Undefined

9. _____ is a measure of the void spaces in a material, and is measured as a fraction, between 0–1, or as a percentage between 0–100%.
   a. Porosity0
   b. Thing
   c. Undefined
   d. Undefined

Chapter 6. NEAR SURFACE FLOW

10. Water of sufficient quality to serve as drinking water is termed _____ whether it is used as such or not.
    a. Potable water0
    b. Thing
    c. Undefined
    d. Undefined

11. A _____ is formed when a thick bed of evaporite minerals found at depth intrudes vertically into surrounding rock strata, forming a diapir.
    a. Thing
    b. Salt dome0
    c. Undefined
    d. Undefined

12. _____ or sulphur is the chemical element that has the symbol S and atomic number 16. It is an abundant, tasteless, multivalent non-metal. _____, in its native form, is a yellow crystalline solid. In nature, it can be found as the pure element or as sulfide and sulfate minerals. It is an essential element for life and is found in two amino acids, cysteine and methionine.
    a. Thing
    b. Sulfur0
    c. Undefined
    d. Undefined

13. In geology, a _____ is a deformational feature consisting of symmetrically-dipping anticlines; their general outline on a geologic map is circular or oval.
    a. Thing
    b. Dome0
    c. Undefined
    d. Undefined

14. A _____ is a naturally occurring substance formed through geological processes that has a characteristic chemical composition, a highly ordered atomic structure and specific physical properties. A rock, by comparison, is an aggregate of minerals and need not have a specific chemical composition. Minerals range in composition from pure elements and simple salts to very complex silicates with thousands of known forms.
    a. Mineral0
    b. Thing
    c. Undefined
    d. Undefined

15. _____ is water located beneath the ground surface in soil pore spaces and in the fractures of geologic formations. _____ is recharged from, and eventually flows to, the surface naturally; natural discharge often occurs at springs and seeps, streams and can often form oases or wetlands.
    a. Groundwater0
    b. Thing
    c. Undefined
    d. Undefined

16. _____ refers to directed, regular, or systematic movement of a group of objects, organisms, or people.
    a. Migration0
    b. Thing
    c. Undefined
    d. Undefined

17. A _____ is an extended period of months or years when a region notes a deficiency in its water supply. Generally, this occurs when a region receives consistently below average precipitation.
    a. Thing
    b. Drought0
    c. Undefined
    d. Undefined

18. In geography, a _____ is a landscape form or region that receives very little precipitation. They are defined as areas that receive an average annual precipitation of less than 250 mm. A _____ where vegetation cover is exceedingly sparse correspond to the 'hyperarid' regions of the earth, where rainfall is exceedingly rare and infrequent.

a. Desert0
b. Place
c. Undefined
d. Undefined

19. _____ is any particulate matter that can be transported by fluid flow and which eventually is deposited as a layer of solid particles on the bed or bottom of a body of water or other liquid.
   a. Thing
   b. Sediment0
   c. Undefined
   d. Undefined

20. _____ is the gas phase of water. _____ is one state of the water cycle within the hydrosphere. _____ can be produced from the evaporation of liquid water or from the sublimation of ice. Under normal atmospheric conditions, _____ is continuously evaporating and condensing.
   a. Thing
   b. Water vapor0
   c. Undefined
   d. Undefined

21. _____ is the gas phase component of a another state of matter which does not completely fill its container. It is distinguished from the pure gas phase by the presence of the same substance in another state of matter. Hence when a liquid has completely evaporated, it is said that the system has been completely transformed to the gas phase.
   a. Thing
   b. Vapor0
   c. Undefined
   d. Undefined

22. _____ is feeding on growing herbage, attached algae, or phytoplankton.
   a. Grazing0
   b. Thing
   c. Undefined
   d. Undefined

23. _____ is a sedimentary rock composed largely of the mineral calcite. _____ often contains variable amounts of silica in the form of chert or flint, as well as varying amounts of clay, silt and sand as disseminations, nodules, or layers within the rock. The primary source of the calcite in _____ is most commonly marine organisms. These organisms secrete shells that settle out of the water column and are deposited on ocean floors as pelagic ooze or alternatively is conglomerated in a coral reef.
   a. Limestone0
   b. Thing
   c. Undefined
   d. Undefined

24. _____ is the production of food, feed, fiber, fuel and other goods by the systematic raizing of plants and animals.
   a. Agriculture0
   b. Thing
   c. Undefined
   d. Undefined

25. A _____ is a natural underground void large enough for a human to enter. Some people suggest that the term '_____' should only apply to cavities that have some part which does not receive daylight; however, in popular usage, the term includes smaller spaces like a sea _____, rock shelters, and grottos.
   a. Cave0
   b. Place
   c. Undefined
   d. Undefined

26. _____ is a highly sought-after precious metal which, for many centuries, has been used as money, a store of value and in jewelery. The metal occurs as nuggets or grains in rocks, underground "veins" and in alluvial deposits. It is one of the coinage metals. Itis dense, soft, shiny and the most malleable and ductile of the known metals.

64 **Chapter 6. NEAR SURFACE FLOW**

    a. Gold0
    c. Undefined
    b. Thing
    d. Undefined

27. _____ is a soft white lustrous transition metal, it has the highest electrical and thermal conductivity for a metal.
    a. Thing
    c. Undefined
    b. Silver0
    d. Undefined

28. A _____ is a wet place where a liquid, usually groundwater, has oozed from the ground to the surface. They are usually not flowing, with the liquid sourced only from underground. The term may also refer to the movement of liquid hydrocarbons to the surface through fractures and fissures in the rock and between geological layers. It may be a significant source of pollution.
    a. Seep0
    c. Undefined
    b. Thing
    d. Undefined

29. _____ is the most commonly used technique within the science of archaeology. It is the exposure, processing and recording of archaeological remains.
    a. Thing
    c. Undefined
    b. Excavation0
    d. Undefined

30. _____ is a chemical element metal. It is a lustrous, silvery soft metal. It and nickel are notable for being the final elements produced by stellar nucleosynthesis, and thus are the heaviest elements which do not require a supernova or similarly cataclysmic event for formation.
    a. Thing
    c. Undefined
    b. Iron0
    d. Undefined

31. An _____ is an underground layer of water-bearing permeable rock or unconsolidated materials from which groundwater can be usefully extracted using a water well.
    a. Thing
    c. Undefined
    b. Aquifer0
    d. Undefined

32. _____ is the science and study of the solid matter that constitute the Earth. Encompassing such things as rocks, soil, and gemstones, _____ studies the composition, structure, physical properties, history, and the processes that shape Earth's components.
    a. Thing
    c. Undefined
    b. Geology0
    d. Undefined

33. _____ is soil or rock derived granular material of a specific grain size. _____ may occur as a soil or alternatively as suspended sediment in a water column of any surface water body. It may also exist as deposition soil at the bottom of a water body.
    a. Thing
    c. Undefined
    b. Silt0
    d. Undefined

34. Water collecting on the ground or in a stream, river, lake, or wetland is called _____; as opposed to groundwater. _____ is naturally replenished by precipitation and naturally lost through discharge to the oceans, evaporation, and sub-surface seepage into the groundwater. _____ is the largest source of fresh water.

Chapter 6. NEAR SURFACE FLOW

a. Surface water0
b. Thing
c. Undefined
d. Undefined

35. _____ is rock that is of a certain particle size range. In geology, _____ is any loose rock that is at least two millimeters in its largest dimension and no more than 75 millimeters.
a. Thing
b. Gravel0
c. Undefined
d. Undefined

36. _____ is a small island located in the middle of San Francisco Bay in California, United States. It served as a lighthouse, then a military fortification, then a military prison followed by a federal prison until 1963, when it became a national recreation area.
a. Place
b. Alcatraz Island0
c. Undefined
d. Undefined

37. An _____ is any piece of land that is completely surrounded by water, above high tide. There are two main types of islands: continental islands and oceanic islands. There are also artificial islands. A grouping of geographically and/or geologically related islands is called an archipelago.
a. Island0
b. Thing
c. Undefined
d. Undefined

38. The _____ is the largest enclosed body of water on Earth by area, variously classed as the world's largest lake or the smallest full-fledged sea. The _____ is a remnant of the Tethys Sea, along with Black, and Aral seas. It became landlocked about 5.5 million years ago.
a. Place
b. Caspian Sea0
c. Undefined
d. Undefined

39. A _____ is a type of hot spring that erupts periodically, ejecting a column of hot water and steam into the air.
a. Geyser0
b. Thing
c. Undefined
d. Undefined

40. _____ is a naturally occurring liquid found in formations in the Earth consisting of a complex mixture of hydrocarbons of various lengths.
a. Petroleum0
b. Thing
c. Undefined
d. Undefined

41. A _____ is a body of water with a current, confined within a bed and banks. Streams are important as conduits in the water cycle, instruments in aquifer recharge, and corridors for fish and wildlife migration.
a. Stream0
b. Thing
c. Undefined
d. Undefined

42. _____ is water saturated or nearly saturated with salt and is a common fluid used in the transport of heat from place to place. It is used because the addition of salt to water lowers the freezing temperature of the solution and a relatively great efficiency in the transport can be obtained for the low cost of the material.
a. Thing
b. Brine0
c. Undefined
d. Undefined

Chapter 6. NEAR SURFACE FLOW

43. _____ is water from a sea or ocean. On average, _____ in the world's oceans has a salinity of ~3.5%, or 35 parts per thousand. This means that every 1 kg of _____ has approximately 35 grams of dissolved salts.
   a. Thing
   b. Seawater0
   c. Undefined
   d. Undefined

44. _____ contains low concentrations of dissolved salts and other total dissolved solids. It is an important renewable resource, necessary for the survival of most terrestrial organisms, and required by humans for drinking and agriculture, among many other uses.
   a. Thing
   b. Fresh water0
   c. Undefined
   d. Undefined

45. A _____ is a tidal phenomenon in which the leading edge of the incoming tide forms a wave of water that travel up a river or narrow bay against the direction of the current. As such, it is a true tidal wave.
   a. Thing
   b. Bore0
   c. Undefined
   d. Undefined

46. In broad terms, the _____ is the direction pointing directly above a particular location. Specifically, in astronomy, geophysics and related sciences, the _____ at a given point is the local vertical direction pointing away from direction of the force of gravity at that location.
   a. Thing
   b. Zenith0
   c. Undefined
   d. Undefined

47. An _____ occurs in recharging aquifers, this happens because the water table at its recharge zone is at a higher elevation than the head of the well.
   a. Thing
   b. Artesian well0
   c. Undefined
   d. Undefined

48. A _____ is a section of a river of relatively steep gradient causing an increase in water flow and turbulence. A _____ is a hydrological feature between a run and a cascade. It is characterized by the river becoming shallower and having some rocks exposed above the flow surface.
   a. Rapid0
   b. Thing
   c. Undefined
   d. Undefined

49. _____ is the native consolidated rock underlying the Earth's surface. Above the _____ is usually an area of broken and weathered unconsolidated rock in the basal subsoil.
   a. Thing
   b. Bedrock0
   c. Undefined
   d. Undefined

50. An _____ is a term for any perforation through the Earth's surface designed to find and release both petroleum oil and gas hydrocarbons.
   a. Oil well0
   b. Thing
   c. Undefined
   d. Undefined

51. _____ is a branch of physics which studies the properties of elastic materials. A material is said to be elastic if it deforms under stress but then returns to its original shape when the stress is removed.

a. Thing
b. Elasticity0
c. Undefined
d. Undefined

52. _____ was an English geologist, credited with creating the first nationwide geologic map. He is known as the "Father of English Geology", however recognition was slow in coming. His work was plagiarised, he was financially ruined, and he spent time in debtors' prison. It was only much later in his life that Smith received recognition for his accomplishments.
   a. William Smith0
   b. Person
   c. Undefined
   d. Undefined

53. A _____ is a movement of an object in a circular motion. A two-dimensional object rotates around a center of _____. A three-dimensional object rotates around a line called an axis. A circular motion about an external point, e.g. the Earth about the Sun, is called an orbit or more properly an orbital revolution.
   a. Thing
   b. Rotation0
   c. Undefined
   d. Undefined

54. _____ is a peninsula in the far north of Russia, part of the Murmansk Oblast. It borders upon the Barents Sea on the North and the White Sea on the East and South. The west border of the _____ stretches along a meridian from the Kola Gulf through the Imandra Lake, Kola Lake, and the Niva River to the Kandalaksha Gulf.
   a. Kola Peninsula0
   b. Place
   c. Undefined
   d. Undefined

55. A _____ is a type of open-pit mine from which rock or minerals are extracted. They are generally used for extracting building materials, such as dimension stone. They are usually shallower than other types of open-pit mines.
   a. Quarry0
   b. Thing
   c. Undefined
   d. Undefined

56. _____ is a gaseous fossil fuel consisting primarily of methane but including significant quantities of ethane, butane, propane, carbon dioxide, nitrogen, helium and hydrogen sulfide.
   a. Thing
   b. Natural gas0
   c. Undefined
   d. Undefined

57. The _____ is defined as the part of the land adjoining or near the ocean. A coastline is properly a line on a map indicating the disposition of a _____, but the word is often used to refer to the _____ itself. The adjective coastal describes something as being on, near to, or associated with a _____.
   a. Place
   b. Coast0
   c. Undefined
   d. Undefined

58. The _____ region of the United States comprises the coasts of states which border the Gulf of Mexico. The states of Texas, Louisiana, Mississippi, Alabama, and Florida are known as the Gulf States. All Gulf States are located in the Southern region of the United States.
   a. Place
   b. Gulf Coast0
   c. Undefined
   d. Undefined

59. _____ is a hydrocolloid gel consisting of fine granular matter, clay, and salt water. The origin of the name refers to "quick" in the older meaning of "alive" rather than "fast," and is thus similar to the origin of the term quicksilver for mercury.

Chapter 6. NEAR SURFACE FLOW

a. Quicksand0
b. Thing
c. Undefined
d. Undefined

60. The _____ is a scientific agency of the United States government. The scientists study the landscape of the United States, its natural resources, and the natural hazards that threaten it. The organization has four major science disciplines, concerning biology, geography, geology, and hydrology.
   a. US Geological Survey0
   b. Person
   c. Undefined
   d. Undefined

61. The _____ occupies a significant portion of southern California and smaller parts of southwestern Utah, southern Nevada, and northwestern Arizona, in the United States. Named after the Mohave tribe of Native Americans, it occupies over 22,000 square miles in a typical Basin and Range topography.
   a. Mojave Desert0
   b. Place
   c. Undefined
   d. Undefined

62. A _____ is a section of land devoted to the production and management of food, either produce or livestock. It is the basic unit in agricultural production.
   a. Farm0
   b. Thing
   c. Undefined
   d. Undefined

63. The _____, is the main U.S. trade association for the oil and natural gas industry, representing about 400 corporations involved in production, refinement, distribution, and many other aspects of the industry. The association's chief functions on behalf of the industry include advocacy and negotiation with governmental, legal, and regulatory agencies; research into economic, toxicological, and environmental effects; establishment and certification of industry standards; and education outreach.
   a. Person
   b. American Petroleum Institute0
   c. Undefined
   d. Undefined

64. _____ is concerned with earth materials that can be utilized for economic and/or industrial purposes. These materials include precious and base metals, nonmetallic minerals, construction-grade stone, petroleum minerals, coal, and water. The term commonly refers to metallic mineral deposits and mineral resources. The techniques employed by other earth science disciplines might all be used to understand, describe, and exploit an ore deposit.
   a. Economic geology0
   b. Thing
   c. Undefined
   d. Undefined

65. _____ is an all-embracing term for the sciences related to the planet Earth. It is arguably a special case in planetary science, being the only known life-bearing planet. There are both reductionist and holistic approaches to _____. The major historic disciplines use physics, geology, geography, mathematics, chemistry, and biology to build a quantitative understanding of the principal areas or spheres of the Earth system.
   a. Earth science0
   b. Thing
   c. Undefined
   d. Undefined

66. _____ is the application of the geologic sciences to engineering practice for the purpose of assuring that the geologic factors affecting the location, design, construction, operation and maintenance of engineering works are recognized and adequately provided for.

Chapter 6. NEAR SURFACE FLOW

a. Thing
c. Undefined
b. Engineering geology0
d. Undefined

67. _____ is the sum of evaporation and plant transpiration. Evaporation accounts for the movement of water to the air from sources such as the soil, canopy interception, and waterbodies. Transpiration accounts for the movement of water within a plant and the subsequent loss of water as vapour through stomata in its leaves.
   a. Evapotranspiration0
   b. Thing
   c. Undefined
   d. Undefined

68. _____ is any product of the condensation of atmospheric water vapor that is deposited on the earth's surface. It occurs when the atmosphere becomes saturated with water vapour and the water condenses and falls out of solution. Air becomes saturated via two processes, cooling and adding moisture.
   a. Thing
   b. Precipitation0
   c. Undefined
   d. Undefined

69. _____ is the natural or artificial removal of surface and sub-surface water from a given area. Many agricultural soils need _____ to improve production or to manage water supplies.
   a. Drainage0
   b. Thing
   c. Undefined
   d. Undefined

70. A _____ is a region of land where water from rain or snow melt drains downhill into a body of water, such as a river, lake, dam, estuary, wetland, sea or ocean. The _____ includes both the streams and rivers that convey the water as well as the land surfaces from which water drains into those channels. The _____ acts like a funnel - collecting all the water within the area covered by the basin and channeling it into a waterway.
   a. Thing
   b. Drainage basin0
   c. Undefined
   d. Undefined

71. _____ is a term used to describe a group of hydrous aluminium phyllosilicate minerals, that are typically less than 2 micrometres in diameter. _____ consists of a variety of phyllosilicate minerals rich in silicon and aluminium oxides and hydroxides which include variable amounts of structural water. Clays are generally formed by the chemical weathering of silicate-bearing rocks by carbonic acid but some are formed by hydrothermal activity.
   a. Clay0
   b. Thing
   c. Undefined
   d. Undefined

72. _____ is the process by which water on the ground surface enters the soil.
   a. Infiltration0
   b. Thing
   c. Undefined
   d. Undefined

73. _____ are regions of land where water from rain or snow melt drains downhill into a body of water, such as a river, lake, dam, estuary, wetland, sea or ocean. It includes both the streams and rivers that convey the water as well as the land surfaces from which water drains into those channels. It acts like a funnel - collecting all the water within the area covered by it and channeling it into a waterway.
   a. Drainage basins0
   b. Thing
   c. Undefined
   d. Undefined

Chapter 6. NEAR SURFACE FLOW

74. _____, located in the northern part of the U.S. state of Utah, is the largest salt lake in the Western Hemisphere, the fourth-largest terminal lake in the world, and the 33rd largest lake on Earth.
    a. Place
    b. Great Salt Lake0
    c. Undefined
    d. Undefined

75. A _____ is a body of water or other liquid of considerable size contained on a body of land. A vast majority are fresh water, and lie in the Northern Hemisphere at higher latitudes. Most have a natural outflow in the form of a river or stream, but some do not, and lose water solely by evaporation and/or underground seepage.
    a. Lake0
    b. Thing
    c. Undefined
    d. Undefined

76. _____ is a term used to describe the flow of water, from rain, snowmelt, or other sources, over the land surface, and is a major component of the water cycle.
    a. Surface runoff0
    b. Thing
    c. Undefined
    d. Undefined

77. _____ is the evaporation of water from aerial parts and of plants, especially leaves but also stems, flowers and fruits. _____ is a side effect of the plant needing to open its stomata in order to obtain carbon dioxide gas from the air for photosynthesis. _____ also cools plants and enables mass flow of mineral nutrients from roots to shoots.
    a. Transpiration0
    b. Thing
    c. Undefined
    d. Undefined

78. _____ is the process by which molecules in a liquid state become a gas.
    a. Evaporation0
    b. Thing
    c. Undefined
    d. Undefined

79. An _____ is a layer of gases that may surround a material body of sufficient mass. The gases are attracted by the gravity of the body, and are retained for a longer duration if gravity is high and the _____'s temperature is low. Some planets consist mainly of various gases, and thus have very deep atmospheres.
    a. Place
    b. Atmosphere0
    c. Undefined
    d. Undefined

80. _____ is a general term for the plant life of a region; it refers to the ground cover provided by plants, and is, by far, the most abundant biotic element of the biosphere. Primeval redwood forests, coastal mangrove stands, sphagnum bogs, desert soil crusts, roadside weed patches, wheat fields, cultivated gardens and lawns; are all encompassed by the term _____.
    a. Place
    b. Vegetation0
    c. Undefined
    d. Undefined

81. _____ is the amount of water present in the soil. It is equivalent to soil water content. _____ may be measured in situ with different instrument, such as Time Domain Reflectometry, neutron probe, frequency domain sensor, tensiometer, capacitance probe, etc. In the laboratory, it is measured gravimetrically; by weighing the moist volume of soil, drying it, and then weighing it again.
    a. Thing
    b. Soil moisture0
    c. Undefined
    d. Undefined

Chapter 6. NEAR SURFACE FLOW

82. The _____ is a physical quantity that describes in which direction and at what rate the pressure changes the most rapidly around a particular location. The _____ is a dimensional quantity expressed in units of pressure per unit length.
    a. Pressure gradient0
    b. Thing
    c. Undefined
    d. Undefined

83. _____, or channel runoff, is the flow of water in streams, rivers, and other channels, and is a major element of the water cycle. It is one component of the runoff of water from the land to waterbodies, the other component being surface runoff. Water flowing in channels comes from surface runoff from adjacent hillslopes, from groundwater flow out of the ground, and from water discharged from pipes.
    a. Thing
    b. Streamflow0
    c. Undefined
    d. Undefined

84. A _____ is one of several large landmasses on Earth. They are generally identified by convention rather than any strict criteria, but seven areas are commonly reckoned as continents – they are: Asia, Africa, North America, South America, Antarctica, Europe, and Australia.
    a. Thing
    b. Continent0
    c. Undefined
    d. Undefined

85. The Earth's water is always in movement, and the _____, describes the continuous movement of water on, above, and below the surface of the Earth. Since the _____ is truly a "cycle," there is no beginning or end. Water can change states among liquid, vapor, and ice at various places in the _____, with these processes happening in the blink of an eye and over millions of years. Although the balance of water on Earth remains fairly constant over time, individual water molecules can come and go in a hurry.
    a. Hydrologic cycle0
    b. Thing
    c. Undefined
    d. Undefined

86. A _____ plots the discharge of a river as a function of time. This activity can be in response to episodal event such as a flood.
    a. Hydrograph0
    b. Thing
    c. Undefined
    d. Undefined

87. _____ is the study of Earth's surface features or those of other planets, moons, and asteroids
    a. Thing
    b. Topography0
    c. Undefined
    d. Undefined

88. _____ is the average and variations of weather over long periods of time. _____ zones can be defined using parameters such as temperature and rainfall.
    a. Thing
    b. Climate0
    c. Undefined
    d. Undefined

89. An _____ is an atom or group of atoms which have lost or gained one or more electrons, making them negatively or positively charged.
    a. Thing
    b. Ion0
    c. Undefined
    d. Undefined

Chapter 6. NEAR SURFACE FLOW

90. _____ is the substance of which physical objects are composed. _____ can be solid, liquid, plasma or gas. It constitutes the observable universe.
    a. Thing
    b. Matter0
    c. Undefined
    d. Undefined

91. _____ is matter that has come from a recently living organism; is capable of decay, or the product of decay; or is composed of organic compounds. The definition of _____ varies upon the subject it is being used for.
    a. Organic matter0
    b. Thing
    c. Undefined
    d. Undefined

92. In biology and ecology, an _____ is a living complex adaptive system of organs that influence each other in such a way that they function in some way as a stable whole.
    a. Organism0
    b. Thing
    c. Undefined
    d. Undefined

93. A _____ is any disturbed state of an astronomical body's atmosphere, especially affecting its surface, and strongly implying severe weather. It may be marked by strong wind, thunder and lightning, heavy precipitation, such as ice, or wind transporting some substance through the atmosphere.
    a. Storm0
    b. Thing
    c. Undefined
    d. Undefined

94. A _____ is an area with a high density of trees, historically, a wooded area set aside for hunting. These plant communities cover large areas of the globe and function as animal habitats, hydrologic flow modulators, and soil conservers, constituting one of the most important aspects of the Earth's biosphere.
    a. Thing
    b. Forest0
    c. Undefined
    d. Undefined

95. _____ is the process of a material being more closely packed together.
    a. Thing
    b. Compaction0
    c. Undefined
    d. Undefined

96. A _____ is a specific layer in the soil which parallels the land surface and possesses physical characteristics which differ from the layers above and beneath.
    a. Soil horizon0
    b. Thing
    c. Undefined
    d. Undefined

97. In the earth sciences, _____ is a measure of the ability of a material to transmit fluids. It is of great importance in determining the flow characteristics of hydrocarbons in oil and gas reservoirs, and of groundwater in aquifers.
    a. Thing
    b. Permeability0
    c. Undefined
    d. Undefined

98. The _____ is the top layer of the soil horizon. The technical definition of it may vary, but it is most commonly described in terms relative to deeper layers.
    a. A horizon0
    b. Thing
    c. Undefined
    d. Undefined

Chapter 6. NEAR SURFACE FLOW

99. _____ flow beneath the water table and gain water froman outflow, groundwater or the water table which creates an increased flow.
   a. Thing
   b. Effluent streams0
   c. Undefined
   d. Undefined

100. A _____ is a solid in which the constituent atoms, molecules, or ions are packed in a regularly ordered, repeating pattern extending in all three spatial dimensions. Most metals encountered in everyday life are polycrystals. Crystals are often symmetrically intergrown to form _____ twins.
   a. Thing
   b. Crystal0
   c. Undefined
   d. Undefined

101. In physics, _____ is defined as the rate of change of displacement or the rate of displacement. Simply put, it is distance per units of time.
   a. Thing
   b. Velocity0
   c. Undefined
   d. Undefined

102. A _____ is a stream or river which flows into a mainstem river, and which does not flow directly into a sea. In orography, they are ordered from those nearest to the source of the river to those nearest to the mouth of the river.
   a. Tributary0
   b. Thing
   c. Undefined
   d. Undefined

103. The _____ is the second-longest named river in North America, with a length of 2320 miles from Lake Itasca to the Gulf of Mexico. It drains most of the area between the Rocky Mountains and the Appalachian Mountains, except for the areas drained by Hudson Bay via the Red River of the North, the Great Lakes and the Rio Grande.
   a. Mississippi River0
   b. Place
   c. Undefined
   d. Undefined

104. The _____ is the ninth largest body of water in the world. It is an ocean basin largely surrounded by the North American continent and the island of Cuba. It is bounded on the northeast, north and northwest by the Gulf Coast of the United States, on the southwest and south by Mexico, and on the southeast by Cuba.
   a. Place
   b. Gulf of Mexico0
   c. Undefined
   d. Undefined

105. A _____ is flat or nearly flat land adjacent to a stream or river that experiences occasional or periodic flooding. It includes the floodway, which consists of the stream channel and adjacent areas that carry flood flows, and the flood fringe, which are areas covered by the flood, but which do not experience a strong current.
   a. Floodplain0
   b. Thing
   c. Undefined
   d. Undefined

106. An _____ plain is a relatively flat and gently sloping landform found at the base of a range of hills or mountains, formed by the deposition of _____ soil over a long period of time by one or more rivers coming from the mountains.
   a. Alluvial0
   b. Thing
   c. Undefined
   d. Undefined

Chapter 6. NEAR SURFACE FLOW

107. The _____ is the set of all extant phenomena in a given atmosphere at a given time. The term usually refers to the activity of these phenomena over short periods, as opposed to the term climate, which refers to the average atmospheric conditions over longer periods of time.
- a. Thing
- b. Weather0
- c. Undefined
- d. Undefined

108. A _____ is a bend in a river. A stream or river flowing through a wide valley or flat plain will tend to form a meandering stream course as it alternatively erodes and deposits sediments along its course. The result is a snaking pattern.
- a. Meander0
- b. Thing
- c. Undefined
- d. Undefined

109. At times when larger waves attack the beach berm, some of the beach material is redistributed offshore to become a _____ possibly visible at low tide.
- a. Longshore bar0
- b. Thing
- c. Undefined
- d. Undefined

110. An _____ is a U-shaped lacustrine water body formed when a wide meander from the mainstem of a river is cut off to create a lake. This landform is called an _____ due to the distinctive curved shape that results from this process.
- a. Oxbow lake0
- b. Thing
- c. Undefined
- d. Undefined

111. _____ refers to the principle that the same processes that shape the universe occurred in the past as they do now, and that the same laws of physics apply in all parts of the knowable universe.
- a. Thing
- b. Uniformitarianism0
- c. Undefined
- d. Undefined

112. A _____ is a landform where the mouth of a river flows into an ocean, sea, desert, estuary or lake. It builds up sediment outwards into the flat area which the river's flow encounters transported by the water and set down as the currents slow.
- a. Thing
- b. Delta0
- c. Undefined
- d. Undefined

113. An _____ is a period of long-term reduction in the temperature of Earth's climate, resulting in an expansion of the continental ice sheets, polar ice sheets and mountain glaciers .
- a. Thing
- b. Ice Age0
- c. Undefined
- d. Undefined

114. A _____ is a large, slow moving river of ice, formed from compacted layers of snow, that slowly deforms and flows in response to gravity. _____ ice is the largest reservoir of fresh water on Earth, and second only to oceans as the largest reservoir of total water. Glaciers cover vast areas of polar regions but are restricted to the highest mountains in the tropics.
- a. Glacier0
- b. Thing
- c. Undefined
- d. Undefined

Chapter 6. NEAR SURFACE FLOW

115. _____ is one of a number of channel types and has a channel that consists of a network of small channels separated by small and often temporary islands called braid bars or, in British usage, aits or eyots.
   a. Thing
   b. Braided stream0
   c. Undefined
   d. Undefined

116. Most often, a _____ refers to an artificial lake, used to store water for various uses. Reservoirs are created first by building a sturdy dam, usually out of cement, earth, rock, or a mixture. Once the dam is completed, a stream is allowed to flow behind it and eventually fill it to capacity.
   a. Thing
   b. Reservoir0
   c. Undefined
   d. Undefined

117. In geology, a _____ is a depression with predominant extent in one direction. The terms U-shaped and V-shaped are descriptive terms of geography to characterize the form of valleys. Most valleys belong to one of these two main types or a mixture of them, at least with respect of the cross section of the slopes or hillsides.
   a. Thing
   b. Valley0
   c. Undefined
   d. Undefined

118. A _____ is a barrier across flowing water that obstructs, directs or slows down the flow, often creating a reservoir, lake or impoundment.
   a. Thing
   b. Dam0
   c. Undefined
   d. Undefined

119. The _____ is a vast yet shallow underground water table aquifer located beneath the Great Plains in the United States.
   a. Thing
   b. Ogallala Aquifer0
   c. Undefined
   d. Undefined

120. The _____ are a subregion of the Great Plains in the central United States, located in eastern Colorado, western Kansas, western Nebraska, central and eastern Montana, eastern New Mexico, western Oklahoma, northwestern Texas, and southeastern Wyoming. In some definitions of the subregion, parts of western South Dakota and North Dakota are included. From east to west, the _____ rise in elevation from around 750 m to over 1800 m.
   a. Place
   b. High Plains0
   c. Undefined
   d. Undefined

121. _____ is the study of the movement, distribution, and quality of water throughout the Earth, and thus addresses both the hydrologic cycle and water resources.
   a. Thing
   b. Hydrology0
   c. Undefined
   d. Undefined

122. _____ is the net action of matter, particles or molecules, heat, momentum, or light whose end is to minimize a concentration gradient.
   a. Thing
   b. Diffusion0
   c. Undefined
   d. Undefined

Chapter 6. NEAR SURFACE FLOW

123. The _____ is the surface where the water pressure is equal to atmospheric pressure. A large amount of water within a body of sand or rock below the _____ is called an aquifer, and the ability of rocks to store such groundwater is dependent on their porosity and permeability.
   a. Water table0
   b. Thing
   c. Undefined
   d. Undefined

124. An _____ is a zone within the earth that restricts the flow of groundwater from one aquifer to another.
   a. Aquitard0
   b. Thing
   c. Undefined
   d. Undefined

125. _____ is a measure of the resistance of a fluid to deform under shear stress. It is commonly perceived as "thickness", or resistance to flow. _____ describes a fluid's internal resistance to flow and may be thought of as a measure of fluid friction.
   a. Viscosity0
   b. Thing
   c. Undefined
   d. Undefined

126. A _____ is a natural depression or hole in the surface topography caused by the removal of soil or bedrock, often both, by water. They may vary in size from less than a meter to several hundred meters both in diameter and depth, and vary in form from soil-lined bowls to bedrock-edged chasms.
   a. Thing
   b. Sinkhole0
   c. Undefined
   d. Undefined

Chapter 7. DRIVING FORCES AND MECHANISMS OF FLUID FLOW

1. _____ is the process of a material being more closely packed together.
   - a. Thing
   - b. Compaction0
   - c. Undefined
   - d. Undefined

2. _____ is any particulate matter that can be transported by fluid flow and which eventually is deposited as a layer of solid particles on the bed or bottom of a body of water or other liquid.
   - a. Sediment0
   - b. Thing
   - c. Undefined
   - d. Undefined

3. _____ rock is one of the three main rock groups. Rock formed from these covers 75% of the Earth's land area, and includes common types such as chalk, limestone, dolomite, sandstone, and shale.
   - a. Thing
   - b. Sedimentary0
   - c. Undefined
   - d. Undefined

4. The term _____ is used to refer to any geographical feature exhibiting subsidence and consequent infilling by sedimentation. As the sediments are buried, they are subjected to increasing pressure and begin the process of lithification.
   - a. Thing
   - b. Sedimentary basin0
   - c. Undefined
   - d. Undefined

5. In geology, a _____ is the outermost layer of a planet, part of its lithosphere. They are generally composed of a less dense material than its deeper layers. Earths' is composed mainly of basalt and granite. It is cooler and more rigid than the deeper layers of the mantle and core.
   - a. Crust0
   - b. Thing
   - c. Undefined
   - d. Undefined

6. An _____ is a volume of rock containing components or minerals in a mode of occurrence that renders it valuable for mining.
   - a. Thing
   - b. Ore0
   - c. Undefined
   - d. Undefined

7. _____ is one of the three main rock groups. _____ covers 75% of the Earth's land area. Four basic processes are involved in the formation of a clastic _____: weathering caused mainly by friction of waves, transportation where the sediment is carried along by a current, deposition and compaction where the sediment is squashed together to form a rock of this kind.
   - a. Thing
   - b. Sedimentary rock0
   - c. Undefined
   - d. Undefined

8. The _____ is used by geologists and other scientists to describe the timing and relationships between events that have occurred during the history of Earth.
   - a. Geological time scale0
   - b. Thing
   - c. Undefined
   - d. Undefined

9. In plate tectonics, a _____ is the normally gently sloping continental shelf area located on the trailing edge of a drifting continent. The _____ is free of the seismic and volcanic activity associated with the subduction, rifting or transform faulting that is the result of plate tectonic activity.

Chapter 7. DRIVING FORCES AND MECHANISMS OF FLUID FLOW

a. Passive margin0
b. Thing
c. Undefined
d. Undefined

10. In geology, a _____ is a place where the Earth's crust and lithosphere are being pulled apart.
a. Rift0
b. Thing
c. Undefined
d. Undefined

11. _____ is a field of study within geology concerned generally with the structures within the crust of the Earth, or other planets, and particularly with the forces and movements that have operated in a region to create these structures.
a. Thing
b. Tectonics0
c. Undefined
d. Undefined

12. A _____ fault is a particular type of fault, or break in the fabric of the Earth's crust with resulting movement of each side against the other, in which a lower stratigraphic position is pushed up and over another. This is the result of compressional forces.
a. Thrust0
b. Thing
c. Undefined
d. Undefined

13. In geology, a _____ generally refers to a linear structural depression that extends laterally over a distance, while being less steep than a trench. It can be a narrow basin or a geologic rift. In meteorolology a _____ is an elongated region of relatively low atmospheric pressure, often associated with fronts.
a. Thing
b. Trough0
c. Undefined
d. Undefined

14. The term _____ is used in geology when one or a stack of originally flat and planar surfaces, such as sedimentary strata, are bent or curved as a result of plastic, i.e. permanent, deformation.
a. Fold0
b. Thing
c. Undefined
d. Undefined

15. In geology, engineering, and surveying, _____ is the motion of a surface as it shifts downward relative to a datum such as sea-level. The opposite of _____ is uplift, which results in an increase in elevation. In meteorology, _____ refers to the downward movement of air.
a. Subsidence0
b. Thing
c. Undefined
d. Undefined

16. _____ are large geologic basins that are below sea level. Geologically, there are other undersea geomorphological features such as the continental shelves, the deep ocean trenches, and the undersea mountain rangeswhich are not considered to be part of the _____.
a. Ocean basins0
b. Thing
c. Undefined
d. Undefined

17. A _____ column is a column of rizing air in the lower altitudes of the Earth's atmosphere. Thermals are created by the uneven heating of the Earth's surface from solar radiation, and are an example of convection. The Sun warms the ground, which in turn warms the air directly above it.

Chapter 7. DRIVING FORCES AND MECHANISMS OF FLUID FLOW

a. Thermal0
b. Thing
c. Undefined
d. Undefined

18. Faults are planar rock fractures, which show evidence of relative movement. Large faults within the Earth's crust are the result of shear motion and active _____ zones are the causal locations of most earthquakes. Earthquakes are caused by energy release during rapid slippage along faults. The largest examples are at tectonic plate boundaries but many faults occur far from active plate boundaries. Since faults do not usually consist of a single, clean fracture, the term _____ zone is used when referring to the zone of complex deformation that is associated with the _____ plane.

a. Fault0
b. Thing
c. Undefined
d. Undefined

19. _____ rocks form when molten rock, magma, cools and solidifies, with or without crystallization, either below the surface as intrusive, plutonic rocks or on the surface as extrusive, volcanic, rocks.

a. Thing
b. Igneous0
c. Undefined
d. Undefined

20. The _____ is the solid outermost shell of a rocky planet. On the Earth, the _____ includes the crust and the uppermost mantle which is joined to the crust across the Mohorovièiæ discontinuity. _____ is underlain by asthenosphere, the weaker, hotter, and deeper part of the upper mantle.

a. Lithosphere0
b. Thing
c. Undefined
d. Undefined

21. The _____ is the extended perimeter of each continent and associated coastal plain, which is covered during interglacial periods such as the current epoch by relatively shallow seas and gulfs. The shelf usually ends at a point of increasing slope.

a. Thing
b. Continental shelf0
c. Undefined
d. Undefined

22. _____ is the process of building mountains, and may be studied as a tectonic structural event, as a geographical event and a chronological event, in that orogenic events cause distinctive structural phenomena and related tectonic activity, affect certain regions of rocks and crust and happen within a time frame.

a. Thing
b. Orogeny0
c. Undefined
d. Undefined

23. The _____ is a geological fault that runs a length of roughly 800 miles through western and southern California in the United States. The fault, a right-lateral strike-slip fault, marks a transform boundary between the Pacific Plate and the North American Plate.

a. San Andreas fault0
b. Thing
c. Undefined
d. Undefined

24. A _____ is a type of excavation or depression in the ground. They are generally defined by being deeper than they are wide, and by being narrow compared to their length.

a. Trench0
b. Thing
c. Undefined
d. Undefined

Chapter 7. DRIVING FORCES AND MECHANISMS OF FLUID FLOW

25. An _____ is any piece of land that is completely surrounded by water, above high tide. There are two main types of islands: continental islands and oceanic islands. There are also artificial islands. A grouping of geographically and/or geologically related islands is called an archipelago.
    a. Island0
    b. Thing
    c. Undefined
    d. Undefined

26. A _____ is a chain of volcanic islands or mountains formed by plate tectonics as an oceanic tectonic plate subducts under another tectonic plate and produces magma.
    a. Thing
    b. Volcanic arc0
    c. Undefined
    d. Undefined

27. In geology, a _____ zone is an area on Earth where two tectonic plates meet and move towards one another, with one sliding underneath the other and moving down into the mantle, at rates typically measured in centimeters per year. An oceanic plate ordinarily slides underneath a continental plate; this often creates an orogenic zone with many volcanoes and earthquakes.
    a. Thing
    b. Subduction0
    c. Undefined
    d. Undefined

28. The _____ is defined as the part of the land adjoining or near the ocean. A coastline is properly a line on a map indicating the disposition of a _____, but the word is often used to refer to the _____ itself. The adjective coastal describes something as being on, near to, or associated with a _____.
    a. Coast0
    b. Place
    c. Undefined
    d. Undefined

29. A _____ is a landform where the mouth of a river flows into an ocean, sea, desert, estuary or lake. It builds up sediment outwards into the flat area which the river's flow encounters transported by the water and set down as the currents slow.
    a. Delta0
    b. Thing
    c. Undefined
    d. Undefined

30. _____ is the geological process whereby material is added to a landform. This is the process by which wind and water create a sediment deposit, through the laying down of granular material that has been eroded and transported from another geographical location.
    a. Deposition0
    b. Thing
    c. Undefined
    d. Undefined

31. In physics, _____ is defined as the rate of change of displacement or the rate of displacement. Simply put, it is distance per units of time.
    a. Velocity0
    b. Thing
    c. Undefined
    d. Undefined

32. The _____ region of the United States comprises the coasts of states which border the Gulf of Mexico. The states of Texas, Louisiana, Mississippi, Alabama, and Florida are known as the Gulf States. All Gulf States are located in the Southern region of the United States.

Chapter 7. DRIVING FORCES AND MECHANISMS OF FLUID FLOW

a. Place
b. Gulf Coast0
c. Undefined
d. Undefined

33. _____ is a measure of the void spaces in a material, and is measured as a fraction, between 0–1, or as a percentage between 0–100%.
a. Thing
b. Porosity0
c. Undefined
d. Undefined

34. A _____ is a geological feature that is also known as a Rip in the earth causing magma to flow out and forming an undersea volcano, it also has geological features, a continuous elevational crest for some distance. Ridges are usually termed hills or mountains as well, depending on size.
a. Thing
b. Ridge0
c. Undefined
d. Undefined

35. _____ is the part of hydrology that deals with the distribution and movement of groundwater in the soil and rocks of the Earth's crust.
a. Thing
b. Hydrogeology0
c. Undefined
d. Undefined

36. In geology, _____ refers to heat sources within the planet. The planet's internal heat was originally generated during its accretion, due to gravitational binding energy, and since then additional heat has continued to be generated by the radioactive decay of elements such as uranium, thorium, and potassium.
a. Thing
b. Geothermal0
c. Undefined
d. Undefined

37. The _____ is the rate of increase in temperature per unit depth in the Earth. It varies with location and is typically measured by determining the bottom open-hole temperature after the drilling of a borehole.
a. Thing
b. Geothermal gradient0
c. Undefined
d. Undefined

38. In geology, a _____ is a depression with predominant extent in one direction. The terms U-shaped and V-shaped are descriptive terms of geography to characterize the form of valleys. Most valleys belong to one of these two main types or a mixture of them, at least with respect of the cross section of the slopes or hillsides.
a. Thing
b. Valley0
c. Undefined
d. Undefined

39. _____ is a fine-grained sedimentary rock whose original constituents were clays or muds. It is characterized by thin laminae breaking with an irregular curving fracture, often splintery and usually parallel to the often-indistinguishable bedding plane.
a. Thing
b. Shale0
c. Undefined
d. Undefined

40. _____ is a sedimentary rock composed mainly of sand-size mineral or rock grains. Most _____ is composed of quartz and/or feldspar because these are the most common minerals in the Earth's crust. Like sand, _____ may be any color, but the most common colors are tan, brown, yellow, red, gray and white.

Chapter 7. DRIVING FORCES AND MECHANISMS OF FLUID FLOW

    a. Thing
    b. Sandstone0
    c. Undefined
    d. Undefined

41. An _____ is an underground layer of water-bearing permeable rock or unconsolidated materials from which groundwater can be usefully extracted using a water well.
    a. Aquifer0
    b. Thing
    c. Undefined
    d. Undefined

42. An _____ is a zone within the earth that restricts the flow of groundwater from one aquifer to another.
    a. Thing
    b. Aquitard0
    c. Undefined
    d. Undefined

43. In the earth sciences, _____ is a measure of the ability of a material to transmit fluids. It is of great importance in determining the flow characteristics of hydrocarbons in oil and gas reservoirs, and of groundwater in aquifers.
    a. Permeability0
    b. Thing
    c. Undefined
    d. Undefined

44. _____ is the work done by a force when the relative positions of objects are changed within a physical system. In other words, it is the work done when an object is moved from one point to another. Conceptually, _____ can be thought of as the energy of an object as a result of the work done to bring it to that position from a reference point.
    a. Potential energy0
    b. Thing
    c. Undefined
    d. Undefined

45. _____ is the third or vertical dimension of land surface. When _____ is described underwater, the term bathymetry is used.
    a. Thing
    b. Terrain0
    c. Undefined
    d. Undefined

46. The _____ is the layer of granitic, sedimentary, and metamorphic rocks which form the continents and the areas of shallow seabed close to their shores, known as continental shelves. It is less dense than the material of the Earth's mantle and thus "floats" on top of it. _____ is also less dense than oceanic crust, though it is considerably thicker. About 40% of the Earth's surface is now underlain by _____.
    a. Thing
    b. Continental crust0
    c. Undefined
    d. Undefined

47. A _____ is a landform that extends above the surrounding terrain in a limited area. A _____ is generally steeper than a hill, but there is no universally accepted standard definition for the height of a _____ or a hill although a _____ usually has an identifiable summit.
    a. Mountain0
    b. Place
    c. Undefined
    d. Undefined

48. A _____ is a group of mountains bordered by lowlands or separated from other mountain ranges by passes or rivers. Individual mountains within the same _____ do not necessarily have the same geology; they may be a mix of different orogeny, for example volcanoes, uplifted mountains or fold mountains and may, therefore, be of different rock.

Chapter 7. DRIVING FORCES AND MECHANISMS OF FLUID FLOW

    a. Mountain range0   b. Thing
    c. Undefined   d. Undefined

49. _____, symbolically represented as K, is a property of vascular plants, soil or rock, that describes the ease with which water can move through pore spaces or fractures
    a. Hydraulic Conductivity0   b. Thing
    c. Undefined   d. Undefined

50. _____, a branch of geology, studies rock layers and layering. It is primarily used in the study of sedimentary and layered volcanic rocks. _____ includes two related subfields: lithologic or lithostratigraphy and biologic _____ or biostratigraphy.
    a. Thing   b. Stratigraphy0
    c. Undefined   d. Undefined

51. The _____ is a major division of the geologic timescale. The _____ is the earliest period in whose rocks are found numerous large, distinctly fossilizable multicellular organisms that are more complex than sponges or medusoids. During this time, roughly fifty separate major groups of organisms or "phyla" emerged suddenly, in most cases without evident precursors. This radiation of animal phyla is referred to as the _____ explosion.
    a. Event   b. Cambrian0
    c. Undefined   d. Undefined

52. _____ is a part of mathematics concerned with questions of size, shape, and relative position of figures and with properties of space. _____ is one of the oldest sciences. Initially a body of practical knowledge concerning lengths, areas, and volumes, in the third century B.C. _____ was put into an axiomatic form by Euclid, whose treatment set a standard for many centuries to follow.
    a. Thing   b. Geometry0
    c. Undefined   d. Undefined

53. The _____ are a broad mountain range in western North America. The _____ stretch more than 4,800 kilometers from northernmost British Columbia, in Canada, to New Mexico, in the United States.
    a. Rocky Mountains0   b. Place
    c. Undefined   d. Undefined

54. _____ is water located beneath the ground surface in soil pore spaces and in the fractures of geologic formations. _____ is recharged from, and eventually flows to, the surface naturally; natural discharge often occurs at springs and seeps, streams and can often form oases or wetlands.
    a. Groundwater0   b. Thing
    c. Undefined   d. Undefined

55. _____ is the study of Earth's surface features or those of other planets, moons, and asteroids
    a. Thing   b. Topography0
    c. Undefined   d. Undefined

56. _____ is the change in direction of a wave due to a change in its speed. This is most commonly seen when a wave passes from one medium to another.

Chapter 7. DRIVING FORCES AND MECHANISMS OF FLUID FLOW

    a. Refraction0
    c. Undefined
    b. Thing
    d. Undefined

57. In physics, _____ is the upward force on an object produced by the surrounding fluid in which it is fully or partially immersed, due to the pressure difference of the fluid between the top and bottom of the object. The net upward _____ force is equal to the magnitude of the weight of fluid displaced by the body.
    a. Buoyancy0
    c. Undefined
    b. Thing
    d. Undefined

58. _____ is the saltiness or dissolved salt content of a body of water. In oceanography, it has been traditional to express halinity not as percent, but as parts per thousand, which is approximately grams of salt per liter of solution.
    a. Salinity0
    c. Undefined
    b. Thing
    d. Undefined

59. In physical geography, a _____ is an environment "at the interface between truly terrestrial ecosystems and aquatic systems making them inherently different from each other yet highly dependent on both". In essence, they are ecotones.
    a. Place
    c. Undefined
    b. Wetland0
    d. Undefined

60. The field of _____ encompasses the analysis of static and dynamic stability of slopes of earth and rock-fill dams, slopes of other types of embankments, excavated slopes, and natural slopes in soil and soft rock.
    a. Thing
    c. Undefined
    b. Slope stability0
    d. Undefined

61. _____ is the accumulation of free salts to such an extent that it leads to degradation of soils and vegetation.
    a. Thing
    c. Undefined
    b. Soil salination0
    d. Undefined

62. _____ are waste types containing radioactive chemical elements that do not have a practical purpose. It is sometimes the product of a nuclear process, such as nuclear fission. However, other industries not directly connected to the nuclear industry can produce large quantities of _____.
    a. Radioactive waste0
    c. Undefined
    b. Thing
    d. Undefined

63. _____ is the study of the movement, distribution, and quality of water throughout the Earth, and thus addresses both the hydrologic cycle and water resources.
    a. Thing
    c. Undefined
    b. Hydrology0
    d. Undefined

64. In organic chemistry, a _____ is an organic compound consisting entirely of hydrogen and carbon. With relation to chemical terminology, aromatic hydrocarbons or arenes, alkanes, alkenes and alkyne-based compounds composed entirely of carbon or hydrogen are referred to as "Pure" hydrocarbons, whereas other hydrocarbons with bonded compounds or impurities of sulphur or nitrogen, are referred to as "impure", and remain somewhat erroneously referred to as hydrocarbons.

Chapter 7. DRIVING FORCES AND MECHANISMS OF FLUID FLOW

a. Thing
b. Hydrocarbon0
c. Undefined
d. Undefined

65. _____ is the extraction of valuable minerals or other geological materials from the earth, usually from an ore body, vein, or seam. Any material that cannot be grown from agricultural processes, or created artificially in a laboratory or factory, is usually extracted from the earth by this method.
a. Mining0
b. Thing
c. Undefined
d. Undefined

66. _____ is the scientific discipline that deals with the measurement and representation of the earth, its gravitational field, and other geodynamic phenomena, such as crustal motion, oceanic tides, and polar motion.
a. Geodesy0
b. Thing
c. Undefined
d. Undefined

67. _____ is the science and study of the solid matter that constitute the Earth. Encompassing such things as rocks, soil, and gemstones, _____ studies the composition, structure, physical properties, history, and the processes that shape Earth's components.
a. Thing
b. Geology0
c. Undefined
d. Undefined

68. The _____ is a physical quantity that describes in which direction and at what rate the pressure changes the most rapidly around a particular location. The _____ is a dimensional quantity expressed in units of pressure per unit length.
a. Thing
b. Pressure gradient0
c. Undefined
d. Undefined

69. _____, in everyday life, is most familiar as the agency that endows objects with weight. _____ is responsible for keeping the Earth and the other planets in their orbits around the Sun; for the formation of tides; and for various other phenomena that we observe. _____ is also the reason for the very existence of the Earth, the Sun, and most macroscopic objects in the universe; without it, matter would not have coalesced into these large masses, and life, as we know it, would not exist.
a. Thing
b. Gravitation0
c. Undefined
d. Undefined

70. _____ in the most general terms refers to the movement of currents within fluids. _____ is one of the major modes of Heat and mass transfer. In fluids, convective heat and mass transfer take place through both diffusion and by advection, in which matter or heat is transported by the larger-scale motion of currents in the fluid.
a. Convection0
b. Thing
c. Undefined
d. Undefined

71. _____ is a measure of the resistance of a fluid to deform under shear stress. It is commonly perceived as "thickness", or resistance to flow. _____ describes a fluid's internal resistance to flow and may be thought of as a measure of fluid friction.
a. Viscosity0
b. Thing
c. Undefined
d. Undefined

Chapter 7. DRIVING FORCES AND MECHANISMS OF FLUID FLOW

72. A _____ is a solid in which the constituent atoms, molecules, or ions are packed in a regularly ordered, repeating pattern extending in all three spatial dimensions. Most metals encountered in everyday life are polycrystals. Crystals are often symmetrically intergrown to form _____ twins.
    a. Thing
    b. Crystal0
    c. Undefined
    d. Undefined

73. The _____ is a large shield covered by a thin layer of soil that forms the nucleus of the North American craton. It has a deep, common, joined bedrock region in eastern and central Canada and stretches North from the Great Lakes to the Arctic Ocean, covering half the country.
    a. Canadian Shield0
    b. Thing
    c. Undefined
    d. Undefined

74. In meteorology, an _____ is a deviation from the normal change of an atmospheric property with altitude. It almost always refers to temperature.
    a. Inversion0
    b. Thing
    c. Undefined
    d. Undefined

75. A _____ is a phenomenon of fluid dynamics which occurs in situations where there are temperature differences within a body of liquid or gas.
    a. Convection cell0
    b. Thing
    c. Undefined
    d. Undefined

76. The _____ is a geologic basin centered on the lower peninsula of the US state of Michigan. The feature is represented by a nearly circular pattern of geologic sedimentary strata in the area with a nearly uniform structural dip toward the center of the peninsula.
    a. Michigan Basin0
    b. Place
    c. Undefined
    d. Undefined

77. _____ is the theory that Earth has been affected by sudden, short-lived, violent events that were sometimes worldwide in scope. The dominant paradigm of geology has been uniformitarianism, but recently a more inclusive and integrated view of geologic events has developed resulting in a gradual change in the scientific consensus, reflecting acceptance of some catastrophic events.
    a. Thing
    b. Catastrophism0
    c. Undefined
    d. Undefined

78. An _____ is the result from the sudden release of stored energy in the Earth's crust that creates seismic waves. At the Earth's surface, earthquakes may manifest themselves by a shaking or displacement of the ground. An _____ is caused by tectonic plates getting stuck and putting a strain on the ground. The strain becomes so great that rocks give way by breaking and sliding along fault planes.
    a. Earthquake0
    b. Thing
    c. Undefined
    d. Undefined

79. _____ is the stress applied to materials resulting in their compaction, decrease of volume.
    a. Compression stress0
    b. Thing
    c. Undefined
    d. Undefined

Chapter 7. DRIVING FORCES AND MECHANISMS OF FLUID FLOW

80. A _____ is a naturally occurring substance formed through geological processes that has a characteristic chemical composition, a highly ordered atomic structure and specific physical properties. A rock, by comparison, is an aggregate of minerals and need not have a specific chemical composition. Minerals range in composition from pure elements and simple salts to very complex silicates with thousands of known forms.
- a. Mineral0
- b. Thing
- c. Undefined
- d. Undefined

81. _____ is a highly sought-after precious metal which, for many centuries, has been used as money, a store of value and in jewelery. The metal occurs as nuggets or grains in rocks, underground "veins" and in alluvial deposits. It is one of the coinage metals. Itis dense, soft, shiny and the most malleable and ductile of the known metals.
- a. Gold0
- b. Thing
- c. Undefined
- d. Undefined

82. The _____ is a mountain range that is almost entirely in the eastern portion of the U.S. state of California. The _____ stretches 400 miles , from Fredonyer Pass in the north to Tehachapi Pass in the south. It is bounded on the west by California's Central Valley, and on the east by the Great Basin.
- a. Sierra Nevada0
- b. Place
- c. Undefined
- d. Undefined

83. _____ is the second most common mineral in the Earth's continental crust. It is made up of a lattice of silica tetrahedra. _____ belongs to the rhombohedral crystal system. In nature _____ crystals are often twinned, distorted, or so intergrown with adjacent crystals of _____ or other minerals as to only show part of this shape, or to lack obvious crystal faces altogether and appear massive.
- a. Thing
- b. Quartz0
- c. Undefined
- d. Undefined

84. In hydrology, the _____ is the volume of water transported by it in a certain amount of time.
- a. River Discharge0
- b. Thing
- c. Undefined
- d. Undefined

85. A _____ is a type of hot spring that erupts periodically, ejecting a column of hot water and steam into the air.
- a. Thing
- b. Geyser0
- c. Undefined
- d. Undefined

86. In geology the term _____ refers to the system of forces that tend to decrease the volume of or shorten rocks. Compressive strength refers to the maximum compressive stress that can be applied to a material before failure occurs.
- a. Thing
- b. Compression0
- c. Undefined
- d. Undefined

87. A _____ is a body of water or other liquid of considerable size contained on a body of land. A vast majority are fresh water, and lie in the Northern Hemisphere at higher latitudes. Most have a natural outflow in the form of a river or stream, but some do not, and lose water solely by evaporation and/or underground seepage.
- a. Lake0
- b. Thing
- c. Undefined
- d. Undefined

Chapter 7. DRIVING FORCES AND MECHANISMS OF FLUID FLOW

88. _____ is any product of the condensation of atmospheric water vapor that is deposited on the earth's surface. It occurs when the atmosphere becomes saturated with water vapour and the water condenses and falls out of solution. Air becomes saturated via two processes, cooling and adding moisture.
- a. Precipitation0
- b. Thing
- c. Undefined
- d. Undefined

89. A _____ is a spring that is produced by the emergence of geothermally-heated groundwater from the earth's crust. They are all over the earth, on every continent and even under the oceans and seas.
- a. Hot spring0
- b. Thing
- c. Undefined
- d. Undefined

90. The _____ is a headwater tributary of the Missouri River, approximately 183 miles long, in the U.S. states of Wyoming and Montana. Its confluence with the Jefferson and Gallatin rivers near Three Forks, Montana form the Missouri River.
- a. Place
- b. Madison River0
- c. Undefined
- d. Undefined

91. A _____ is a body of water with a current, confined within a bed and banks. Streams are important as conduits in the water cycle, instruments in aquifer recharge, and corridors for fish and wildlife migration.
- a. Thing
- b. Stream0
- c. Undefined
- d. Undefined

92. _____ is a rock composed of angular fragments of rocks or minerals in a matrix, that is a cementing material, that may be similar or different in composition to the fragments.
- a. Thing
- b. Breccia0
- c. Undefined
- d. Undefined

93. _____ is the net movement of water across a partially permeable membrane from a region of high solvent potential to an area of low solvent potential, up a solute concentration gradient. It is a physical process in which a solvent moves, without input of energy, across a semi permeable membrane separating two solutions of different concentrations._____ releases energy, and can be made to do work, as when a growing tree-root splits a stone.
- a. Thing
- b. Osmosis0
- c. Undefined
- d. Undefined

94. An _____ is an atom or group of atoms which have lost or gained one or more electrons, making them negatively or positively charged.
- a. Thing
- b. Ion0
- c. Undefined
- d. Undefined

95. In chemistry, a _____ is defined as a sufficiently stable electrically neutral group of at least two atoms in a definite arrangement held together by strong chemical bonds.
- a. Thing
- b. Molecule0
- c. Undefined
- d. Undefined

Chapter 7. DRIVING FORCES AND MECHANISMS OF FLUID FLOW

96. _____ contains low concentrations of dissolved salts and other total dissolved solids. It is an important renewable resource, necessary for the survival of most terrestrial organisms, and required by humans for drinking and agriculture, among many other uses.
- a. Thing
- b. Fresh water0
- c. Undefined
- d. Undefined

97. _____ is a separation process that uses pressure to force a solvent through a membrane that retains the solute on one side and allows the pure solvent to pass to the other side. More formally, it is the process of forcing a solvent from a region of high solute concentration through a membrane to a region of low solute concentration by applying a pressure in excess of the osmotic pressure.
- a. Reverse osmosis0
- b. Thing
- c. Undefined
- d. Undefined

98. _____ is water from a sea or ocean. On average, _____ in the world's oceans has a salinity of ~3.5%, or 35 parts per thousand. This means that every 1 kg of _____ has approximately 35 grams of dissolved salts.
- a. Seawater0
- b. Thing
- c. Undefined
- d. Undefined

99. _____ is the hydrostatic pressure produced by a solution in a space divided by a semipermeable membrane due to a differential in the concentrations of solute.
- a. Thing
- b. Osmotic pressure0
- c. Undefined
- d. Undefined

100. _____ is a term used to describe a group of hydrous aluminium phyllosilicate minerals, that are typically less than 2 micrometres in diameter. _____ consists of a variety of phyllosilicate minerals rich in silicon and aluminium oxides and hydroxides which include variable amounts of structural water. Clays are generally formed by the chemical weathering of silicate-bearing rocks by carbonic acid but some are formed by hydrothermal activity.
- a. Thing
- b. Clay0
- c. Undefined
- d. Undefined

101. An _____ phenomenon is an observed event which deviates from what is expected according to existing rules or scientific theory.
- a. Thing
- b. Anomalous0
- c. Undefined
- d. Undefined

102. _____ refers to directed, regular, or systematic movement of a group of objects, organisms, or people.
- a. Migration0
- b. Thing
- c. Undefined
- d. Undefined

103. In thermal physics, _____ is the passage of thermal energy from a hot to a cold body. When a physical body, e.g. an object or fluid, is at a different temperature than its surroundings or another body, transfer of thermal energy, also known as _____, occurs in such a way that the body and the surroundings reach thermal equilibrium.
- a. Heat transfer0
- b. Thing
- c. Undefined
- d. Undefined

104. _____ refers to things having to do with the land or with the planet Earth.

a. Terrestrial0 b. Thing
c. Undefined d. Undefined

Chapter 8. ABNORMAL FLUID PRESSURES

1. Overburden, or _____ pressure, is a term used in geology to denote the pressure imposed on a stratigraphic layer by the weight of overlying layers of material.
   - a. Lithostatic0
   - b. Thing
   - c. Undefined
   - d. Undefined

2. _____ is a term used in geology to denote the pressure imposed on a stratigraphic layer by the weight of overlying layers of material.
   - a. Event
   - b. Lithostatic pressure0
   - c. Undefined
   - d. Undefined

3. _____ rock is one of the three main rock groups. Rock formed from these covers 75% of the Earth's land area, and includes common types such as chalk, limestone, dolomite, sandstone, and shale.
   - a. Sedimentary0
   - b. Thing
   - c. Undefined
   - d. Undefined

4. The term _____ is used to refer to any geographical feature exhibiting subsidence and consequent infilling by sedimentation. As the sediments are buried, they are subjected to increasing pressure and begin the process of lithification.
   - a. Sedimentary basin0
   - b. Thing
   - c. Undefined
   - d. Undefined

5. _____ is any particulate matter that can be transported by fluid flow and which eventually is deposited as a layer of solid particles on the bed or bottom of a body of water or other liquid.
   - a. Thing
   - b. Sediment0
   - c. Undefined
   - d. Undefined

6. _____ is a naturally occurring liquid found in formations in the Earth consisting of a complex mixture of hydrocarbons of various lengths.
   - a. Thing
   - b. Petroleum0
   - c. Undefined
   - d. Undefined

7. _____ is the theory that Earth has been affected by sudden, short-lived, violent events that were sometimes worldwide in scope. The dominant paradigm of geology has been uniformitarianism, but recently a more inclusive and integrated view of geologic events has developed resulting in a gradual change in the scientific consensus, reflecting acceptance of some catastrophic events.
   - a. Thing
   - b. Catastrophism0
   - c. Undefined
   - d. Undefined

8. The _____ is defined as the part of the land adjoining or near the ocean. A coastline is properly a line on a map indicating the disposition of a _____, but the word is often used to refer to the _____ itself. The adjective coastal describes something as being on, near to, or associated with a _____.
   - a. Place
   - b. Coast0
   - c. Undefined
   - d. Undefined

9. The _____ region of the United States comprises the coasts of states which border the Gulf of Mexico. The states of Texas, Louisiana, Mississippi, Alabama, and Florida are known as the Gulf States. All Gulf States are located in the Southern region of the United States.

Chapter 8. ABNORMAL FLUID PRESSURES

a. Place
b. Gulf Coast0
c. Undefined
d. Undefined

10. _____ is the part of hydrology that deals with the distribution and movement of groundwater in the soil and rocks of the Earth's crust.
    a. Thing
    b. Hydrogeology0
    c. Undefined
    d. Undefined

11. The _____ is used by geologists and other scientists to describe the timing and relationships between events that have occurred during the history of Earth.
    a. Thing
    b. Geological time scale0
    c. Undefined
    d. Undefined

12. An _____ phenomenon is an observed event which deviates from what is expected according to existing rules or scientific theory.
    a. Anomalous0
    b. Thing
    c. Undefined
    d. Undefined

13. The _____ is a physical quantity that describes in which direction and at what rate the pressure changes the most rapidly around a particular location. The _____ is a dimensional quantity expressed in units of pressure per unit length.
    a. Thing
    b. Pressure gradient0
    c. Undefined
    d. Undefined

14. The carbonate mineral _____ is a chemical or biochemical calcium carbonate and is one of the most widely distributed minerals on the Earth's surface. It is a common constituent of sedimentary rocks, limestone in particular. It is also the primary mineral in metamorphic marble
    a. Calcite0
    b. Thing
    c. Undefined
    d. Undefined

15. _____ is a fine-grained sedimentary rock whose original constituents were clays or muds. It is characterized by thin laminae breaking with an irregular curving fracture, often splintery and usually parallel to the often-indistinguishable bedding plane.
    a. Thing
    b. Shale0
    c. Undefined
    d. Undefined

16. _____ is a measure of the void spaces in a material, and is measured as a fraction, between 0–1, or as a percentage between 0–100%.
    a. Thing
    b. Porosity0
    c. Undefined
    d. Undefined

17. _____ is any product of the condensation of atmospheric water vapor that is deposited on the earth's surface. It occurs when the atmosphere becomes saturated with water vapour and the water condenses and falls out of solution. Air becomes saturated via two processes, cooling and adding moisture.

Chapter 8. ABNORMAL FLUID PRESSURES

    a. Precipitation0   b. Thing
    c. Undefined   d. Undefined

18. In the earth sciences, _____ is a measure of the ability of a material to transmit fluids. It is of great importance in determining the flow characteristics of hydrocarbons in oil and gas reservoirs, and of groundwater in aquifers.
    a. Permeability0   b. Thing
    c. Undefined   d. Undefined

19. Most often, a _____ refers to an artificial lake, used to store water for various uses. Reservoirs are created first by building a sturdy dam, usually out of cement, earth, rock, or a mixture. Once the dam is completed, a stream is allowed to flow behind it and eventually fill it to capacity.
    a. Thing   b. Reservoir0
    c. Undefined   d. Undefined

20. Faults are planar rock fractures, which show evidence of relative movement. Large faults within the Earth's crust are the result of shear motion and active _____ zones are the causal locations of most earthquakes. Earthquakes are caused by energy release during rapid slippage along faults. The largest examples are at tectonic plate boundaries but many faults occur far from active plate boundaries. Since faults do not usually consist of a single, clean fracture, the term _____ zone is used when referring to the zone of complex deformation that is associated with the _____ plane.
    a. Thing   b. Fault0
    c. Undefined   d. Undefined

21. An _____ is a zone within the earth that restricts the flow of groundwater from one aquifer to another.
    a. Aquitard0   b. Thing
    c. Undefined   d. Undefined

22. _____ are naturally occurring substances that are considered valuable in their relatively unmodified or natural form. Its value rests in the amount of the material available and the demand for the certain material.
    a. Natural resources0   b. Thing
    c. Undefined   d. Undefined

23. _____ is the discipline concerned with the questions of how one should live ; what sorts of things exist and what are their essential natures ; what counts as genuine knowledge; and what are the correct principles of reasoning.
    a. Thing   b. Philosophy0
    c. Undefined   d. Undefined

24. _____ refers to the cyclic rizing and falling of Earth's ocean surface caused by the tidal forces of the Moon and the sun acting on the oceans. They cause changes in the depth of the marine and estuarine water bodies and produce oscillating currents known as tidal streams, making prediction of tides important for coastal navigation.
    a. Thing   b. Tide0
    c. Undefined   d. Undefined

25. _____ are the cyclic rizing and falling of Earth's ocean surface caused by the tidal forces of the Moon and the sun acting on the oceans. _____ cause changes in the depth of the marine and estuarine water bodies and produce oscillating currents known as tidal streams, making prediction of _____ important for coastal navigation.

Chapter 8. ABNORMAL FLUID PRESSURES

    a. Tides0   b. Thing
    c. Undefined   d. Undefined

26. An _____ is an underground layer of water-bearing permeable rock or unconsolidated materials from which groundwater can be usefully extracted using a water well.
    a. Aquifer0   b. Thing
    c. Undefined   d. Undefined

27. A _____ column is a column of rizing air in the lower altitudes of the Earth's atmosphere. Thermals are created by the uneven heating of the Earth's surface from solar radiation, and are an example of convection. The Sun warms the ground, which in turn warms the air directly above it.
    a. Thing   b. Thermal0
    c. Undefined   d. Undefined

28. _____ is water located beneath the ground surface in soil pore spaces and in the fractures of geologic formations. _____ is recharged from, and eventually flows to, the surface naturally; natural discharge often occurs at springs and seeps, streams and can often form oases or wetlands.
    a. Thing   b. Groundwater0
    c. Undefined   d. Undefined

29. An _____ is the result from the sudden release of stored energy in the Earth's crust that creates seismic waves. At the Earth's surface, earthquakes may manifest themselves by a shaking or displacement of the ground. An _____ is caused by tectonic plates getting stuck and putting a strain on the ground. The strain becomes so great that rocks give way by breaking and sliding along fault planes.
    a. Thing   b. Earthquake0
    c. Undefined   d. Undefined

30. In geology, a _____ is the outermost layer of a planet, part of its lithosphere. They are generally composed of a less dense material than its deeper layers.Earths' is composed mainly of basalt and granite. It is cooler and more rigid than the deeper layers of the mantle and core.
    a. Crust0   b. Thing
    c. Undefined   d. Undefined

31. In geology, _____ is soil at or below the freezing point of water for two or more years. Ice is not always present, as may be in the case of nonporous bedrock, but it frequently occurs and it may be in amounts exceeding the potential hydraulic saturation of the ground material. Most _____ is located in high latitudes, but alpine _____ exists at high altitudes.
    a. Permafrost0   b. Thing
    c. Undefined   d. Undefined

32. A _____ is a section of a river of relatively steep gradient causing an increase in water flow and turbulence. A _____ is a hydrological feature between a run and a cascade. It is characterized by the river becoming shallower and having some rocks exposed above the flow surface.
    a. Rapid0   b. Thing
    c. Undefined   d. Undefined

33. _____ is the condition of a system in which competing influences are balanced.

Chapter 8. ABNORMAL FLUID PRESSURES 95

    a. Thing
    c. Undefined
    b. Equilibrium0
    d. Undefined

34. _____ is the study of Earth's surface features or those of other planets, moons, and asteroids
    a. Thing
    c. Undefined
    b. Topography0
    d. Undefined

35. _____ is the net action of matter, particles or molecules, heat, momentum, or light whose end is to minimize a concentration gradient.
    a. Diffusion0
    c. Undefined
    b. Thing
    d. Undefined

36. _____, symbolically represented as K, is a property of vascular plants, soil or rock, that describes the ease with which water can move through pore spaces or fractures
    a. Thing
    c. Undefined
    b. Hydraulic Conductivity0
    d. Undefined

37. In geology, _____ refers to heat sources within the planet. The planet's internal heat was originally generated during its accretion, due to gravitational binding energy, and since then additional heat has continued to be generated by the radioactive decay of elements such as uranium, thorium, and potassium.
    a. Geothermal0
    c. Undefined
    b. Thing
    d. Undefined

38. The _____ is the rate of increase in temperature per unit depth in the Earth. It varies with location and is typically measured by determining the bottom open-hole temperature after the drilling of a borehole.
    a. Thing
    c. Undefined
    b. Geothermal gradient0
    d. Undefined

39. _____ is displacement of solids by the agents of ocean currents, wind, water, or ice by downward or down-slope movement in response to gravity or by living organisms.
    a. Erosion0
    c. Undefined
    b. Thing
    d. Undefined

40. _____ is a small island located in the middle of San Francisco Bay in California, United States. It served as a lighthouse, then a military fortification, then a military prison followed by a federal prison until 1963, when it became a national recreation area.
    a. Alcatraz Island0
    c. Undefined
    b. Place
    d. Undefined

41. _____ is the process of a material being more closely packed together.
    a. Thing
    c. Undefined
    b. Compaction0
    d. Undefined

Chapter 8. ABNORMAL FLUID PRESSURES

42. _____ is a term used to describe a group of hydrous aluminium phyllosilicate minerals, that are typically less than 2 micrometres in diameter. _____ consists of a variety of phyllosilicate minerals rich in silicon and aluminium oxides and hydroxides which include variable amounts of structural water. Clays are generally formed by the chemical weathering of silicate-bearing rocks by carbonic acid but some are formed by hydrothermal activity.
- a. Thing
- b. Clay0
- c. Undefined
- d. Undefined

43. _____ is a sedimentary rock composed mainly of sand-size mineral or rock grains. Most _____ is composed of quartz and/or feldspar because these are the most common minerals in the Earth's crust. Like sand, _____ may be any color, but the most common colors are tan, brown, yellow, red, gray and white.
- a. Sandstone0
- b. Thing
- c. Undefined
- d. Undefined

44. The _____ covers roughly the time span between the demise of the non-avian dinosaurs and beginning of the most recent Ice Age. Each epoch of the _____ was marked by striking developments in mammalian life. The earliest recognizable hominoid relatives of humans appeared. Tectonic activity continued as Gondwana finally split completely apart.
- a. Thing
- b. Tertiary0
- c. Undefined
- d. Undefined

45. _____ is the saltiness or dissolved salt content of a body of water. In oceanography, it has been traditional to express halinity not as percent, but as parts per thousand, which is approximately grams of salt per liter of solution.
- a. Thing
- b. Salinity0
- c. Undefined
- d. Undefined

46. In physics, _____ is the upward force on an object produced by the surrounding fluid in which it is fully or partially immersed, due to the pressure difference of the fluid between the top and bottom of the object. The net upward _____ force is equal to the magnitude of the weight of fluid displaced by the body.
- a. Thing
- b. Buoyancy0
- c. Undefined
- d. Undefined

47. In physics, _____ is defined as the rate of change of displacement or the rate of displacement. Simply put, it is distance per units of time.
- a. Thing
- b. Velocity0
- c. Undefined
- d. Undefined

48. A _____ is a naturally occurring substance formed through geological processes that has a characteristic chemical composition, a highly ordered atomic structure and specific physical properties. A rock, by comparison, is an aggregate of minerals and need not have a specific chemical composition. Minerals range in composition from pure elements and simple salts to very complex silicates with thousands of known forms.
- a. Thing
- b. Mineral0
- c. Undefined
- d. Undefined

49. _____ are hydrous aluminium phyllosilicates, sometimes with variable amounts of iron, magnesium, alkali metals, alkaline earths and other cations. Clays have structures similar to the micas and therefore form flat hexagonal sheets. _____ are common weathering products and low temperature hydrothermal alteration products.

Chapter 8. ABNORMAL FLUID PRESSURES

a. Clay minerals0
b. Thing
c. Undefined
d. Undefined

50. A _____ is a solid in which the constituent atoms, molecules, or ions are packed in a regularly ordered, repeating pattern extending in all three spatial dimensions. Most metals encountered in everyday life are polycrystals. Crystals are often symmetrically intergrown to form _____ twins.
   a. Thing
   b. Crystal0
   c. Undefined
   d. Undefined

51. A _____ is a unique arrangement of atoms in a crystal. It is composed of a unit cell, a set of atoms arranged in a particular way, which is periodically repeated in three dimensions on a lattice. The spacing between unit cells in various directions is called its lattice parameters. The symmetry properties of the crystal are embodied in its space group.
   a. Crystal structure0
   b. Thing
   c. Undefined
   d. Undefined

52. _____ is one of the allotropes of carbon. It holds the distinction of being the most stable form of solid carbon ever discovered. It may be considered to be the highest grade of coal, just above anthracite, although it is not normally used as fuel because it is hard to ignite.
   a. Thing
   b. Graphite0
   c. Undefined
   d. Undefined

53. _____ is a mixture of organic chemical compounds that make up a portion of the organic matter in sedimentary rocks. It is insoluble in normal organic solvents because of the huge molecular weight of its component compounds. The soluble portion is known as bitumen.
   a. Kerogen0
   b. Thing
   c. Undefined
   d. Undefined

54. _____ is matter that has come from a recently living organism; is capable of decay, or the product of decay; or is composed of organic compounds. The definition of _____ varies upon the subject it is being used for.
   a. Organic matter0
   b. Thing
   c. Undefined
   d. Undefined

55. In biology and ecology, an _____ is a living complex adaptive system of organs that influence each other in such a way that they function in some way as a stable whole.
   a. Organism0
   b. Thing
   c. Undefined
   d. Undefined

56. In organic chemistry, a _____ is a salt of carbonic acid.
   a. Thing
   b. Carbonate0
   c. Undefined
   d. Undefined

57. _____ is the change in direction of a wave due to a change in its speed. This is most commonly seen when a wave passes from one medium to another.
   a. Refraction0
   b. Thing
   c. Undefined
   d. Undefined

Chapter 8. ABNORMAL FLUID PRESSURES

58. _____, a branch of geology, studies rock layers and layering. It is primarily used in the study of sedimentary and layered volcanic rocks. _____ includes two related subfields: lithologic or lithostratigraphy and biologic _____ or biostratigraphy.
   a. Thing
   b. Stratigraphy0
   c. Undefined
   d. Undefined

59. The law of _____, also known as law of mass/matter conservation, states that the mass of a closed system of substances will remain constant, regardless of the processes acting inside the system. An equivalent statement is that matter cannot be created nor destroyed, although it may change form.
   a. Thing
   b. Conservation of mass0
   c. Undefined
   d. Undefined

60. _____ is a part of mathematics concerned with questions of size, shape, and relative position of figures and with properties of space. _____ is one of the oldest sciences. Initially a body of practical knowledge concerning lengths, areas, and volumes, in the third century B.C. _____ was put into an axiomatic form by Euclid, whose treatment set a standard for many centuries to follow.
   a. Geometry0
   b. Thing
   c. Undefined
   d. Undefined

Chapter 9. ENVIRONMENTAL HYDROGEOLOGY

1. In geology, engineering, and surveying, _____ is the motion of a surface as it shifts downward relative to a datum such as sea-level. The opposite of _____ is uplift, which results in an increase in elevation. In meteorology, _____ refers to the downward movement of air.
   a. Thing
   b. Subsidence0
   c. Undefined
   d. Undefined

2. _____ is the process of a material being more closely packed together.
   a. Compaction0
   b. Thing
   c. Undefined
   d. Undefined

3. _____ is water located beneath the ground surface in soil pore spaces and in the fractures of geologic formations. _____ is recharged from, and eventually flows to, the surface naturally; natural discharge often occurs at springs and seeps, streams and can often form oases or wetlands.
   a. Thing
   b. Groundwater0
   c. Undefined
   d. Undefined

4. _____ is the extraction of valuable minerals or other geological materials from the earth, usually from an ore body, vein, or seam. Any material that cannot be grown from agricultural processes, or created artificially in a laboratory or factory, is usually extracted from the earth by this method.
   a. Mining0
   b. Thing
   c. Undefined
   d. Undefined

5. An _____ is an underground layer of water-bearing permeable rock or unconsolidated materials from which groundwater can be usefully extracted using a water well.
   a. Thing
   b. Aquifer0
   c. Undefined
   d. Undefined

6. Most often, a _____ refers to an artificial lake, used to store water for various uses. Reservoirs are created first by building a sturdy dam, usually out of cement, earth, rock, or a mixture. Once the dam is completed, a stream is allowed to flow behind it and eventually fill it to capacity.
   a. Thing
   b. Reservoir0
   c. Undefined
   d. Undefined

7. _____ is a naturally occurring liquid found in formations in the Earth consisting of a complex mixture of hydrocarbons of various lengths.
   a. Thing
   b. Petroleum0
   c. Undefined
   d. Undefined

8. An _____ is often thought of as being an underground "lake" of oil, but it is actually composed of hydrocarbons contained in porous rock formations.
   a. Thing
   b. Oil reservoir0
   c. Undefined
   d. Undefined

9. In geology the term _____ refers to the system of forces that tend to decrease the volume of or shorten rocks. Compressive strength refers to the maximum compressive stress that can be applied to a material before failure occurs.

Chapter 9. ENVIRONMENTAL HYDROGEOLOGY

    a. Compression0
    b. Thing
    c. Undefined
    d. Undefined

10. _____, in everyday life, is most familiar as the agency that endows objects with weight. _____ is responsible for keeping the Earth and the other planets in their orbits around the Sun; for the formation of tides; and for various other phenomena that we observe. _____ is also the reason for the very existence of the Earth, the Sun, and most macroscopic objects in the universe; without it, matter would not have coalesced into these large masses, and life, as we know it, would not exist.
    a. Thing
    b. Gravitation0
    c. Undefined
    d. Undefined

11. In the earth sciences, _____ is a measure of the ability of a material to transmit fluids. It is of great importance in determining the flow characteristics of hydrocarbons in oil and gas reservoirs, and of groundwater in aquifers.
    a. Thing
    b. Permeability0
    c. Undefined
    d. Undefined

12. _____ refers to the area of the Central Valley of California that lies south of the Sacramento-San Joaquin Delta in Stockton. Although most of the valley is rural, it does contain major urban cities such as Stockton, Fresno, Modesto, Bakersfield, and Merced.
    a. Place
    b. San Joaquin Valley0
    c. Undefined
    d. Undefined

13. In geology, a _____ is a depression with predominant extent in one direction. The terms U-shaped and V-shaped are descriptive terms of geography to characterize the form of valleys. Most valleys belong to one of these two main types or a mixture of them, at least with respect of the cross section of the slopes or hillsides.
    a. Valley0
    b. Thing
    c. Undefined
    d. Undefined

14. _____ is the study of the three dimensional distribution of rock bodies and their planar or folded surfaces, and their internal fabrics.
    a. Structural geology0
    b. Thing
    c. Undefined
    d. Undefined

15. An _____ is a zone within the earth that restricts the flow of groundwater from one aquifer to another.
    a. Thing
    b. Aquitard0
    c. Undefined
    d. Undefined

16. _____ is a term used to describe a group of hydrous aluminium phyllosilicate minerals, that are typically less than 2 micrometres in diameter. _____ consists of a variety of phyllosilicate minerals rich in silicon and aluminium oxides and hydroxides which include variable amounts of structural water. Clays are generally formed by the chemical weathering of silicate-bearing rocks by carbonic acid but some are formed by hydrothermal activity.
    a. Clay0
    b. Thing
    c. Undefined
    d. Undefined

Chapter 9. ENVIRONMENTAL HYDROGEOLOGY

17. _____ is a sedimentary rock composed mainly of sand-size mineral or rock grains. Most _____ is composed of quartz and/or feldspar because these are the most common minerals in the Earth's crust. Like sand, _____ may be any color, but the most common colors are tan, brown, yellow, red, gray and white.
 a. Sandstone0   b. Thing
 c. Undefined   d. Undefined

18. _____, symbolically represented as K, is a property of vascular plants, soil or rock, that describes the ease with which water can move through pore spaces or fractures
 a. Hydraulic Conductivity0   b. Thing
 c. Undefined   d. Undefined

19. A _____ is a section of a river of relatively steep gradient causing an increase in water flow and turbulence. A _____ is a hydrological feature between a run and a cascade. It is characterized by the river becoming shallower and having some rocks exposed above the flow surface.
 a. Rapid0   b. Thing
 c. Undefined   d. Undefined

20. Mean _____ is the average height of the sea, with reference to a suitable reference surface.
 a. Thing   b. Sea level0
 c. Undefined   d. Undefined

21. A _____, is a site for the disposal of waste materials by burial and is the oldest form of waste treatment.
 a. Thing   b. Landfill0
 c. Undefined   d. Undefined

22. A _____ is a natural or artificial slope or wall, usually earthen and often parallels the course of a river.
 a. Thing   b. Levee0
 c. Undefined   d. Undefined

23. _____ transport is a transportation of goods through a pipe. Most commonly, liquid and gases are sent, but pneumatic tubes that transport solid capsules using compressed air have also been used..
 a. Pipeline0   b. Thing
 c. Undefined   d. Undefined

24. A _____ is a barrier across flowing water that obstructs, directs or slows down the flow, often creating a reservoir, lake or impoundment.
 a. Thing   b. Dam0
 c. Undefined   d. Undefined

25. _____ is the part of hydrology that deals with the distribution and movement of groundwater in the soil and rocks of the Earth's crust.
 a. Thing   b. Hydrogeology0
 c. Undefined   d. Undefined

26. An _____ plain is a relatively flat and gently sloping landform found at the base of a range of hills or mountains, formed by the deposition of _____ soil over a long period of time by one or more rivers coming from the mountains.

Chapter 9. ENVIRONMENTAL HYDROGEOLOGY

    a. Thing
    c. Undefined
    b. Alluvial0
    d. Undefined

27. The _____ is the average height of the sea, with reference to a suitable reference surface. To extend this definition far from the sea means comparing the local height of the mean sea surface with a "level" reference surface, or datum, called the geoid.
    a. Sea-level0
    c. Undefined
    b. Thing
    d. Undefined

28. _____ is the natural or artificial removal of surface and sub-surface water from a given area. Many agricultural soils need _____ to improve production or to manage water supplies.
    a. Drainage0
    c. Undefined
    b. Thing
    d. Undefined

29. An _____ is the result from the sudden release of stored energy in the Earth's crust that creates seismic waves. At the Earth's surface, earthquakes may manifest themselves by a shaking or displacement of the ground. An _____ is caused by tectonic plates getting stuck and putting a strain on the ground. The strain becomes so great that rocks give way by breaking and sliding along fault planes.
    a. Earthquake0
    c. Undefined
    b. Thing
    d. Undefined

30. In meteorology, a _____ is an area of low atmospheric pressure characterized by inward spiraling winds that rotate counter clockwise in the northern hemisphere and clockwise in the southern hemisphere of the Earth.
    a. Thing
    c. Undefined
    b. Cyclone0
    d. Undefined

31. _____ is the study of Earth's surface features or those of other planets, moons, and asteroids
    a. Topography0
    c. Undefined
    b. Thing
    d. Undefined

32. A _____ is a landform that extends above the surrounding terrain in a limited area. A _____ is generally steeper than a hill, but there is no universally accepted standard definition for the height of a _____ or a hill although a _____ usually has an identifiable summit.
    a. Mountain0
    c. Undefined
    b. Place
    d. Undefined

33. _____ is a field of study within geology concerned generally with the structures within the crust of the Earth, or other planets, and particularly with the forces and movements that have operated in a region to create these structures.
    a. Tectonics0
    c. Undefined
    b. Thing
    d. Undefined

34. The _____ is a mountain range that is almost entirely in the eastern portion of the U.S. state of California. The _____ stretches 400 miles , from Fredonyer Pass in the north to Tehachapi Pass in the south. It is bounded on the west by California's Central Valley, and on the east by the Great Basin.

Chapter 9. ENVIRONMENTAL HYDROGEOLOGY

    a. Place
    b. Sierra Nevada0
    c. Undefined
    d. Undefined

35. In geology, a _____ generally refers to a linear structural depression that extends laterally over a distance, while being less steep than a trench. It can be a narrow basin or a geologic rift. In meteorolology a _____ is an elongated region of relatively low atmospheric pressure, often associated with fronts.
    a. Trough0
    b. Thing
    c. Undefined
    d. Undefined

36. A _____ is a body of water with a current, confined within a bed and banks. Streams are important as conduits in the water cycle, instruments in aquifer recharge, and corridors for fish and wildlife migration.
    a. Thing
    b. Stream0
    c. Undefined
    d. Undefined

37. _____ is any particulate matter that can be transported by fluid flow and which eventually is deposited as a layer of solid particles on the bed or bottom of a body of water or other liquid.
    a. Sediment0
    b. Thing
    c. Undefined
    d. Undefined

38. A _____ is a body of water or other liquid of considerable size contained on a body of land. A vast majority are fresh water, and lie in the Northern Hemisphere at higher latitudes. Most have a natural outflow in the form of a river or stream, but some do not, and lose water solely by evaporation and/or underground seepage.
    a. Lake0
    b. Thing
    c. Undefined
    d. Undefined

39. The _____ is used by geologists and other scientists to describe the timing and relationships between events that have occurred during the history of Earth.
    a. Geological time scale0
    b. Thing
    c. Undefined
    d. Undefined

40. _____ is soil or rock derived granular material of a specific grain size. _____ may occur as a soil or alternatively as suspended sediment in a water column of any surface water body. It may also exist as deposition soil at the bottom of a water body.
    a. Thing
    b. Silt0
    c. Undefined
    d. Undefined

41. _____ is any product of the condensation of atmospheric water vapor that is deposited on the earth's surface. It occurs when the atmosphere becomes saturated with water vapour and the water condenses and falls out of solution. Air becomes saturated via two processes, cooling and adding moisture.
    a. Thing
    b. Precipitation0
    c. Undefined
    d. Undefined

42. _____ is the average and variations of weather over long periods of time. _____ zones can be defined using parameters such as temperature and rainfall.

Chapter 9. ENVIRONMENTAL HYDROGEOLOGY

a. Climate0
b. Thing
c. Undefined
d. Undefined

43. An alluvial fan is a fan-shaped deposit formed where a fast flowing stream flattens, slows, and spreads typically at the exit of a canyon onto a flatter plain. A convergence of neighboring _____ into a single apron of deposits against a slope is called a bajada, or compound alluvial fan.

a. Thing
b. Alluvial fans0
c. Undefined
d. Undefined

44. _____ is the artificial application of water to the soil usually for assisting in growing crops. In crop production it is mainly used to replace missing rainfall in periods of drought, but also to protect plants against frost.

a. Irrigation0
b. Thing
c. Undefined
d. Undefined

45. _____ is the production of food, feed, fiber, fuel and other goods by the systematic raizing of plants and animals.

a. Agriculture0
b. Thing
c. Undefined
d. Undefined

46. _____ are artificial channels for water. There are two main types of _____: irrigation _____, which are used for the delivery of water, and waterways, which are transportation _____ used for passage of goods and people, often connected to existing lakes, rivers, or oceans.

a. Thing
b. Canals0
c. Undefined
d. Undefined

47. _____ is a highly sought-after precious metal which, for many centuries, has been used as money, a store of value and in jewelery. The metal occurs as nuggets or grains in rocks, underground "veins" and in alluvial deposits. It is one of the coinage metals. Itis dense, soft, shiny and the most malleable and ductile of the known metals.

a. Gold0
b. Thing
c. Undefined
d. Undefined

48. Water collecting on the ground or in a stream, river, lake, or wetland is called _____; as opposed to groundwater. _____ is naturally replenished by precipitation and naturally lost through discharge to the oceans, evaporation, and sub-surface seepage into the groundwater. _____ is the largest source of fresh water.

a. Thing
b. Surface water0
c. Undefined
d. Undefined

49. A _____ is an extended period of months or years when a region notes a deficiency in its water supply. Generally, this occurs when a region receives consistently below average precipitation.

a. Thing
b. Drought0
c. Undefined
d. Undefined

50. A _____ is a landform where the mouth of a river flows into an ocean, sea, desert, estuary or lake. It builds up sediment outwards into the flat area which the river's flow encounters transported by the water and set down as the currents slow.

Chapter 9. ENVIRONMENTAL HYDROGEOLOGY

    a. Delta0
    c. Undefined
    b. Thing
    d. Undefined

51. The _____ is an agency under the U.S. Department of the Interior and oversees water resource management, specifically as it applies to the oversight and/or operation of numerous water diversion, delivery, storage and hydroelectric power generation projects it built throughout the western United States.
    a. Bureau of Reclamation0
    c. Undefined
    b. Person
    d. Undefined

52. _____ is the net action of matter, particles or molecules, heat, momentum, or light whose end is to minimize a concentration gradient.
    a. Thing
    c. Undefined
    b. Diffusion0
    d. Undefined

53. _____ is the state of extreme dryness, or the process of extreme drying. A desiccant is a hygroscopic substance that induces or sustains such a state in its local vicinity in a moderately-well sealed container.
    a. Thing
    c. Undefined
    b. Desiccation0
    d. Undefined

54. A _____ is a naturally occurring substance formed through geological processes that has a characteristic chemical composition, a highly ordered atomic structure and specific physical properties. A rock, by comparison, is an aggregate of minerals and need not have a specific chemical composition. Minerals range in composition from pure elements and simple salts to very complex silicates with thousands of known forms.
    a. Mineral0
    c. Undefined
    b. Thing
    d. Undefined

55. _____ is a very soft phyllosilicate mineral that typically forms in microscopic crystals, forming a clay. It is the main constituent of the volcanic ash weathering product, bentonite.
    a. Thing
    c. Undefined
    b. Montmorillonite0
    d. Undefined

56. _____ is the geological process whereby material is added to a landform. This is the process by which wind and water create a sediment deposit, through the laying down of granular material that has been eroded and transported from another geographical location.
    a. Thing
    c. Undefined
    b. Deposition0
    d. Undefined

57. An _____ is a chemical compound containing an oxygen atom and other elements. Most of the earth's crust consists of them. They result when elements are oxidized by air.
    a. Thing
    c. Undefined
    b. Oxide0
    d. Undefined

58. In biology and ecology, an _____ is a living complex adaptive system of organs that influence each other in such a way that they function in some way as a stable whole.

Chapter 9. ENVIRONMENTAL HYDROGEOLOGY

a. Thing
b. Organism0
c. Undefined
d. Undefined

59. _____ is a chemical element. An abundant nonmetallic, tetravalent element, _____ has several allotropic forms. This element is the basis of the chemistry of all known life.
   a. Carbon0
   b. Thing
   c. Undefined
   d. Undefined

60. _____ is a chemical compound, normally in a gaseous state, and is composed of one carbon and two oxygen atoms. It is often referred to by its formula CO2. It is present in the Earth's atmosphere at a concentration of approximately .000383 by volume and is an important greenhouse gas due to its ability to absorb many infrared wavelengths of sunlight, and due to the length of time it stays in the atmosphere.
   a. Thing
   b. Carbon dioxide0
   c. Undefined
   d. Undefined

61. _____ refers to the reduction of the body of a formerly living organism into simpler forms of matter.
   a. Decomposition0
   b. Thing
   c. Undefined
   d. Undefined

62. _____ is an accumulation of partially decayed vegetation matter. It forms in wetlands.
   a. Peat0
   b. Thing
   c. Undefined
   d. Undefined

63. An _____ is a natural unit consisting of all plants, animals and micro organisms in an area functioning together with all the non living physical factors of the environment.
   a. Thing
   b. Ecosystem0
   c. Undefined
   d. Undefined

64. In geography, _____ latitudes of the globe lie between the tropics and the polar circles. The changes in these regions between summer and winter are generally subtle: warm or cool, rather than extreme hot or cold.
   a. Thing
   b. Temperate0
   c. Undefined
   d. Undefined

65. _____ is the native consolidated rock underlying the Earth's surface. Above the _____ is usually an area of broken and weathered unconsolidated rock in the basal subsoil.
   a. Bedrock0
   b. Thing
   c. Undefined
   d. Undefined

66. A _____ is a geological feature that is also known as a Rip in the earth causing magma to flow out and forming an undersea volcano, it also has geological features, a continuous elevational crest for some distance. Ridges are usually termed hills or mountains as well, depending on size.
   a. Thing
   b. Ridge0
   c. Undefined
   d. Undefined

Chapter 9. ENVIRONMENTAL HYDROGEOLOGY

67. _____ is a sedimentary rock composed largely of the mineral calcite. _____ often contains variable amounts of silica in the form of chert or flint, as well as varying amounts of clay, silt and sand as disseminations, nodules, or layers within the rock. The primary source of the calcite in _____ is most commonly marine organisms. These organisms secrete shells that settle out of the water column and are deposited on ocean floors as pelagic ooze or alternatively is conglomerated in a coral reef.
   a. Thing
   b. Limestone0
   c. Undefined
   d. Undefined

68. _____ contains low concentrations of dissolved salts and other total dissolved solids. It is an important renewable resource, necessary for the survival of most terrestrial organisms, and required by humans for drinking and agriculture, among many other uses.
   a. Fresh water0
   b. Thing
   c. Undefined
   d. Undefined

69. _____ is one of the four seasons of temperate zones. Almost all English-language calendars, going by astronomy, state that _____ begins on the _____ solstice, and ends on the spring equinox. Calculated more by the weather, it begins and ends earlier and is the season with the shortest days and the lowest temperatures.
   a. Winter0
   b. Thing
   c. Undefined
   d. Undefined

70. _____ is a ductile metal with excellent electrical conductivity, and finds extensive use as an electrical conductor, heat conductor, as a building material, and as a component of various alloys.
   a. Copper0
   b. Thing
   c. Undefined
   d. Undefined

71. _____ is the theory that Earth has been affected by sudden, short-lived, violent events that were sometimes worldwide in scope. The dominant paradigm of geology has been uniformitarianism, but recently a more inclusive and integrated view of geologic events has developed resulting in a gradual change in the scientific consensus, reflecting acceptance of some catastrophic events.
   a. Thing
   b. Catastrophism0
   c. Undefined
   d. Undefined

72. A _____ is an intrusion into a cross-cutting fissure, meaning a _____ cuts across other pre-existing layers or bodies of rock, this means that a _____ is always younger than the rocks that contain it. The thickness is usually much smaller than the other two dimensions. Thickness can vary from sub-centimeter scale to many meters in thickness and the lateral dimensions can extend over many kilometers.
   a. Dike0
   b. Thing
   c. Undefined
   d. Undefined

73. In physical geography, a _____ is an environment "at the interface between truly terrestrial ecosystems and aquatic systems making them inherently different from each other yet highly dependent on both". In essence, they are ecotones.
   a. Wetland0
   b. Place
   c. Undefined
   d. Undefined

Chapter 9. ENVIRONMENTAL HYDROGEOLOGY

74. _____ ecology is the study of renewing a degraded, damaged, or destroyed ecosystem through active human intervention. It specifically refers to the scientific study that has evolved as recently as the 1980's.
- a. Restoration0
- b. Thing
- c. Undefined
- d. Undefined

75. A _____ is a natural depression or hole in the surface topography caused by the removal of soil or bedrock, often both, by water. They may vary in size from less than a meter to several hundred meters both in diameter and depth, and vary in form from soil-lined bowls to bedrock-edged chasms.
- a. Thing
- b. Sinkhole0
- c. Undefined
- d. Undefined

76. _____ is a three-dimensional landscape shaped by the dissolution of a soluble layer or layers of bedrock, usually carbonate rock such as limestone or dolomite. These landscapes display distinctive surface features and underground drainages, and in some examples there may be little or no surface drainage. Some areas of _____ are underlain by thousands of caves.
- a. Karst topography0
- b. Thing
- c. Undefined
- d. Undefined

77. A _____ is a natural underground void large enough for a human to enter. Some people suggest that the term '_____' should only apply to cavities that have some part which does not receive daylight; however, in popular usage, the term includes smaller spaces like a sea _____, rock shelters, and grottos.
- a. Cave0
- b. Place
- c. Undefined
- d. Undefined

78. In organic chemistry, a _____ is a salt of carbonic acid.
- a. Carbonate0
- b. Thing
- c. Undefined
- d. Undefined

79. An _____ is a period of long-term reduction in the temperature of Earth's climate, resulting in an expansion of the continental ice sheets, polar ice sheets and mountain glaciers .
- a. Ice Age0
- b. Thing
- c. Undefined
- d. Undefined

80. _____ is the process of breaking down rocks, soils and their minerals through direct contact with the atmosphere. _____ occurs without movement. Two main classifications of _____ processes exist. Mechanical or physical _____ involves the breakdown of rocks and soils through direct contact with atmospheric conditions. The second classification, chemical _____, involves the direct effect of atmospheric chemicals in the breakdown of rocks, soils and minerals.
- a. Thing
- b. Weathering0
- c. Undefined
- d. Undefined

81. _____ is an alpine ski resort in _____, Colorado in the Rocky Mountains. Located just off U.S. Highway 40, the resort is about an hour and a half's drive from Denver, Colorado.
- a. Place
- b. Winter Park0
- c. Undefined
- d. Undefined

Chapter 9. ENVIRONMENTAL HYDROGEOLOGY

82. _____ is a term used in geology to denote the pressure imposed on a stratigraphic layer by the weight of overlying layers of material.
   a. Event
   b. Lithostatic pressure0
   c. Undefined
   d. Undefined

83. _____ are where one sedimetary deposit ends and another one begins. The rock is prone to breakage at these points because of the weakness between the layers.
   a. Bedding planes0
   b. Thing
   c. Undefined
   d. Undefined

84. _____ is the name of a sedimentary carbonate rock and a mineral, both composed of calcium magnesium carbonate found in crystals. _____ rock is composed predominantly of the mineral _____. Limestone that is partially replaced by _____ is referred to as dolomitic limestone.
   a. Dolomite0
   b. Thing
   c. Undefined
   d. Undefined

85. _____ has the symbol Mg. It is the ninth most abundant element in the universe by mass. It constitutes about 2% of the Earth's crust by mass, and it is the third most abundant element dissolved in seawater. It is essential to all living cells, and is the 11th most abundant element by mass in the human body.
   a. Thing
   b. Magnesium0
   c. Undefined
   d. Undefined

86. _____ are a class of sedimentary rocks composed primarily of carbonate minerals. The two major types are limestone and dolomite, composed of calcite and the mineral dolomite respectively. Chalk and tufa are also minor sedimentary carbonates.
   a. Thing
   b. Carbonate rocks0
   c. Undefined
   d. Undefined

87. A _____ is a type of speleothem that hangs from the ceiling or wall of limestone caves. Stalactites are formed by the deposition of calcium carbonate and other minerals, which is precipitated from mineralized water solutions. The corresponding formation on the floor underneath a _____ is known as a stalagmite.
   a. Thing
   b. Stalactite0
   c. Undefined
   d. Undefined

88. A _____ is a type of speleothem that rises from the floor of a limestone cave due to the dripping of mineralized solutions and the deposition of calcium carbonate. The corresponding formation on the ceiling of a cave is known as a stalactite. If these formations grow together, meeting in the middle, the result is known as a column.
   a. Thing
   b. Stalagmite0
   c. Undefined
   d. Undefined

89. _____ rocks are rocks formed from fragments of pre-existing rock.
   a. Clastic0
   b. Thing
   c. Undefined
   d. Undefined

90. _____ is the measurement of the number of occurrences of a repeated event per unit of time. It is also defined as the rate of change of phase of a sinusoidal waveform.

Chapter 9. ENVIRONMENTAL HYDROGEOLOGY

a. Frequency0
b. Thing
c. Undefined
d. Undefined

91. _____ is the process by which water on the ground surface enters the soil.
a. Thing
b. Infiltration0
c. Undefined
d. Undefined

92. The _____ is defined as the part of the land adjoining or near the ocean. A coastline is properly a line on a map indicating the disposition of a _____, but the word is often used to refer to the _____ itself. The adjective coastal describes something as being on, near to, or associated with a _____.
a. Place
b. Coast0
c. Undefined
d. Undefined

93. An _____ is a body of igneous rock that has crystallized from a molten magma below the surface of the Earth.
a. Intrusion0
b. Thing
c. Undefined
d. Undefined

94. _____ is a natural process that occurs in virtually all coastal aquifers. It consists in salt water flowing inland in freshwater aquifers. This behavior is caused by the fact that sea water has a higher density than freshwater.
a. Thing
b. Saltwater intrusion0
c. Undefined
d. Undefined

95. A _____ is one of the major divisions of the year, generally based on yearly periodic changes in weather. They are recognized as: spring, summer, autumn, and winter.
a. Season0
b. Thing
c. Undefined
d. Undefined

96. In physics, _____ is defined as the rate of change of displacement or the rate of displacement. Simply put, it is distance per units of time.
a. Velocity0
b. Thing
c. Undefined
d. Undefined

97. The _____ is the layer of granitic, sedimentary, and metamorphic rocks which form the continents and the areas of shallow seabed close to their shores, known as continental shelves. It is less dense than the material of the Earth's mantle and thus "floats" on top of it. _____ is also less dense than oceanic crust, though it is considerably thicker. About 40% of the Earth's surface is now underlain by _____.
a. Thing
b. Continental crust0
c. Undefined
d. Undefined

98. _____ is water saturated or nearly saturated with salt and is a common fluid used in the transport of heat from place to place. It is used because the addition of salt to water lowers the freezing temperature of the solution and a relatively great efficiency in the transport can be obtained for the low cost of the material.
a. Brine0
b. Thing
c. Undefined
d. Undefined

Chapter 9. ENVIRONMENTAL HYDROGEOLOGY

99. In geology, a _____ is the outermost layer of a planet, part of its lithosphere. They are generally composed of a less dense material than its deeper layers. Earths' is composed mainly of basalt and granite. It is cooler and more rigid than the deeper layers of the mantle and core.
  a. Crust0
  b. Thing
  c. Undefined
  d. Undefined

100. _____ is water from a sea or ocean. On average, _____ in the world's oceans has a salinity of ~3.5%, or 35 parts per thousand. This means that every 1 kg of _____ has approximately 35 grams of dissolved salts.
  a. Seawater0
  b. Thing
  c. Undefined
  d. Undefined

101. The _____ is the surface where the water pressure is equal to atmospheric pressure. A large amount of water within a body of sand or rock below the _____ is called an aquifer, and the ability of rocks to store such groundwater is dependent on their porosity and permeability.
  a. Thing
  b. Water table0
  c. Undefined
  d. Undefined

102. A _____ is one of several large landmasses on Earth. They are generally identified by convention rather than any strict criteria, but seven areas are commonly reckoned as continents – they are: Asia, Africa, North America, South America, Antarctica, Europe, and Australia.
  a. Continent0
  b. Thing
  c. Undefined
  d. Undefined

103. _____ refers to the cyclic rizing and falling of Earth's ocean surface caused by the tidal forces of the Moon and the sun acting on the oceans. They cause changes in the depth of the marine and estuarine water bodies and produce oscillating currents known as tidal streams, making prediction of tides important for coastal navigation.
  a. Tide0
  b. Thing
  c. Undefined
  d. Undefined

104. _____ are the cyclic rizing and falling of Earth's ocean surface caused by the tidal forces of the Moon and the sun acting on the oceans. _____ cause changes in the depth of the marine and estuarine water bodies and produce oscillating currents known as tidal streams, making prediction of _____ important for coastal navigation.
  a. Thing
  b. Tides0
  c. Undefined
  d. Undefined

105. _____ is the condition of a system in which competing influences are balanced.
  a. Thing
  b. Equilibrium0
  c. Undefined
  d. Undefined

106. _____ occurs when compression due to gravity is balanced by a pressure gradient which creates a pressure gradient force in the opposite direction. The balance of these two forces is known as the hydrostatic balance.
  a. Thing
  b. Hydrostatic equilibrium0
  c. Undefined
  d. Undefined

107. A _____ is the fringe of land at the edge of a large body of water, such as an ocean, sea, or lake. A strict definition is the strip of land along a water body that is alternately exposed and covered by waves and tides.

Chapter 9. ENVIRONMENTAL HYDROGEOLOGY

    a. Thing
    b. Shoreline0
    c. Undefined
    d. Undefined

108. _____ refers to things having to do with the land or with the planet Earth.
    a. Terrestrial0
    b. Thing
    c. Undefined
    d. Undefined

109. A _____ is a tropical or subtropical woodland ecosystem. They are characterized by the trees being sufficiently small or widely spaced so that the canopy does not close. It is often believed that they are characterized by widely spaced, scattered trees, however in many _____ communities tree densities are higher and trees are more regularly spaced than in forest communities.
    a. Savanna0
    b. Place
    c. Undefined
    d. Undefined

110. _____ is the increase in the population of cities in proportion to the region's rural population. _____ is studied in terms of its effects on the ecology and economy of a region.
    a. Urbanization0
    b. Thing
    c. Undefined
    d. Undefined

111. A _____ is a wetland that features temporary or permanent inundation of large areas of land by shallow bodies of water, generally with a substantial number of hummocks, or dry-land protrusions, and covered by aquatic vegetation, or vegetation that tolerates periodical inundation.
    a. Thing
    b. Swamp0
    c. Undefined
    d. Undefined

112. _____ is the saltiness or dissolved salt content of a body of water. In oceanography, it has been traditional to express halinity not as percent, but as parts per thousand, which is approximately grams of salt per liter of solution.
    a. Salinity0
    b. Thing
    c. Undefined
    d. Undefined

113. An _____ is a term for any perforation through the Earth's surface designed to find and release both petroleum oil and gas hydrocarbons.
    a. Thing
    b. Oil well0
    c. Undefined
    d. Undefined

114. _____ is rock that is of a certain particle size range. In geology, _____ is any loose rock that is at least two millimeters in its largest dimension and no more than 75 millimeters.
    a. Thing
    b. Gravel0
    c. Undefined
    d. Undefined

115. Water of sufficient quality to serve as drinking water is termed _____ whether it is used as such or not.
    a. Thing
    b. Potable water0
    c. Undefined
    d. Undefined

Chapter 9. ENVIRONMENTAL HYDROGEOLOGY

116. _____ is a fossil fuel formed in swamp ecosystems where plant remains were saved by water and mud from oxidization and biodegradation. It is a sedimentary rock, but the harder forms, such as anthracite _____, can be regarded as metamorphic rocks because of later exposure to elevated temperature and pressure. It is composed primarily of carbon along with assorted other elements, including sulfur.
- a. Thing
- b. Coal0
- c. Undefined
- d. Undefined

117. In physics, a _____ states that a particular measurable property of an isolated physical system does not change as the system evolves. Any particular _____ is a mathematical identity to certain symmetry of a physical system.
- a. Thing
- b. Conservation law0
- c. Undefined
- d. Undefined

118. _____ is the introduction of substances or energy into the environment, resulting in deleterious effects of such a nature as to endanger human health, harm living resources and ecosystems, and impair or interfere with amenities and other legitimate uses of the environment.
- a. Thing
- b. Pollution0
- c. Undefined
- d. Undefined

119. _____ is the process by which molecules in a liquid state become a gas.
- a. Evaporation0
- b. Thing
- c. Undefined
- d. Undefined

120. _____ is a fine-grained sedimentary rock whose original constituents were clays or muds. It is characterized by thin laminae breaking with an irregular curving fracture, often splintery and usually parallel to the often-indistinguishable bedding plane.
- a. Thing
- b. Shale0
- c. Undefined
- d. Undefined

121. _____ refers to directed, regular, or systematic movement of a group of objects, organisms, or people.
- a. Migration0
- b. Thing
- c. Undefined
- d. Undefined

122. _____ is the accumulation of free salts to such an extent that it leads to degradation of soils and vegetation.
- a. Soil salination0
- b. Thing
- c. Undefined
- d. Undefined

123. _____ is the science and study of the solid matter that constitute the Earth. Encompassing such things as rocks, soil, and gemstones, _____ studies the composition, structure, physical properties, history, and the processes that shape Earth's components.
- a. Thing
- b. Geology0
- c. Undefined
- d. Undefined

124. _____ is a soft, white, porous sedimentary rock, a form of limestone composed of the mineral calcite. It forms under relatively deep marine conditions from the gradual accumulation of minute calcite plates shed from micro-organisms called coccolithophores. It is common to find flint nodules embedded in it.

Chapter 9. ENVIRONMENTAL HYDROGEOLOGY

a. Thing
b. Chalk0
c. Undefined
d. Undefined

125. _____ is a shallow, productive estuary through which water draining approximately forty percent of California, flowing in the Sacramento and San Joaquin rivers from the Sierra Nevada mountains, enters the Pacific Ocean. Technically, both rivers flow into Suisun Bay, which flows through the Carquinez Strait to meet with the Napa River at the entrance to San Pablo Bay, which connects at its south end to _____.
a. Place
b. San Francisco Bay0
c. Undefined
d. Undefined

126. _____ is the substance of which physical objects are composed. _____ can be solid, liquid, plasma or gas. It constitutes the observable universe.
a. Thing
b. Matter0
c. Undefined
d. Undefined

127. _____ refers to a sediment, sedimentary rock, or soil type which is formed from or contains a high proportion of calcium carbonate in the form of calcite or aragonite.
a. Thing
b. Calcareous0
c. Undefined
d. Undefined

128. _____ is the second most common mineral in the Earth's continental crust. It is made up of a lattice of silica tetrahedra. _____ belongs to the rhombohedral crystal system. In nature _____ crystals are often twinned, distorted, or so intergrown with adjacent crystals of _____ or other minerals as to only show part of this shape, or to lack obvious crystal faces altogether and appear massive.
a. Quartz0
b. Thing
c. Undefined
d. Undefined

129. _____ is a small island located in the middle of San Francisco Bay in California, United States. It served as a lighthouse, then a military fortification, then a military prison followed by a federal prison until 1963, when it became a national recreation area.
a. Place
b. Alcatraz Island0
c. Undefined
d. Undefined

130. _____ is the sum of evaporation and plant transpiration. Evaporation accounts for the movement of water to the air from sources such as the soil, canopy interception, and waterbodies. Transpiration accounts for the movement of water within a plant and the subsequent loss of water as vapour through stomata in its leaves.
a. Thing
b. Evapotranspiration0
c. Undefined
d. Undefined

131. _____ is an excavation activity or operation usually carried out at least partly underwater, in shallow seas or fresh water areas with the purpose of gathering up bottom sediments and disposing of them at a different location.
a. Dredging0
b. Thing
c. Undefined
d. Undefined

Chapter 9. ENVIRONMENTAL HYDROGEOLOGY

132. The _____ is the second-largest of the world's oceanic divisions; with a total area of about 106.4 million square kilometres, it covers approximately one-fifth of the Earth's surface. The _____ occupies an elongated, S-shaped basin extending longitudinally between the Americas to the west, and Eurasia and Africa to the east.
   a. Atlantic Ocean0
   b. Place
   c. Undefined
   d. Undefined

133. The _____ of the USA is the working arm of the United States National Academy of Sciences and the United States National Academy of Engineering, carrying out most of the studies done in their names.
   a. National Research Council0
   b. Person
   c. Undefined
   d. Undefined

134. _____ are unicellular microorganisms. They are typically a few micrometres long and have many shapes including curved rods, spheres, rods, and spirals.
   a. Thing
   b. Bacteria0
   c. Undefined
   d. Undefined

135. The _____ is an agency of the federal government of the United States charged with protecting human health and with safeguarding the natural environment: air, water, and land.
   a. Person
   b. Environmental Protection Agency0
   c. Undefined
   d. Undefined

136. The _____ was a United States chemical weapons manufacturing center located in the Denver Metropolitan Area in Commerce City, Colorado. The site was operated by the United States Army throughout the later 20th century and was controversial among local residents until its closure.
   a. Place
   b. Rocky Mountain Arsenal0
   c. Undefined
   d. Undefined

137. _____ are dangerous compounds that cause contamination and are dangerous to human health and the environement.
   a. Hazardous Chemicals0
   b. Thing
   c. Undefined
   d. Undefined

138. The _____ comprises the companies that produce industrial chemicals. It is central to modern world economy, converting raw materials into more than 70,000 different products. Polymers and plastics, especially polyethylene, polypropylene, polyvinyl chloride, polyethylene terephthalate, polystyrene and polycarbonate comprise about 80% of the industry's output worldwide.
   a. Chemical industry0
   b. Thing
   c. Undefined
   d. Undefined

139. _____ is a solid carbonaceous material derived from destructive distillation of low-ash, low-sulfur bituminous coal. The volatile constituents of the coal, including water, coal-gas and coal-tar, are driven off by baking in an airless oven at temperatures as high as 1,000 degrees Celsius so that the fixed carbon and residual ash are fused together.
   a. Coke0
   b. Thing
   c. Undefined
   d. Undefined

Chapter 9. ENVIRONMENTAL HYDROGEOLOGY

140. A _____ is an organism that requires organic substrates to get its carbon for growth and development. It is known as a consumer in the food chain
    a. Heterotroph0
    b. Thing
    c. Undefined
    d. Undefined

141. The U.S Environmental Protection Agency defines a _____ as "any substance or mixture of substances intended for preventing, destroying, repelling, or lessening the damage of any pest".
    a. Thing
    b. Pesticide0
    c. Undefined
    d. Undefined

142. _____ is a body of law, which is a system of complex and interlocking statutes, common law, treaties, conventions, regulations and policies which seek to protect the natural environment which may be affected, impacted or endangered by human activities.
    a. Thing
    b. Environmental law0
    c. Undefined
    d. Undefined

143. _____ is a chemical, physical, or biological agent that modifies the natural characteristics of the atmosphere. The atmosphere is a complex, dynamic natural gaseous system that is essential to support life on planet Earth. Stratospheric ozone depletion due to _____ has long been recognized as a threat to human health as well as to the Earth's ecosystems. Worldwide _____ is responsible for large numbers of deaths and cases of respiratory disease.
    a. Air pollution0
    b. Thing
    c. Undefined
    d. Undefined

144. _____ is a neighborhood in Niagara Falls, New York, United States of America. It officially covers 36 square blocks in the far southeastern corner of the city, along 99th Street and Read Avenue. Two bodies of water define the northern and southern boundaries of the neighborhood: Bergholtz Creek to the north and the Niagara River one-quarter mile to the south.
    a. Place
    b. Love Canal0
    c. Undefined
    d. Undefined

145. The _____ was enacted by the United States Congress in response to the Love Canal disaster. The Act was created to protect people, families, communities and others from heavily contaminated toxic waste sites that have been abandoned. It paid for toxic waste cleanups at sites where no other responsible parties could pay for a cleanup by assessing a tax on petroleum and chemical industries.
    a. Comprehensive Environmental Response, Compensation, and Liability Act0
    b. Thing
    c. Undefined
    d. Undefined

146. _____ is waste that poses substantial or potential threats to public health or the environment. Many types of businesses generate _____. Some are small companies that may be located in a community.
    a. Thing
    b. Hazardous waste0
    c. Undefined
    d. Undefined

147. Ocean _____ are any more or less continuous, directed movement of ocean water that flows in one of the Earth's oceans. They are rivers of hot or cold water within the ocean. They are generated from the forces acting upon the water like the earth's rotation, the wind, the temperature and salinity differences and the gravitation of the moon.

Chapter 9. ENVIRONMENTAL HYDROGEOLOGY 117

a. Thing
b. Currents0
c. Undefined
d. Undefined

148. _____ is a general term for a variety of phenomena resulting from the presence and flow of charge. This includes many well-known physical phenomena such as lightning, electromagnetic fields and electric currents, and is put to use in industrial applications such as electronics and electric power.
a. Thing
b. Electricity0
c. Undefined
d. Undefined

149. A _____ is a type of excavation or depression in the ground. They are generally defined by being deeper than they are wide, and by being narrow compared to their length.
a. Trench0
b. Thing
c. Undefined
d. Undefined

150. _____ is the common name for the group of compounds classified as polychlorinated dibenzodioxins PCDDs. They are members of the family of halogenated organic compounds, have been shown to bioaccumulate in humans and wildlife due to their lipophilic properties, and are known teratogens, mutagens, and suspected human carcinogens.
a. Dioxin0
b. Thing
c. Undefined
d. Undefined

151. An _____ is any member of a large class of chemical compounds whose molecules contain carbon.
a. Organic compound0
b. Thing
c. Undefined
d. Undefined

152. A _____ is a chemical substance of two or more different chemically bonded chemical elements, with a fixed ratio determining the composition. The ratio of each element is usually expressed by chemical formula.
a. Chemical compound0
b. Thing
c. Undefined
d. Undefined

153. A _____ is a pesticide used to kill unwanted plants. They kill specific targets while leaving the desired crop relatively unharmed.
a. Herbicide0
b. Thing
c. Undefined
d. Undefined

154. _____ is the liquid produced when water percolates through any permeable material. It can contain either dissolved or suspended material, or usually both. This liquid is most commonly found in association with landfills, where rain percolates through the waste and reacts with the products of decomposition, chemicals and other materials in the waste to produce the _____.
a. Thing
b. Leachate0
c. Undefined
d. Undefined

155. The term _____ refers to any substance, radionuclide or radiation which is an agent directly involved in the promotion of cancer or in the facilitation of its propagation.
a. Carcinogen0
b. Thing
c. Undefined
d. Undefined

Chapter 9. ENVIRONMENTAL HYDROGEOLOGY

156. _____ is a measure of the degree to which something is toxic or poisonous. _____ can refer to the effect on a whole organism, such as a human or a bacterium or a plant, or to a substructure, such as a cell or an organ.
   a. Thing
   b. Toxicity0
   c. Undefined
   d. Undefined

157. A _____ is a poisonous substance produced by living cells or organisms.
   a. Toxin0
   b. Thing
   c. Undefined
   d. Undefined

158. _____ as used in physics, is energy in the form of waves or moving subatomic particles.
   a. Radiation0
   b. Thing
   c. Undefined
   d. Undefined

159. _____, sometimes simply called space, refers to the relatively empty regions of the universe outside the atmospheres of celestial bodies. _____ is used to distinguish it from airspace. Contrary to popular understanding, _____ is not actually empty but contains a low density of particles, predominantly hydrogen plasma, as well as electromagnetic radiation, dark matter and dark energy.
   a. Outer space0
   b. Thing
   c. Undefined
   d. Undefined

160. _____ is the elevation of an object from a known level or datum. Common datums are mean sea level and the surface of the World Geodetic System geoid, used by Global Positioning System. In aviation, _____ is measured in feet. For non-aviation uses, _____ may be measured in other units such as metres or miles.
   a. Thing
   b. Altitude0
   c. Undefined
   d. Undefined

161. An _____ is a layer of gases that may surround a material body of sufficient mass. The gases are attracted by the gravity of the body, and are retained for a longer duration if gravity is high and the _____'s temperature is low. Some planets consist mainly of various gases, and thus have very deep atmospheres.
   a. Atmosphere0
   b. Place
   c. Undefined
   d. Undefined

162. The term _____ refers to any substance, radionuclide or radiation which is an agent directly involved in the promotion of cancer or in the facilitation of its propagation.
   a. Carcinogens0
   b. Thing
   c. Undefined
   d. Undefined

163. A _____ is an organism that feeds on another living organism or organisms known as prey. A _____ may or may not kill their prey prior to or during the act of feeding on them.
   a. Thing
   b. Predator0
   c. Undefined
   d. Undefined

164. _____ refers to all species of microscopic fungi that grow in the form of multicellular filaments, called hyphae.
   a. Mold0
   b. Thing
   c. Undefined
   d. Undefined

Chapter 9. ENVIRONMENTAL HYDROGEOLOGY

165. _____ are naturally occurring substances that are considered valuable in their relatively unmodified or natural form. Its value rests in the amount of the material available and the demand for the certain material.
   a. Natural resources0
   b. Thing
   c. Undefined
   d. Undefined

166. _____ is a New York City-based, non-profit, non-partisan environmental advocacy group, with offices in Washington, D.C., San Francisco, Los Angeles, Chicago and Beijing. Founded in 1970, today has 1.2 million members and online activists nationwide, and a staff of more than 300 scientists, attorneys, and other specialists.
   a. Natural Resources Defense Council0
   b. Person
   c. Undefined
   d. Undefined

167. _____ systems are a diverse group of air pollution control devices that can be used to remove particulates and/or gases from industrial exhaust streams. Recently, the term is used to describe systems that inject a dry reagent or slurry into a dirty exhaust stream to "scrub out" acid gases. Scrubbers are one of the primary devices that control gaseous emissions, especially acid gases.
   a. Thing
   b. Scrubber0
   c. Undefined
   d. Undefined

168. A _____, the key component of a septic system, is a small scale sewage treatment system common in areas with no connection to main sewerage pipes provided by private corporations or local governments.
   a. Thing
   b. Septic tank0
   c. Undefined
   d. Undefined

169. In ethology, sociobiology and behavioral ecology, the term _____ refers to any geographical area that an animal of a particular species consistently defends against conspecifics.
   a. Territory0
   b. Thing
   c. Undefined
   d. Undefined

170. _____ is the discipline concerned with the questions of how one should live ; what sorts of things exist and what are their essential natures ; what counts as genuine knowledge; and what are the correct principles of reasoning.
   a. Thing
   b. Philosophy0
   c. Undefined
   d. Undefined

171. A _____ is a massive, luminous ball of plasma. Stars group together to form galaxies, and they dominate the visible universe. The nearest _____ to Earth is the Sun, which is the source of most of the energy on Earth, including daylight. Other stars are visible in the night sky, when they are not outshone by the Sun. A _____ shines because nuclear fusion in its core releases energy which traverses the _____'s interior and then radiates into outer space.
   a. Thing
   b. Star0
   c. Undefined
   d. Undefined

172. _____ is a body of techniques for investigating phenomena and acquiring new knowledge, as well as for correcting and integrating previous knowledge. It is based on gathering observable, empirical and measurable evidence subject to specific principles of reasoning,
   a. Thing
   b. Scientific method0
   c. Undefined
   d. Undefined

Chapter 9. ENVIRONMENTAL HYDROGEOLOGY

173. _____ is a chemical element in the periodic table that has the symbol Hg and atomic number 80. A heavy, silvery transition metal, _____ is one of five elements that are liquid at or near room temperature and pressure.
   a. Mercury0
   b. Thing
   c. Undefined
   d. Undefined

174. An _____ is a type of atom that is defined by its atomic number; that is, by the number of protons in its nucleus.
   a. Thing
   b. Element0
   c. Undefined
   d. Undefined

175. _____ is displacement of solids by the agents of ocean currents, wind, water, or ice by downward or down-slope movement in response to gravity or by living organisms.
   a. Thing
   b. Erosion0
   c. Undefined
   d. Undefined

176. _____ is deterioration of essential properties in a material due to reactions with its surroundings. In the most common use of the word, this means a loss of an electron of metals reacting with water or oxygen.
   a. Thing
   b. Corrosion0
   c. Undefined
   d. Undefined

177. _____ is a small scale sewage treatment system common in areas with no connection to main sewerage pipes provided by private corporations or local governments
   a. Thing
   b. Septic system0
   c. Undefined
   d. Undefined

178. The _____ is the portion of Earth between the land surface and the phreatic zone or zone of saturation.
   a. Vadose Zone0
   b. Thing
   c. Undefined
   d. Undefined

179. A _____ is a biological agent that causes disease or illness to its host.
   a. Pathogen0
   b. Thing
   c. Undefined
   d. Undefined

180. _____ is a chemical element which has the symbol N and atomic number 7. Elemental _____ is a colorless, odourless, tasteless and mostly inert diatomic gas at standard conditions, constituting 78.1% by volume of Earth's atmosphere.
   a. Thing
   b. Nitrogen0
   c. Undefined
   d. Undefined

181. A _____, in inorganic chemistry, is a salt of phosphoric acid. In organic chemistry it is an ester of phosphoric acid.
   a. Phosphate0
   b. Thing
   c. Undefined
   d. Undefined

182. _____ is the process of reducing nitrate and nitrite, highly oxidised forms of nitrogen available for consumption by many groups of organisms, into gaseous nitrogen, which is far less accessible to life forms but makes up the bulk of our atmosphere. The process is performed by heterotrophic bacteria from all main proteolytic groups.

Chapter 9. ENVIRONMENTAL HYDROGEOLOGY

a. Thing
c. Undefined
b. Denitrification0
d. Undefined

183. A _____ is an organism that is microscopic. They can be bacteria, fungi, archaea or protists, but not viruses and prions, which are generally classified as non-living. Micro-organisms are generally single-celled, or unicellular organisms.
a. Thing
c. Undefined
b. Microorganism0
d. Undefined

184. _____ bacteria are a commonly-used bacterial indicator of sanitary quality of foods and water.
a. Thing
c. Undefined
b. Coliform0
d. Undefined

185. _____ is a facultatively-anaerobic, rod-shaped, gram-negative, non-sporulating bacteria. They are capable of growth in the presence of bile salts or similar surface agents, oxidase negative, and produce acid and gas from lactose within 48 hours at 44 ± 0.5°C.
a. Fecal coliform bacteria0
c. Undefined
b. Thing
d. Undefined

186. _____ rock is one of the three main rock groups. Rock formed from these covers 75% of the Earth's land area, and includes common types such as chalk, limestone, dolomite, sandstone, and shale.
a. Sedimentary0
c. Undefined
b. Thing
d. Undefined

187. _____ is one of the three main rock groups. _____ covers 75% of the Earth's land area. Four basic processes are involved in the formation of a clastic _____: weathering caused mainly by friction of waves, transportation where the sediment is carried along by a current, deposition and compaction where the sediment is squashed together to form a rock of this kind.
a. Thing
c. Undefined
b. Sedimentary rock0
d. Undefined

188. _____ is a chemical element. It is a soft silvery-white metallic alkali metal that occurs naturally bound to other elements in seawater and many minerals. It oxidizes rapidly in air and is very reactive, especially towards water. In many respects, it and sodium are chemically similar, although organisms in general, and animal cells in particular, treat them very differently.
a. Thing
c. Undefined
b. Potassium0
d. Undefined

189. _____ is a layman's term used to describe newborns with cyanotic conditions, such as • Cyanotic heart defects • Tetralogy of Fallot   • Dextro-Transposition of the great arteries   • Hypoplastic left heart syndrome • Methemoglobinemia   • Respiratory distress syndrome
a. Thing
c. Undefined
b. Blue baby0
d. Undefined

Chapter 9. ENVIRONMENTAL HYDROGEOLOGY

190. A _____ is a region of land where water from rain or snow melt drains downhill into a body of water, such as a river, lake, dam, estuary, wetland, sea or ocean. The _____ includes both the streams and rivers that convey the water as well as the land surfaces from which water drains into those channels. The _____ acts like a funnel - collecting all the water within the area covered by the basin and channeling it into a waterway.
   a. Thing
   b. Drainage basin0
   c. Undefined
   d. Undefined

191. _____ is an s-triazine-ring herbicide that is used globally to stop pre- and post-emergence broadleaf and grassy weeds in major crops. _____ binds to the plastoquinone-binding protein in photosystem II, inhibiting electron transport. _____ is one of the most widely used herbicides and according to the Environmental Protection Agency.
   a. Atrazine0
   b. Thing
   c. Undefined
   d. Undefined

192. A _____ in a general sense is a plant that is considered by the user of the term to be a nuisance, and normally applied to unwanted plants in human made settings like a garden, lawn, or agricultural areas but also to parks, woods and other natural areas.
   a. Weed0
   b. Thing
   c. Undefined
   d. Undefined

193. In organic chemistry, a _____ is an organic compound consisting entirely of hydrogen and carbon. With relation to chemical terminology, aromatic hydrocarbons or arenes, alkanes, alkenes and alkyne-based compounds composed entirely of carbon or hydrogen are referred to as "Pure" hydrocarbons, whereas other hydrocarbons with bonded compounds or impurities of sulphur or nitrogen, are referred to as "impure", and remain somewhat erroneously referred to as hydrocarbons.
   a. Thing
   b. Hydrocarbon0
   c. Undefined
   d. Undefined

194. _____ is a chlorinated hydrocarbon originally produced by Bayer AG as an insecticide. The molecule has a ring structure based on naphthalene. _____ is closely related to aldrin which itself breaks down to form _____.
   a. Thing
   b. Dieldrin0
   c. Undefined
   d. Undefined

195. The _____ is a major north-flowing river in Africa, generally regarded as the longest river in the world. The _____ has two major tributaries, the White Nile and Blue Nile, the latter being the source of most of the Nile's water and fertile soil, but the former being the longer of the two. It ends in a large delta that empties into the Mediterranean Sea.
   a. Place
   b. Nile River0
   c. Undefined
   d. Undefined

196. The term _____ refers to water and can be either a noun or an adjective. Dictionary definitions do not specify what kind of water, although in both general use and in the sciences, the implication is often that of fresh water.
   a. Thing
   b. Aquatic0
   c. Undefined
   d. Undefined

197. _____ is feeding on growing herbage, attached algae, or phytoplankton.

Chapter 9. ENVIRONMENTAL HYDROGEOLOGY

a. Thing
b. Grazing0
c. Undefined
d. Undefined

198. A _____ is a section of land devoted to the production and management of food, either produce or livestock. It is the basic unit in agricultural production.
a. Farm0
b. Thing
c. Undefined
d. Undefined

199. A _____ is a body of comparatively shallow salt or brackish water separated from the deeper sea by a shallow or exposed sandbank, coral reef, or similar feature. Thus, the enclosed body of water behind a barrier reef or barrier islands or enclosed by an atoll reef is called a _____.
a. Place
b. Lagoon0
c. Undefined
d. Undefined

200. _____ is the reprocessing of materials into new products. It prevents useful material resources being wasted, reduces the consumption of raw materials and reduces energy usage, and hence greenhouse gas emissions, compared to virgin production.
a. Recycling0
b. Thing
c. Undefined
d. Undefined

201. _____ is the process of extracting a substance from a solid by dissolving it in a liquid.
a. Thing
b. Leaching0
c. Undefined
d. Undefined

202. A _____ is a geological phenomenon which includes a wide range of ground movement, such as rock falls, deep failure of slopes and shallow debris flows. Although gravity's action on an over-steepened slope is the primary reason for a _____, there are other contributing factors affecting the original slope stability.
a. Thing
b. Landslide0
c. Undefined
d. Undefined

203. A _____ is flat or nearly flat land adjacent to a stream or river that experiences occasional or periodic flooding. It includes the floodway, which consists of the stream channel and adjacent areas that carry flood flows, and the flood fringe, which are areas covered by the flood, but which do not experience a strong current.
a. Thing
b. Floodplain0
c. Undefined
d. Undefined

204. _____ is the study of the movement, distribution, and quality of water throughout the Earth, and thus addresses both the hydrologic cycle and water resources.
a. Hydrology0
b. Thing
c. Undefined
d. Undefined

205. The _____ enacted in 1976, is a Federal law of the United States It states that RCRA's goals are:to protect the public from harm caused by waste disposal to encourage reuse, reduction, and recycling to clean up spilled or improperly stored wastes.

Chapter 9. ENVIRONMENTAL HYDROGEOLOGY

    a. Resource Conservation and Recovery Act0
    b. Thing
    c. Undefined
    d. Undefined

206. The _____ is the largest of the Earth's oceanic divisions. It extends from the Arctic in the north to the Antarctic in the south, bounded by Asia and Australia on the west and the Americas on the east. At 169.2 million square kilometres in area, this largest division of the World Ocean – and, in turn, the hydrosphere – covers about 46% of the Earth's water surface and about 32% of its total surface area, making it larger than all of the Earth's land area combined.
    a. Place
    b. Pacific Ocean0
    c. Undefined
    d. Undefined

207. _____ is the gas phase component of a another state of matter which does not completely fill its container. It is distinguished from the pure gas phase by the presence of the same substance in another state of matter. Hence when a liquid has completely evaporated, it is said that the system has been completely transformed to the gas phase.
    a. Vapor0
    b. Thing
    c. Undefined
    d. Undefined

208. _____ is a reaction force applied by a stretched string, rope or a similar object on the objects which stretch it. The direction of the force of it is parallel to the string, towards the string.
    a. Tension0
    b. Thing
    c. Undefined
    d. Undefined

209. _____ is a chemical element metal. It is a lustrous, silvery soft metal. It and nickel are notable for being the final elements produced by stellar nucleosynthesis, and thus are the heaviest elements which do not require a supernova or similarly cataclysmic event for formation.
    a. Iron0
    b. Thing
    c. Undefined
    d. Undefined

210. _____ is a sedimentary rock which has a composition intermediate in grain size between the coarser sandstones and the finer mudstones and shales.
    a. Thing
    b. Siltstone0
    c. Undefined
    d. Undefined

211. The _____ covers roughly the time span between the demise of the non-avian dinosaurs and beginning of the most recent Ice Age. Each epoch of the _____ was marked by striking developments in mammalian life. The earliest recognizable hominoid relatives of humans appeared. Tectonic activity continued as Gondwana finally split completely apart.
    a. Thing
    b. Tertiary0
    c. Undefined
    d. Undefined

212. The _____ on the geologic timescale had been intended to cover the world's recent period of repeated glaciations. The _____ follows the Pliocene and is followed by the Holocene. The _____ is the third epoch of the Neogene period or 6th epoch of the Cenozoic era. The end of the _____ corresponds with the end of the Paleolithic age used in archaeology. The _____ is divided into the Early _____, Middle _____ and Late _____, and numerous faunal stages.
    a. Thing
    b. Pleistocene0
    c. Undefined
    d. Undefined

Chapter 9. ENVIRONMENTAL HYDROGEOLOGY

213. _____ or sediments are deposited by a river or other running water. _____ is typically made up of a variety of materials, including fine particles of silt and clay and larger particles of sand and gravel.
- a. Thing
- b. Alluvial soil0
- c. Undefined
- d. Undefined

214. _____ is an absorbent aluminium phyllosilicate generally impure clay consisting mostly of montmorillonite.
- a. Thing
- b. Bentonite0
- c. Undefined
- d. Undefined

215. _____, is a general term which covers carbon materials mostly derived from charcoal. It is a material with an exceptionally high surface area. Just one gram of _____ has a surface area of approximately 500 m2, typically determined by nitrogen gas adsorption, and includes a large amount of microporosity.
- a. Activated charcoal0
- b. Thing
- c. Undefined
- d. Undefined

216. _____ is a steel-gray, lustrous, hard metal that takes a high polish and has a high melting point. It is also odourless, tasteless, and malleable
- a. Chromium0
- b. Thing
- c. Undefined
- d. Undefined

217. _____ are organic chemical compounds that have high enough vapour pressures under normal conditions to significantly vaporize and enter the atmosphere.
- a. Thing
- b. Volatile organic compounds0
- c. Undefined
- d. Undefined

218. _____ are the materials left over after the process of separating the valuable fraction from the worthless fraction of an ore. _____ represent external costs of mining. As mining techniques and the price of minerals improve, it is not unusual for _____ to be reprocessed using new methods, or more thoroughly with old methods, to recover additional minerals.
- a. Thing
- b. Tailings0
- c. Undefined
- d. Undefined

219. _____ or sulphur is the chemical element that has the symbol S and atomic number 16. It is an abundant, tasteless, multivalent non-metal. _____, in its native form, is a yellow crystalline solid. In nature, it can be found as the pure element or as sulfide and sulfate minerals. It is an essential element for life and is found in two amino acids, cysteine and methionine.
- a. Thing
- b. Sulfur0
- c. Undefined
- d. Undefined

220. The mineral _____ is iron disulfide, FeS2. It has isometric crystals that usually appear as cubes. Its metallic luster and pale-to-normal, brass-yellow hue have earned it a nickname due to many miners mistaking it for the real thing.
- a. Thing
- b. Pyrite0
- c. Undefined
- d. Undefined

221. An _____ is a volume of rock containing components or minerals in a mode of occurrence that renders it valuable for mining.

Chapter 9. ENVIRONMENTAL HYDROGEOLOGY

    a. Ore0
    b. Thing
    c. Undefined
    d. Undefined

222. _____ is a strong mineral acid. It is soluble in water at all concentrations. _____ has many applications, and is one of the top products of the chemical industry. Principal uses include ore processing, fertilizer manufacturing, oil refining, wastewater processing, and chemical synthesis.
    a. Sulfuric acid0
    b. Thing
    c. Undefined
    d. Undefined

223. _____, also known by many other names is the chemical compound with the formula CCl_4. It is a reagent in synthetic chemistry and was formerly widely used in fire extinguishers and as a precursor to refrigerants. It is a colorless liquid with a "sweet" smell that can be detected at low levels.
    a. Carbon tetrachloride0
    b. Thing
    c. Undefined
    d. Undefined

224. _____ is a measure of the resistance of a fluid to deform under shear stress. It is commonly perceived as "thickness", or resistance to flow. _____ describes a fluid's internal resistance to flow and may be thought of as a measure of fluid friction.
    a. Viscosity0
    b. Thing
    c. Undefined
    d. Undefined

225. An _____ is any piece of land that is completely surrounded by water, above high tide. There are two main types of islands: continental islands and oceanic islands. There are also artificial islands. A grouping of geographically and/or geologically related islands is called an archipelago.
    a. Thing
    b. Island0
    c. Undefined
    d. Undefined

226. _____ is a measure of the void spaces in a material, and is measured as a fraction, between 0–1, or as a percentage between 0–100%.
    a. Porosity0
    b. Thing
    c. Undefined
    d. Undefined

227. _____ is an organic chemical compound with the formula C_6H_6. It is sometimes abbreviated Ph-H. _____ is a colorless and flammable liquid with a sweet smell and a relatively high melting point. It is carcinogenic and its use as additive in gasoline is now limited, but it is an important industrial solvent and precursor in the production of drugs, plastics, synthetic rubber, and dyes.
    a. Thing
    b. Benzene0
    c. Undefined
    d. Undefined

228. _____ is the process by which organic substances are broken down by other living organisms.
    a. Thing
    b. Biodegradation0
    c. Undefined
    d. Undefined

229. In physics, _____ is the upward force on an object produced by the surrounding fluid in which it is fully or partially immersed, due to the pressure difference of the fluid between the top and bottom of the object. The net upward _____ force is equal to the magnitude of the weight of fluid displaced by the body.

Chapter 9. ENVIRONMENTAL HYDROGEOLOGY

    a. Buoyancy0
    b. Thing
    c. Undefined
    d. Undefined

230. An _____ is a long period of time with different technical and colloquial meanings, and usages in language. It begins with some beginning event known as an epoch, epochal date, epochal event or epochal moment.
    a. Era0
    b. Thing
    c. Undefined
    d. Undefined

231. _____ is a technique used in the oil and gas industry for recording rock and fluid properties to find hydrocarbon zones in the geological formations within the Earth's crust.
    a. Thing
    b. Well logs0
    c. Undefined
    d. Undefined

232. _____ is the physical, chemical and biological characteristics of water, characterized through the methods of hydrometry.
    a. Thing
    b. Water quality0
    c. Undefined
    d. Undefined

233. A _____ is a type of underground carriage system for transporting sewage from houses or industry to treatment or disposal.
    a. Sanitary sewer0
    b. Thing
    c. Undefined
    d. Undefined

234. In chemistry, a _____ is defined as a sufficiently stable electrically neutral group of at least two atoms in a definite arrangement held together by strong chemical bonds.
    a. Thing
    b. Molecule0
    c. Undefined
    d. Undefined

235. An _____ is an atom or group of atoms which have lost or gained one or more electrons, making them negatively or positively charged.
    a. Ion0
    b. Thing
    c. Undefined
    d. Undefined

236. _____ between members of a species is the driving force behind evolution and natural selection; especially for resources such as food, water, territory, and sunlight results in the ultimate survival and dominance of the variation of the species best suited for survival.
    a. Competition0
    b. Thing
    c. Undefined
    d. Undefined

237. _____ is a field of geology which focuses on the study of rocks and the conditions by which they form. There are three branches of _____, corresponding to the three types of rocks: igneous, metamorphic, and sedimentary. _____ utilizes the classical fields of mineralogy, petrography, optical mineralogy, and chemical analyses to describe the composition and texture of rocks.
    a. Thing
    b. Petrology0
    c. Undefined
    d. Undefined

128 Chapter 9. ENVIRONMENTAL HYDROGEOLOGY

238. A _____ is a process that results in the interconversion of chemical substances. The substance or substances initially involved in a _____ are called reactants. Chemical reactions are characterized by a chemical change, and they yield one or more products which are, in general, different from the reactants.
- a. Chemical reaction0
- b. Thing
- c. Undefined
- d. Undefined

239. A _____ is any aspect of an object or substance that can be measured or perceived without changing its identity. Physical properties can be intensive or extensive. An intensive property does not depend on the size or amount of matter in the object, while an extensive property does.
- a. Thing
- b. Physical property0
- c. Undefined
- d. Undefined

240. _____ is a part of mathematics concerned with questions of size, shape, and relative position of figures and with properties of space. _____ is one of the oldest sciences. Initially a body of practical knowledge concerning lengths, areas, and volumes, in the third century B.C. _____ was put into an axiomatic form by Euclid, whose treatment set a standard for many centuries to follow.
- a. Geometry0
- b. Thing
- c. Undefined
- d. Undefined

241. _____ is the reduction in amplitude and intensity of a signal.
- a. Thing
- b. Attenuation0
- c. Undefined
- d. Undefined

242. _____ are hydrous aluminium phyllosilicates, sometimes with variable amounts of iron, magnesium, alkali metals, alkaline earths and other cations. Clays have structures similar to the micas and therefore form flat hexagonal sheets. _____ are common weathering products and low temperature hydrothermal alteration products.
- a. Clay minerals0
- b. Thing
- c. Undefined
- d. Undefined

243. _____ : a _____ is an ion with a positive charge. It is the inverse anion.
- a. Thing
- b. Cation0
- c. Undefined
- d. Undefined

244. An _____ is a negetive ion.
- a. Anion0
- b. Thing
- c. Undefined
- d. Undefined

245. _____ is a chemical element in the periodic table that has the symbol Cd and atomic number 48. A relatively rare, soft, bluish-white, transition metal, _____ is known to cause cancer and occurs with zinc ores. _____ is used largely in batteries and pigments, for example in plastic products..
- a. Thing
- b. Cadmium0
- c. Undefined
- d. Undefined

246. _____ is a chemical element in the periodic table that has the symbol Zn and atomic number 30. In some historical and sculptural contexts, it is known as spelter.

Chapter 9. ENVIRONMENTAL HYDROGEOLOGY

a. Zinc0
b. Thing
c. Undefined
d. Undefined

247. _____ is matter that has come from a recently living organism; is capable of decay, or the product of decay; or is composed of organic compounds. The definition of _____ varies upon the subject it is being used for.
a. Organic matter0
b. Thing
c. Undefined
d. Undefined

248. In soil science, cation exchange capacity is the _____ capacity of soil for positively charged ions. Soils can be considered as natural weak cation exchangers.
a. Ion exchange0
b. Thing
c. Undefined
d. Undefined

249. _____ is water that has a high mineral content. This content usually consists of high levels of metal ions, mainly calcium and magnesium in the form of carbonates, but may include several other metals as well as bicarbonates and sulfates.
a. Thing
b. Hard water0
c. Undefined
d. Undefined

250. A _____ is an area of flat, low-lying land adjacent to a seacoast and separated from the interior by other features.
a. Coastal plain0
b. Thing
c. Undefined
d. Undefined

251. _____ is the term used to describe types of water that contain few or no calcium or magnesium ions. The term is usually relative to hard water, which does contain significant amounts of such ions.
a. Soft water0
b. Thing
c. Undefined
d. Undefined

252. The _____ is a fundamental subatomic particle that carries a negative electric charge.
a. Thing
b. Electron0
c. Undefined
d. Undefined

253. The term _____ refers to several types of chemical compounds containing sulfur in its lowest oxidation number of −2.
a. Thing
b. Sulfide0
c. Undefined
d. Undefined

254. A _____ is a mineral containing sulfide as the major anion. Closely related and often included within the sulfide class are selenide and telluride minerals.
a. Sulfide mineral0
b. Thing
c. Undefined
d. Undefined

Chapter 9. ENVIRONMENTAL HYDROGEOLOGY

255. The _____ is the part of the earth, including air, land, surface rocks, and water, within which life occurs, and which biotic processes in turn alter or transform. From the broadest biophysiological point of view, the _____ is the global ecological system integrating all living beings and their relationships, including their interaction with the elements of the lithosphere, hydrosphere, and atmosphere. This _____ is postulated to have evolved, beginning through a process of biogenesis or biopoesis, at least some 3.5 billion years ago.
- a. Thing
- b. Biosphere0
- c. Undefined
- d. Undefined

256. _____ is an effect within the surface layer of a liquid that causes that layer to behave as an elastic sheet. This effect allows insects to walk on water. It allows small metal objects such as needles, razor blades, or foil fragments to float on the surface of water, and causes capillary action.
- a. Thing
- b. Surface tension0
- c. Undefined
- d. Undefined

257. An _____ organism is an organism that has an oxygen based metabolism
- a. Aerobic0
- b. Thing
- c. Undefined
- d. Undefined

258. _____ is concerned with earth materials that can be utilized for economic and/or industrial purposes. These materials include precious and base metals, nonmetallic minerals, construction-grade stone, petroleum minerals, coal, and water. The term commonly refers to metallic mineral deposits and mineral resources. The techniques employed by other earth science disciplines might all be used to understand, describe, and exploit an ore deposit.
- a. Thing
- b. Economic geology0
- c. Undefined
- d. Undefined

259. _____ is a term used to describe the flow of water, from rain, snowmelt, or other sources, over the land surface, and is a major component of the water cycle.
- a. Thing
- b. Surface runoff0
- c. Undefined
- d. Undefined

260. _____ is a broadly useful concept that expresses how fast something moves through a system in equilibrium. It is the average time a substance spends within a specified region of space, such as a reservoir.
- a. Residence time0
- b. Thing
- c. Undefined
- d. Undefined

261. A _____ is a volume of sedimentary rock in which a mineral cement fills the porosity. They are often ovoid or spherical in shape, although irregular shapes also occur. They form within layers of sedimentary strata that have already been deposited. They usually form early in the burial history of the sediment, before the rest of the sediment is hardened into rock.
- a. Thing
- b. Concretion0
- c. Undefined
- d. Undefined

Chapter 9. ENVIRONMENTAL HYDROGEOLOGY

262. Faults are planar rock fractures, which show evidence of relative movement. Large faults within the Earth's crust are the result of shear motion and active _____ zones are the causal locations of most earthquakes. Earthquakes are caused by energy release during rapid slippage along faults. The largest examples are at tectonic plate boundaries but many faults occur far from active plate boundaries. Since faults do not usually consist of a single, clean fracture, the term _____ zone is used when referring to the zone of complex deformation that is associated with the _____ plane.
- a. Fault0
- b. Thing
- c. Undefined
- d. Undefined

263. The _____ region of the United States comprises the coasts of states which border the Gulf of Mexico. The states of Texas, Louisiana, Mississippi, Alabama, and Florida are known as the Gulf States. All Gulf States are located in the Southern region of the United States.
- a. Gulf Coast0
- b. Place
- c. Undefined
- d. Undefined

Chapter 10. PETROLEUM MIGRATION

1. A chemical compound composed only of the elements carbon and hydrogen is called _____.
   - a. Thing
   - b. Hydrocarbon10
   - c. Undefined
   - d. Undefined

2. _____ refers to any of a group of naturally occurring substances made up of hydrocarbons. These substances may be gaseous, liquid, or semi-solid.
   - a. Petroleum10
   - b. 1509 Istanbul earthquake
   - c. Undefined
   - d. Undefined

3. _____ occurs when living things move from one biome to another. In most cases organisms migrate to avoid local shortages of food, usually caused by winter. Animals may also migrate to a certain location to breed, as is the case with some fish.
   - a. Thing
   - b. Migration10
   - c. Undefined
   - d. Undefined

4. _____ refers to a crack or break in a rock. To break in random places instead of cleaving.
   - a. Fracture10
   - b. 1509 Istanbul earthquake
   - c. Undefined
   - d. Undefined

5. A _____ is the outer layer of a planet, part of its lithosphere. Planetary _____ is generally composed of a less dense material than that of its deeper layers. The _____ of the Earth is composed mainly of basalt and granite.
   - a. Crust10
   - b. Thing
   - c. Undefined
   - d. Undefined

6. _____ refers to a naturally formed aggregate of usually inorganic materials from within the Earth.
   - a. 1509 Istanbul earthquake
   - b. Rock10
   - c. Undefined
   - d. Undefined

7. _____ refers to a permeable rock containing oil or gas.
   - a. 1509 Istanbul earthquake
   - b. Reservoir rock10
   - c. Undefined
   - d. Undefined

8. All processes that adds snow or ice to a glacier or to floating ice or snow cove are referred to as _____.
   - a. AASHTO Soil Classification System
   - b. Accumulation10
   - c. Undefined
   - d. Undefined

9. _____ refers to a place in which water is stored, including the oceans, glaciers and polar ice, groundwater, lakes and rivers, the atmosphere, and the biosphere. A source or place of residence for elements in a chemical cycle or hydrologic cycle.
   - a. 1509 Istanbul earthquake
   - b. Reservoir10
   - c. Undefined
   - d. Undefined

10. Aggregates of minerals or rock fragments are called _____.
    - a. Rocks10
    - b. 1509 Istanbul earthquake
    - c. Undefined
    - d. Undefined

Chapter 10. PETROLEUM MIGRATION

11. An _____ is any member of a large class of chemical compounds whose molecules contain carbon, with the exception of carbides, carbonates, carbon oxides and gases containing carbon.
    a. Organic compound10
    b. Thing
    c. Undefined
    d. Undefined

12. An electrically neutral substance that consists of two or more elements combined in specific, constant proportions is a _____. A _____ typically has physical characteristics different from those of its constituent elements.
    a. 1509 Istanbul earthquake
    b. Compound10
    c. Undefined
    d. Undefined

13. _____ refers to an element that occurs in minute quantities in rocks or plant or animal tissue. Some are essential for human health.
    a. Trace element10
    b. 1509 Istanbul earthquake
    c. Undefined
    d. Undefined

14. _____ is a chemical element in the periodic table that has the symbol H and atomic number 1. At standard temperature and pressure it is a colorless, odorless, nonmetallic, univalent, tasteless, highly flammable diatomic gas.
    a. Thing
    b. Hydrogen10
    c. Undefined
    d. Undefined

15. _____ refers to the smallest possible unit of a substance that has the properties of that substance.
    a. 1509 Istanbul earthquake
    b. Molecule10
    c. Undefined
    d. Undefined

16. A chemical _____, often called simply _____, is a chemical substance that cannot be divided or changed into other chemical substances by any ordinary chemical technique. An _____ is a class of substances that contain the same number of protons in all its atoms.
    a. Thing
    b. Element10
    c. Undefined
    d. Undefined

17. _____ is a chemical element in the periodic table that has the symbol C and atomic number 6. An abundant nonmetallic, tetravalent element, _____ has several allotropic forms.
    a. Thing
    b. Carbon10
    c. Undefined
    d. Undefined

18. _____ is the chemical element in the periodic table that has the symbol S and atomic number 16. It is an abundant, tasteless, odorless, multivalent non-metal. _____, in its native form, is a yellow crystaline solid. In nature, it can be found as the pure element or as sulfide and sulfate minerals.
    a. Thing
    b. Sulfur10
    c. Undefined
    d. Undefined

19. _____ is a chemical element in the periodic table. It has the symbol O and atomic number 8. _____ is the second most common element on Earth, composing around 46% of the mass of Earth's crust and 28% of the mass of Earth as a whole, and is the third most common element in the universe.

Chapter 10. PETROLEUM MIGRATION

    a. Oxygen10
    c. Undefined
    b. Thing
    d. Undefined

20. A gaseous mixture of naturally occurring hydrocarbons is _____.
    a. 1509 Istanbul earthquake
    c. Undefined
    b. Natural gas10
    d. Undefined

21. _____ is an atmospheric gas comprized of one carbon and two oxygen atoms. A very widely known chemical compound, it is frequently called by its formula CO_2. In its solid state, it is commonly known as dry ice.
    a. Thing
    c. Undefined
    b. Carbon dioxide10
    d. Undefined

22. One of the minerals that is abundant in the hot water that seeps through hydrothermal vents is _____.
    a. Sulfide10
    c. Undefined
    b. Thing
    d. Undefined

23. _____ is a chemical element; it is a colorless, odorless, tasteless, non-toxic, and nearly inert monatomic that heads the noble gas series in the periodic table. Its atomic number is 2 and its boiling and melting points are the lowest among the elements. It exists only as a gas except in extreme conditions.
    a. Thing
    c. Undefined
    b. Helium10
    d. Undefined

24. A transition in a rock's mineralogy to a denser, more closely packed crystal structure, signaled by a change in seismic-wave velocity is referred to as the _____.
    a. Phase change10
    c. Undefined
    b. 1509 Istanbul earthquake
    d. Undefined

25. The release of gases and water vapor from molten rocks, leading to the formation of the earth's atmosphere and oceans is _____.
    a. AASHTO Soil Classification System
    c. Undefined
    b. Outgassing10
    d. Undefined

26. The middle layer of the Earth, lying just below the crust and consisting of relatively dense rocks is called the _____. The _____ is divided into two sections, the upper _____ and the lower _____; the lower _____ has greater density than the upper _____.
    a. Mantle10
    c. Undefined
    b. 1509 Istanbul earthquake
    d. Undefined

27. Rocks formed by solidification of sediments formed and transported at the Earth's surface are referred to as _____.
    a. Sedimentary rocks10
    c. Undefined
    b. 1509 Istanbul earthquake
    d. Undefined

28. _____ is one of the three main rock groups and is formed in three main ways—by the deposition of the weathered remains of other rocks; by the deposition of the results of biogenic activity; and by precipitation from solution.

Chapter 10. PETROLEUM MIGRATION

a. Event
b. Sedimentary rock10
c. Undefined
d. Undefined

29. _____ is the part of hydrology that deals with the distribution and movement of groundwater in the soil and rocks of the Earth's crust (commonly in aquifers).
a. Thing
b. Hydrogeology10
c. Undefined
d. Undefined

30. _____ is a chemical element in the periodic table that has the symbol Au and atomic number 79. A soft, shiny, yellow, dense, malleable, ductile (trivalent and univalent) transition metal, _____ does not react with most chemicals but is attacked by chlorine, fluorine and aqua regia.
a. Thing
b. Gold10
c. Undefined
d. Undefined

31. The relationship between distance on a map and the distance on the terrain being represented by that map is a _____.
a. 1509 Istanbul earthquake
b. Scale10
c. Undefined
d. Undefined

32. The study of rock strata, especially of their distribution, deposition, and age is called _____.
a. Stratigraphic10
b. 1509 Istanbul earthquake
c. Undefined
d. Undefined

33. The undifferentiated rocks that underlie the rocks of interest in an area are referred to as _____.
a. 1509 Istanbul earthquake
b. Basement10
c. Undefined
d. Undefined

34. _____ refers to a body of water found on the Earth's surface and confined to a narrow topographic depression, down which it flows and transports rock particles, sediment, and dissolved particles. Rivers, creeks, brooks, and runs are all streams.
a. 1509 Istanbul earthquake
b. Stream10
c. Undefined
d. Undefined

35. _____ refers to the reduction of the body of a formerly living organism into simpler forms of matter.
a. Thing
b. Decomposition10
c. Undefined
d. Undefined

36. A body of rock identified by lithic characteristics and stratigraphic position and is mappable at the earth's surface or traceable in the subsurface is a _____.
a. Formation10
b. 1509 Istanbul earthquake
c. Undefined
d. Undefined

37. A mineral or fuel deposit, known or not yet discovered, that may be or become available for human exploitation is called a _____.

Chapter 10. PETROLEUM MIGRATION

    a. 1509 Istanbul earthquake   b. Resource10
    c. Undefined   d. Undefined

38. Ability to do work is referred to as _____. Most evident in glacial systems as radiant _____ from the sun and as latent _____ required to melt ice to water.
    a. AASHTO Soil Classification System   b. Energy10
    c. Undefined   d. Undefined

39. _____ is any particulate matter that can be transported by fluid flow and which eventually is deposited as a layer of solid particles on the bed or bottom of a body of water or other liquid.
    a. Sediment10   b. Thing
    c. Undefined   d. Undefined

40. A rock in which hydrocarbons originate is referred to as a _____.
    a. Source rock10   b. 1509 Istanbul earthquake
    c. Undefined   d. Undefined

41. The set of processes that cause physical and chemical changes in sediment after it has been deposited and buried under another layer of sediment is _____. _____ may culminate in lithification.
    a. Diagenesis10   b. 1509 Istanbul earthquake
    c. Undefined   d. Undefined

42. _____ refers to the height of floodwaters in feet or meters above an established datum plane.
    a. Stage10   b. 1509 Istanbul earthquake
    c. Undefined   d. Undefined

43. The scientific study of the Earth, its origins and evolution, the materials that make it up, and the processes that act on it is called _____.
    a. 1509 Istanbul earthquake   b. Geology10
    c. Undefined   d. Undefined

44. A solid, waxy, organic substance that forms when pressure and heat from the Earth act on the remains of plants and animals is _____. _____ converts to various liquid and gaseous hydrocarbons at a depth of 7 or more kilometers and a temperature between 50° and 100°C.
    a. Kerogen10   b. 1509 Istanbul earthquake
    c. Undefined   d. Undefined

45. _____ is a measure, in kelvins (K), of temperature for thermodynamics. The (unattainable) temperature of 0 K is called "absolute zero", and coincides with the minimum molecular activity of matter, which is zero, except for the residual quantum mechanical zero-point energy.
    a. Thing   b. Absolute temperature10
    c. Undefined   d. Undefined

46. _____ refers to a process leading to chemical changes in matter; involves the making and/or breaking of chemical bonds.

Chapter 10. PETROLEUM MIGRATION

a. Chemical reaction10
b. Thing
c. Undefined
d. Undefined

47. The _____ is the threshold energy, or the energy that must be overcome in order for a chemical reaction to occur. _____ may otherwise be denoted as the minimum energy necessary for a specific chemical reaction to occur.
a. Thing
b. Activation energy10
c. Undefined
d. Undefined

48. In biology, _____ is the process by which novel traits arise in populations and are passed on from generation to generation. Its action over large stretches of time explains the origin of new species and ultimately the vast diversity of the biological world.
a. Evolution10
b. Concept
c. Undefined
d. Undefined

49. _____ refers to a sedimentary rock composed of detrital sediment particles less than 0.004 millimeters in diameter. _____ tends to be red, brown, black, or gray, and usually originate in relatively still waters.
a. 1509 Istanbul earthquake
b. Shale10
c. Undefined
d. Undefined

50. The angle formed by the inclined plane of a geological structure and the horizontal plane of the Earth's surface is referred to as a _____.
a. Dip10
b. 1509 Istanbul earthquake
c. Undefined
d. Undefined

51. The vertical drop in a stream's elevation over a given horizontal distance, expressed as an angle is referred to as a _____.
a. 1509 Istanbul earthquake
b. Gradient10
c. Undefined
d. Undefined

52. _____ refers to the beginning or source area for a stream. Also called the headwaters.
a. 1509 Istanbul earthquake
b. Head10
c. Undefined
d. Undefined

53. _____ refers to a timeline based on a stratigraphic succession that provides a chronological record of the history of a region. The entire span of time since the Earth formed.
a. 1509 Istanbul earthquake
b. Geologic time10
c. Undefined
d. Undefined

54. The branch of geology that studies the physics of the Earth, using the physical principles underlying such phenomena as seismic waves, heat flow, gravity, and magnetism to investigate planetary properties is called _____.
a. 1509 Istanbul earthquake
b. Geophysics10
c. Undefined
d. Undefined

55. A piece of one rock unit contained within another is called _____. Inclusions are used in relative dating. The rock mass adjacent to the one containing the _____ must have been there first in order to provide the fragment.

Chapter 10. PETROLEUM MIGRATION

   a. Inclusion10
   c. Undefined
   b. AASHTO Soil Classification System
   d. Undefined

56. The quantity of water in a stream that passes a given point in a period of time is referred to as _____.
   a. Discharge10
   c. Undefined
   b. 1509 Istanbul earthquake
   d. Undefined

57. Water stored beneath the surface in open pore spaces and fractures in rock is called _____.
   a. 1509 Istanbul earthquake
   c. Undefined
   b. Groundwater10
   d. Undefined

58. The scientific study of the geological processes that deform the Earth's crust and create mountains is _____.
   a. Structural geology10
   c. Undefined
   b. 1509 Istanbul earthquake
   d. Undefined

59. The processes by which crustal forces cause a rock formation to break and slip along a fault are called _____.
   a. 1509 Istanbul earthquake
   c. Undefined
   b. Faulting10
   d. Undefined

60. The force acting on a rock or another solid to deform it, measured in kilograms per square centimeter or pounds per square inch is _____.
   a. 1509 Istanbul earthquake
   c. Undefined
   b. Stress10
   d. Undefined

61. A concave fold, the central part of which contains the youngest section of roc is called the _____.
   a. 1509 Istanbul earthquake
   c. Undefined
   b. Syncline10
   d. Undefined

62. _____ is a term used for ionic compounds composed of positively charged cations and negatively charged anions, so that the product is neutral and without a net charge.
   a. Salt10
   c. Undefined
   b. Thing
   d. Undefined

63. An _____ is an underground layer of water-bearing permeable rock, or unconsolidated materials (gravel, sand, silt, or clay) from which groundwater can be usefully extracted using a water well.
   a. Thing
   c. Undefined
   b. Aquifer10
   d. Undefined

64. A movement within the Earth's crust or mantle, caused by the sudden rupture or repositioning of underground rocks as they release stress is an _____.
   a. Earthquake10
   c. Undefined
   b. AASHTO Soil Classification System
   d. Undefined

65. A fracture dividing a rock into two sections that have visibly moved relative to each other is a _____.

Chapter 10. PETROLEUM MIGRATION

a. 1509 Istanbul earthquake
b. Fault10
c. Undefined
d. Undefined

66. _____ refers to a rock in which most of the mineral grains are less than 1 millimeter across or less than 1/16 mm.
a. Fine-grained rock10
b. 1509 Istanbul earthquake
c. Undefined
d. Undefined

67. Gravity is called the _____.
a. Driving force10
b. 1509 Istanbul earthquake
c. Undefined
d. Undefined

68. The capability of a given substance to allow the passage of a fluid is called _____. _____ depends on the size of and the degree of connection among a substance's pores.
a. Permeability10
b. 1509 Istanbul earthquake
c. Undefined
d. Undefined

69. A numerical expression of the amount of energy released by an earthquake, determined by measuring earthquake waves on standardized recording instruments is called a _____. The number scale for magnitudes is logarithmic rather than arithmetic. Therefore, deflections on a seismograph for a _____ 5 earthquake, for example, are 10 times greater than those for a _____ 4 earthquake, 100 times greater than for a _____ 3 earthquake, and so on.
a. Magnitude10
b. 1509 Istanbul earthquake
c. Undefined
d. Undefined

70. Stored energy as a result of location or spatial arrangement is referred to as _____.
a. Thing
b. Potential energy10
c. Undefined
d. Undefined

71. A geologic structure that allows for significant amounts of oil and gas to accumulate is called _____.
a. AASHTO Soil Classification System
b. Oil trap10
c. Undefined
d. Undefined

72. _____ refers to the altitude, or vertical distance, above or below sea level.
a. AASHTO Soil Classification System
b. Elevation10
c. Undefined
d. Undefined

73. The force of attraction exerted by one body in the universe on another is _____. _____ is directly proportional to the product of the masses of the two attracted bodies. The force of attraction exerted by the Earth on bodies on or near its surface, tending to pull them toward the Earth's center.
a. Gravity10
b. 1509 Istanbul earthquake
c. Undefined
d. Undefined

74. _____ refers to a person who studies the geology and management of underground and related aspects of surface waters.

Chapter 10. PETROLEUM MIGRATION

    a. Hydrogeologist10
    c. Undefined
    b. 1509 Istanbul earthquake
    d. Undefined

75. The _____ is a geologic period that extends from about 299.0 Ma to 248.0 Ma. It is the last period of the Palaeozoic Era. As with most older geologic periods, the strata that define the _____ are well identified, but the exact date of the period's start is uncertain by a few million years.
    a. Permian10
    b. Thing
    c. Undefined
    d. Undefined

76. A round or oval depression in the Earth's surface, containing the youngest section of rock in its lowest, central part is a _____.
    a. 1509 Istanbul earthquake
    b. Basin10
    c. Undefined
    d. Undefined

77. _____ refers to a clastic rock composed of particles that range in diameter from 1/16 millimeter to 2 millimeters in diameter. Sandstones make up about 25% of all sedimentary rocks.
    a. 1509 Istanbul earthquake
    b. Sandstone10
    c. Undefined
    d. Undefined

78. _____ refers to an area underlain by one or more oil pools.
    a. Oil field10
    b. AASHTO Soil Classification System
    c. Undefined
    d. Undefined

79. Turbidity current deposit characterized by graded bedding is called _____.
    a. 1509 Istanbul earthquake
    b. Turbidite10
    c. Undefined
    d. Undefined

80. _____ refers to a feature on the surface of the planet Mars that very closely resembles certain types of stream channels on Earth.
    a. 1509 Istanbul earthquake
    b. Channel10
    c. Undefined
    d. Undefined

81. A _____ is a bend in a river, also known as an oxbow loop. A stream or river flowing through a wide valley or flat plain will tend to form a meandering stream course as it alternatively erodes and deposites sediments along its course.
    a. Meander10
    b. Thing
    c. Undefined
    d. Undefined

82. _____ refers to a long, narrow trough bounded by normal faults. It represents a region where divergence is taking place.
    a. 1509 Istanbul earthquake
    b. Rift10
    c. Undefined
    d. Undefined

83. _____, a branch of geology, is basically the study of rock layers and layering. It is primarily used in the study of sedimentary and layered volcanic rocks.

Chapter 10. PETROLEUM MIGRATION

a. Stratigraphy10   b. Thing
c. Undefined   d. Undefined

84. _____ refers to a portion of a rock unit that possesses a distinctive set of characteristics that distinguishes it from other parts of the same unit.
   a. Facies10
   b. 1509 Istanbul earthquake
   c. Undefined
   d. Undefined

85. The percentage of a soil, rock, or sediment's volume that is made up of pores is _____.
   a. 1509 Istanbul earthquake
   b. Porosity10
   c. Undefined
   d. Undefined

86. A fold in rock connecting two vertically offset, horizontal sections of sedimentary rocks is called the _____.
   a. 1509 Istanbul earthquake
   b. Monocline10
   c. Undefined
   d. Undefined

87. Any place where bedrock is visible on the surface of the Earth is referred to as _____.
   a. AASHTO Soil Classification System
   b. Outcrop10
   c. Undefined
   d. Undefined

88. A high mountain peak that forms when the walls of three or more cirques intersect is called a _____.
   a. Horn10
   b. 1509 Istanbul earthquake
   c. Undefined
   d. Undefined

89. A high mountain pass that forms when part of an arête erodes is referred to as a _____.
   a. 1509 Istanbul earthquake
   b. Col10
   c. Undefined
   d. Undefined

90. Dominantly unsorted and unstratified drift, generally unconsolidated deposited directly by and underneath a glacier without subsequent reworking by meltwater, and consisting of a hetergeneous mixture of clay, silt, sand, gravel, stones, and boulders is called _____.
   a. 1509 Istanbul earthquake
   b. Till10
   c. Undefined
   d. Undefined

91. _____ refers to an atom or molecule that has gained or lost one or more electrons, thus acquiring an electrical charge.
   a. Thing
   b. Ion10
   c. Undefined
   d. Undefined

Chapter 11. HEAT TRANSPORT

1. Gradual loss of heat from Earth's interior out into space is called _____.
   a. 1509 Istanbul earthquake
   b. Heat flow11
   c. Undefined
   d. Undefined

2. Ability to do work is referred to as _____. Most evident in glacial systems as radiant _____ from the sun and as latent _____ required to melt ice to water.
   a. AASHTO Soil Classification System
   b. Energy11
   c. Undefined
   d. Undefined

3. A device that converts heat energy into mechanical energy is called the _____.
   a. Heat engine11
   b. 1509 Istanbul earthquake
   c. Undefined
   d. Undefined

4. _____ refers to huge slabs of rock that make up the Earth's crust. They can be continental or oceanic.
   a. Tectonic plate11
   b. Thing
   c. Undefined
   d. Undefined

5. General term for the processes of folding, faulting, shearing, compression, or extension of rocks as the result of various natural forces is called _____.
   a. 1509 Istanbul earthquake
   b. Deformation11
   c. Undefined
   d. Undefined

6. A movement within the Earth's crust or mantle, caused by the sudden rupture or repositioning of underground rocks as they release stress is an _____.
   a. Earthquake11
   b. AASHTO Soil Classification System
   c. Undefined
   d. Undefined

7. An episode of mountain building is called _____.
   a. AASHTO Soil Classification System
   b. Orogeny11
   c. Undefined
   d. Undefined

8. _____ refers to rigid parts of the Earth's crust and part of the Earth's upper mantle that moves and adjoins each other along zones of seismic activity.
   a. Plate11
   b. 1509 Istanbul earthquake
   c. Undefined
   d. Undefined

9. A nearly flat erosional surface presumably produced as mass wasting, sheet erosion, and stream erosion reduce a region almost to base level is referred to as _____.
   a. Peneplain11
   b. 1509 Istanbul earthquake
   c. Undefined
   d. Undefined

10. _____ is the displacement of solids (soil, mud, rock, and other particles) by the agents of wind, water, ice, movement in response to gravity, or living organisms.
    a. Thing
    b. Erosion11
    c. Undefined
    d. Undefined

Chapter 11. HEAT TRANSPORT

11. The vertical difference between the summit of a mountain and the adjacent valley or plain is referred to as a _____.
    a. 1509 Istanbul earthquake
    b. Relief11
    c. Undefined
    d. Undefined

12. The force of attraction exerted by one body in the universe on another is _____. _____ is directly proportional to the product of the masses of the two attracted bodies. The force of attraction exerted by the Earth on bodies on or near its surface, tending to pull them toward the Earth's center.
    a. Gravity11
    b. 1509 Istanbul earthquake
    c. Undefined
    d. Undefined

13. Weather condition of an area including especially prevailing temperature and average daily/yearly rainfall over a long period of time is called _____.
    a. Thing
    b. Climate11
    c. Undefined
    d. Undefined

14. A geosystem that includes all parts of the Earth system and all the interactions among these components needed to describe how climate behaves in space and time is a _____.
    a. Climate system11
    b. 1509 Istanbul earthquake
    c. Undefined
    d. Undefined

15. Energy derived from the Sun, including energy from solar generating systems, hydroelectric systems, and wind power is called _____.
    a. Solar energy11
    b. 1509 Istanbul earthquake
    c. Undefined
    d. Undefined

16. _____ refers to earth's crust, which is formed at mid-oceanic ridges, typically 5 to 10 kilometers thick with a density of 3.0 grams per centimeter cubed.
    a. Oceanic crust11
    b. AASHTO Soil Classification System
    c. Undefined
    d. Undefined

17. A _____ is the outer layer of a planet, part of its lithosphere. Planetary _____ is generally composed of a less dense material than that of its deeper layers. The _____ of the Earth is composed mainly of basalt and granite.
    a. Crust11
    b. Thing
    c. Undefined
    d. Undefined

18. _____ refers to the process of emplacement of magma in pre-existing rock. Also, the term refers to igneous rock mass so formed within the surrounding rock.
    a. AASHTO Soil Classification System
    b. Intrusion11
    c. Undefined
    d. Undefined

19. _____ refers to pertaining to magma.
    a. 1509 Istanbul earthquake
    b. Magmatic11
    c. Undefined
    d. Undefined

Chapter 11. HEAT TRANSPORT

20. _____ refers to a process leading to chemical changes in matter; involves the making and/or breaking of chemical bonds.
   a. Chemical reaction11
   b. Thing
   c. Undefined
   d. Undefined

21. The process by which conditions within the Earth, below the zone of diagenesis, alter the mineral content, chemical composition, and structure of solid rock without melting it is called _____. Igneous, sedimentary, and metamorphic rocks may all undergo _____.
   a. Metamorphism11
   b. 1509 Istanbul earthquake
   c. Undefined
   d. Undefined

22. The set of processes that cause physical and chemical changes in sediment after it has been deposited and buried under another layer of sediment is _____. _____ may culminate in lithification.
   a. Diagenesis11
   b. 1509 Istanbul earthquake
   c. Undefined
   d. Undefined

23. _____ refers to any condensed water falling from the atmosphere to the surface of the earth. Common types include rain, snow, sleet, and hail.
   a. 1509 Istanbul earthquake
   b. Precipitation11
   c. Undefined
   d. Undefined

24. The same as a mineral reserve except that it refers only to a metal-bearing deposit is referred to as _____.
   a. Ore deposit11
   b. AASHTO Soil Classification System
   c. Undefined
   d. Undefined

25. The part of an ore, usually metallic, that is economically desirable is called _____.
   a. Ore mineral11
   b. AASHTO Soil Classification System
   c. Undefined
   d. Undefined

26. A naturally occurring, usually inorganic, solid consisting of either a single element or a compound, and having a definite chemical composition and a systematic internal arrangement of atoms is referred to as a _____.
   a. Mineral11
   b. 1509 Istanbul earthquake
   c. Undefined
   d. Undefined

27. A mineral deposit that can be mined for a profit is called _____.
   a. AASHTO Soil Classification System
   b. Ore11
   c. Undefined
   d. Undefined

28. A region of considerable extent where the combination of deposition and subsidence has formed thick accumulations of sediment and sedimentary rock is called _____.
   a. 1509 Istanbul earthquake
   b. Sedimentary basin11
   c. Undefined
   d. Undefined

29. A rock in which hydrocarbons originate is referred to as a _____.

Chapter 11. HEAT TRANSPORT

a. Source rock11
b. 1509 Istanbul earthquake
c. Undefined
d. Undefined

30. A body of rock identified by lithic characteristics and stratigraphic position and is mappable at the earth's surface or traceable in the subsurface is a _____.
a. 1509 Istanbul earthquake
b. Formation11
c. Undefined
d. Undefined

31. Aggregates of minerals or rock fragments are called _____.
a. 1509 Istanbul earthquake
b. Rocks11
c. Undefined
d. Undefined

32. A round or oval depression in the Earth's surface, containing the youngest section of rock in its lowest, central part is a _____.
a. 1509 Istanbul earthquake
b. Basin11
c. Undefined
d. Undefined

33. _____ refers to a naturally formed aggregate of usually inorganic materials from within the Earth.
a. Rock11
b. 1509 Istanbul earthquake
c. Undefined
d. Undefined

34. Water stored beneath the surface in open pore spaces and fractures in rock is called _____.
a. Groundwater11
b. 1509 Istanbul earthquake
c. Undefined
d. Undefined

35. A chemical compound composed only of the elements carbon and hydrogen is called _____.
a. Thing
b. Hydrocarbon11
c. Undefined
d. Undefined

36. _____ refers to the transfer of heat through matter by molecular activity.
a. 1509 Istanbul earthquake
b. Conduction11
c. Undefined
d. Undefined

37. _____ is the transfer of heat by currents within a fluid. It may arise from temperature differences either within the fluid or between the fluid and its boundary, other sources of density variations (such as variable salinity), or from the application of an external motive force.
a. Convection11
b. Event
c. Undefined
d. Undefined

38. The _____ is the solid outermost shell of a rocky planet. On the Earth, the _____ includes the crust and the uppermost layer of the mantle (the upper mantle or lower _____) which is joined to the crust.
a. Thing
b. Lithosphere11
c. Undefined
d. Undefined

Chapter 11. HEAT TRANSPORT

39. _____ is a form of energy present in any electric field or magnetic field, or in any volume containing electromagnetic radiation. The SI unit of electrical energy is the joule, while the unit used by electrical utility companies is the watt-hour (W·h) or the kilowatt-hour (kW·h).
   a. Electromagnetic energy11
   b. Thing
   c. Undefined
   d. Undefined

40. _____ is a physical or chemical phenomenon or a process in which atoms, molecules, or ions enter some bulk phase - gas, liquid or solid material. In nutrition, amino acids are broken down through digestion, which begins in the stomach.
   a. Absorption11
   b. Thing
   c. Undefined
   d. Undefined

41. Movement of heat from one place to another is a _____.
   a. Heat transfer11
   b. 1509 Istanbul earthquake
   c. Undefined
   d. Undefined

42. Earth's _____ is a layer of gases surrounding the planet Earth and retained by the Earth's gravity. It contains roughly 78% nitrogen and 21% oxygen, with trace amounts of other gases.
   a. Atmosphere11
   b. Thing
   c. Undefined
   d. Undefined

43. _____ refers to the gradual increase in temperature with depth in the crust. The average is 30°C per kilometer in the upper crust.
   a. Geothermal gradient11
   b. 1509 Istanbul earthquake
   c. Undefined
   d. Undefined

44. _____ is the naturally hot interior of Earth. The heat is maintained by naturally occurring nuclear reactions in Earth's interior.
   a. Geothermal11
   b. Thing
   c. Undefined
   d. Undefined

45. The vertical drop in a stream's elevation over a given horizontal distance, expressed as an angle is referred to as a _____.
   a. 1509 Istanbul earthquake
   b. Gradient11
   c. Undefined
   d. Undefined

46. The zone of convergence of two tectonic plates, one of which usually overrides the other is referred to as the _____.
   a. Subduction zone11
   b. 1509 Istanbul earthquake
   c. Undefined
   d. Undefined

47. The downward movement of a plate into the mantle that occurs in trenches, which are also known as _____ zones.
   a. Subduction11
   b. Thing
   c. Undefined
   d. Undefined

Chapter 11. HEAT TRANSPORT

48. A term used to describe the property of releasing energy or particles from an unstable atom is called _____.
   a. Radioactive11
   b. Thing
   c. Undefined
   d. Undefined

49. _____ refers to the mechanism by which the earth is believed to have formed from a small nucleus by additions of solid bodies, such as meteorites, asteroids, or planetesimals. Also used in plate tectonics to indicate the addition of terranes to a continent.
   a. AASHTO Soil Classification System
   b. Accretion11
   c. Undefined
   d. Undefined

50. A chemical _____, often called simply _____, is a chemical substance that cannot be divided or changed into other chemical substances by any ordinary chemical technique. An _____ is a class of substances that contain the same number of protons in all its atoms.
   a. Thing
   b. Element11
   c. Undefined
   d. Undefined

51. _____ is a chemical element with the symbol Ag. A soft white lustrous transition metal, it has the highest electrical and thermal conductivity of any metal and occurs in minerals and in free form.
   a. Silver11
   b. Thing
   c. Undefined
   d. Undefined

52. The percentage of a soil, rock, or sediment's volume that is made up of pores is _____.
   a. Porosity11
   b. 1509 Istanbul earthquake
   c. Undefined
   d. Undefined

53. _____ refers to the solid matter in which a fossil or crystal is embedded.
   a. Matrix11
   b. 1509 Istanbul earthquake
   c. Undefined
   d. Undefined

54. The amount of energy required to raise the temperature of 1 gram of a substance by 1 °C is _____.
   a. Thing
   b. Specific heat11
   c. Undefined
   d. Undefined

55. The ability of a given stream to carry sediment, measured as the maximum quantity it can transport past a given point on the channel bank in a given amount of time is called _____.
   a. 1509 Istanbul earthquake
   b. Capacity11
   c. Undefined
   d. Undefined

56. The spontaneous nuclear disintegration of atoms of certain isotopes is _____.
   a. Radioactivity11
   b. 1509 Istanbul earthquake
   c. Undefined
   d. Undefined

57. Earth's crust that includes both the continents and the continental shelves is the _____.
   a. 1509 Istanbul earthquake
   b. Continental crust11
   c. Undefined
   d. Undefined

Chapter 11. HEAT TRANSPORT

58. Describing a substance in which the atoms are arranged in a regular, repeating, orderly pattern is called _____.
    a. Crystalline11
    b. 1509 Istanbul earthquake
    c. Undefined
    d. Undefined

59. _____ refers to the water that lies beneath the ground surface, filling the cracks, crevices, and pore space of rocks.
    a. Ground water11
    b. 1509 Istanbul earthquake
    c. Undefined
    d. Undefined

60. _____ refers to the beginning or source area for a stream. Also called the headwaters.
    a. Head11
    b. 1509 Istanbul earthquake
    c. Undefined
    d. Undefined

61. _____ refers to a body of water found on the Earth's surface and confined to a narrow topographic depression, down which it flows and transports rock particles, sediment, and dissolved particles. Rivers, creeks, brooks, and runs are all streams.
    a. 1509 Istanbul earthquake
    b. Stream11
    c. Undefined
    d. Undefined

62. _____ is a term used for ionic compounds composed of positively charged cations and negatively charged anions, so that the product is neutral and without a net charge.
    a. Salt11
    b. Thing
    c. Undefined
    d. Undefined

63. A mineral or fuel deposit, known or not yet discovered, that may be or become available for human exploitation is called a _____.
    a. Resource11
    b. 1509 Istanbul earthquake
    c. Undefined
    d. Undefined

64. The branch of geology that studies the physics of the Earth, using the physical principles underlying such phenomena as seismic waves, heat flow, gravity, and magnetism to investigate planetary properties is called _____.
    a. Geophysics11
    b. 1509 Istanbul earthquake
    c. Undefined
    d. Undefined

65. The study of water's properties, circulation, and distribution is referred to as _____.
    a. Hydrology11
    b. 1509 Istanbul earthquake
    c. Undefined
    d. Undefined

66. _____ is the part of hydrology that deals with the distribution and movement of groundwater in the soil and rocks of the Earth's crust (commonly in aquifers).
    a. Thing
    b. Hydrogeology11
    c. Undefined
    d. Undefined

67. The movement of surface water into rock or soil through cracks and pore spaces is called _____.

Chapter 11. HEAT TRANSPORT

    a. Infiltration11
    b. AASHTO Soil Classification System
    c. Undefined
    d. Undefined

68. Usually slow but effective process of weathering and erosion in which rocks are dissolved by water is a _____.
    a. Solution11
    b. 1509 Istanbul earthquake
    c. Undefined
    d. Undefined

69. _____ refers to the curve that describes how temperature increases with depth in the Earth.
    a. 1509 Istanbul earthquake
    b. Geotherm11
    c. Undefined
    d. Undefined

70. _____ refers both to animals and plants, of having a resemblance in structure, due to descent from a common progenitor with subsequent modification.
    a. Homogeneous11
    b. Thing
    c. Undefined
    d. Undefined

71. The time between winter and summer is _____.
    a. 1509 Istanbul earthquake
    b. Spring11
    c. Undefined
    d. Undefined

72. A spring in which the water is 6-9°C warmer than the mean annual air temperature of its locality is called _____.
    a. Hot spring11
    b. 1509 Istanbul earthquake
    c. Undefined
    d. Undefined

73. The capability of a given substance to allow the passage of a fluid is called _____. _____ depends on the size of and the degree of connection among a substance's pores.
    a. Permeability11
    b. 1509 Istanbul earthquake
    c. Undefined
    d. Undefined

74. _____ refers to two parallel rows of standing stones or a grand ceremonial way bordered by ditches and banks of earth leading to a ceremonial centre such as at Stonehenge.
    a. AASHTO Soil Classification System
    b. Avenue11
    c. Undefined
    d. Undefined

75. The set of geological processes that result in the expulsion of lava, pyroclastics, and gases at the Earth's surface is referred to as _____.
    a. Volcanism11
    b. 1509 Istanbul earthquake
    c. Undefined
    d. Undefined

76. An area in the upper mantle, ranging from 100 to 200 kilometers in width, from which magma rises in a plume to form volcanoes. A _____ may endure for 10 million years or more.
    a. 1509 Istanbul earthquake
    b. Hot spot11
    c. Undefined
    d. Undefined

Chapter 11. HEAT TRANSPORT

77. _____ refers to the process by which solid, liquid, and gaseous materials are ejected into the earth's atmosphere and onto the earth's surface by volcanic activity. Eruptions range from the quiet overflow of liquid rock to the tremendously violent expulsion of pyroclastics.
- a. Eruption11
- b. AASHTO Soil Classification System
- c. Undefined
- d. Undefined

78. _____ refers to a vent or opening through which issue steam, hydrogen sulfide, or other gases. The craters of many dormant volcanoes contain active fumaroles.
- a. Fumarole11
- b. 1509 Istanbul earthquake
- c. Undefined
- d. Undefined

79. _____ refers to a natural spring marked by the intermittent escape of hot water and steam.
- a. Geyser11
- b. 1509 Istanbul earthquake
- c. Undefined
- d. Undefined

80. An opening in the Earth's surface through which lava, gases, and hot particles are expelled is a _____. Also called volcanic _____ and volcano.
- a. 1509 Istanbul earthquake
- b. Vent11
- c. Undefined
- d. Undefined

81. A large mass of rock projecting above surrounding terrain is called a _____.
- a. 1509 Istanbul earthquake
- b. Mountain11
- c. Undefined
- d. Undefined

82. A sedimentary rock formed from the accumulation of carbonate minerals precipitated organically or inorganically is _____.
- a. 1509 Istanbul earthquake
- b. Carbonate rock11
- c. Undefined
- d. Undefined

83. A nearly flat surface separating two beds of sedimentary rock is a _____. Each _____ marks the end of one deposit and the beginning of another having different characteristics.
- a. Bedding plane11
- b. 1509 Istanbul earthquake
- c. Undefined
- d. Undefined

84. _____ refers to a clastic rock composed of particles that range in diameter from 1/16 millimeter to 2 millimeters in diameter. Sandstones make up about 25% of all sedimentary rocks.
- a. Sandstone11
- b. 1509 Istanbul earthquake
- c. Undefined
- d. Undefined

85. _____ is a sedimentary rock composed largely of the mineral calcite (calcium carbonate: $CaCO_3$). _____ often contains variable amounts of silica in the form of chert or flint, as well as varying amounts of clay, silt and sand as disseminations, nodules, or layers within the rock.
- a. Limestone11
- b. Thing
- c. Undefined
- d. Undefined

86. The quantity of water in a stream that passes a given point in a period of time is referred to as _____.

Chapter 11. HEAT TRANSPORT

a. Discharge11
b. 1509 Istanbul earthquake
c. Undefined
d. Undefined

87. One of several minerals containing one central carbon atom with strong covalent bonds to three oxygen atoms and typically having ionic bonds to one or more positive ions is _____.
a. 1509 Istanbul earthquake
b. Carbonate11
c. Undefined
d. Undefined

88. The division of sediment or sedimentary rock into parallel layers that can be distinguished from each other by such features as chemical composition and grain size is _____.
a. Bedding11
b. 1509 Istanbul earthquake
c. Undefined
d. Undefined

89. A fracture dividing a rock into two sections that have visibly moved relative to each other is a _____.
a. 1509 Istanbul earthquake
b. Fault11
c. Undefined
d. Undefined

90. _____ refers to a crack or break in a rock. To break in random places instead of cleaving.
a. 1509 Istanbul earthquake
b. Fracture11
c. Undefined
d. Undefined

91. A form of chemical weathering in which water molecules, sometimes in combination with acid or another compound in the environment, attract and remove oppositely charged ions or ion groups from a mineral or rock is a _____.
a. Dissolution11
b. 1509 Istanbul earthquake
c. Undefined
d. Undefined

92. One of several minerals containing positive sulfur ions bonded to negative oxygen ions is _____.
a. Sulfate11
b. 1509 Istanbul earthquake
c. Undefined
d. Undefined

93. _____ refers to general term referring to the rock underlying other unconsolidated material, i.e. soil.
a. Bedrock11
b. 1509 Istanbul earthquake
c. Undefined
d. Undefined

94. A coarse-grained, nonfoliated metamorphic rock derived from limestone or dolostone is referred to as _____.
a. 1509 Istanbul earthquake
b. Marble11
c. Undefined
d. Undefined

95. _____ refers to the height of floodwaters in feet or meters above an established datum plane.
a. 1509 Istanbul earthquake
b. Stage11
c. Undefined
d. Undefined

96. Group of organisms of the same species occupying a certain area and sharing a common gene pool is referred to as _____.

Chapter 11. HEAT TRANSPORT

    a. Thing
    c. Undefined
    b. Population11
    d. Undefined

97. _____ occurs when living things move from one biome to another. In most cases organisms migrate to avoid local shortages of food, usually caused by winter. Animals may also migrate to a certain location to breed, as is the case with some fish.
    a. Thing
    c. Undefined
    b. Migration11
    d. Undefined

98. A chain of volcanoes fueled by magma that rises from an underlying subducting plate is called a _____.
    a. 1509 Istanbul earthquake
    c. Undefined
    b. Volcanic arc11
    d. Undefined

99. _____ refers to a group of closely spaced mountains or parallel ridges.
    a. 1509 Istanbul earthquake
    c. Undefined
    b. Mountain range11
    d. Undefined

100. The extent to which a given substance allows water to flow through it, determined by such factors as sorting and grain size and shape is called _____.
    a. Hydraulic conductivity11
    c. Undefined
    b. 1509 Istanbul earthquake
    d. Undefined

101. A numerical expression of the amount of energy released by an earthquake, determined by measuring earthquake waves on standardized recording instruments is called a _____. The number scale for magnitudes is logarithmic rather than arithmetic. Therefore, deflections on a seismograph for a _____ 5 earthquake, for example, are 10 times greater than those for a _____ 4 earthquake, 100 times greater than for a _____ 3 earthquake, and so on.
    a. Magnitude11
    c. Undefined
    b. 1509 Istanbul earthquake
    d. Undefined

102. Material is in _____ if it is adjusted to the physical and chemical conditions of its environment so that it does not change or alter with time.
    a. AASHTO Soil Classification System
    c. Undefined
    b. Equilibrium11
    d. Undefined

103. _____ refers to a basic unit of the geologic time scale that is a subdivision of an era. Periods may be divided into smaller units called epochs.
    a. Period11
    c. Undefined
    b. 1509 Istanbul earthquake
    d. Undefined

104. A member of a group of easily combustible, organic sedimentary rocks composed mostly of plant remains and containing a high proportion of carbon is called _____.
    a. Coal11
    c. Undefined
    b. 1509 Istanbul earthquake
    d. Undefined

105. _____ refers to an atom or molecule that has gained or lost one or more electrons, thus acquiring an electrical charge.

Chapter 11. HEAT TRANSPORT

a. Thing
b. Ion11
c. Undefined
d. Undefined

106. _____ refers to a feature on the surface of the planet Mars that very closely resembles certain types of stream channels on Earth.
a. 1509 Istanbul earthquake
b. Channel11
c. Undefined
d. Undefined

107. With reference to groundwater, the area over which infiltration and resupply of a given aquifer occurs is a _____.
a. Recharge area11
b. Thing
c. Undefined
d. Undefined

108. Any relatively sunken part of the Earth's surface, especially a low-lying area surrounded by higher ground is called a _____.
a. Depression11
b. 1509 Istanbul earthquake
c. Undefined
d. Undefined

109. _____ refers to the addition of new water to an aquifer or to the zone of saturation.
a. Recharge11
b. 1509 Istanbul earthquake
c. Undefined
d. Undefined

Chapter 12. EARTHQUAKES, STRESS, AND FLUIDS

1. A movement within the Earth's crust or mantle, caused by the sudden rupture or repositioning of underground rocks as they release stress is an _____.
   a. Earthquake12
   b. AASHTO Soil Classification System
   c. Undefined
   d. Undefined

2. The force acting on a rock or another solid to deform it, measured in kilograms per square centimeter or pounds per square inch is _____.
   a. Stress12
   b. 1509 Istanbul earthquake
   c. Undefined
   d. Undefined

3. A _____ is the outer layer of a planet, part of its lithosphere. Planetary _____ is generally composed of a less dense material than that of its deeper layers. The _____ of the Earth is composed mainly of basalt and granite.
   a. Crust12
   b. Thing
   c. Undefined
   d. Undefined

4. _____ refers to the conversion of moderately cohesive, unconsolidated sediment into a fluid, water-saturated mass.
   a. Liquefaction12
   b. 1509 Istanbul earthquake
   c. Undefined
   d. Undefined

5. The quantity of water in a stream that passes a given point in a period of time is referred to as _____.
   a. Discharge12
   b. 1509 Istanbul earthquake
   c. Undefined
   d. Undefined

6. _____ is any particulate matter that can be transported by fluid flow and which eventually is deposited as a layer of solid particles on the bed or bottom of a body of water or other liquid.
   a. Sediment12
   b. Thing
   c. Undefined
   d. Undefined

7. The time between winter and summer is _____.
   a. Spring12
   b. 1509 Istanbul earthquake
   c. Undefined
   d. Undefined

8. Water stored beneath the surface in open pore spaces and fractures in rock is called _____.
   a. 1509 Istanbul earthquake
   b. Groundwater12
   c. Undefined
   d. Undefined

9. A numerical expression of the amount of energy released by an earthquake, determined by measuring earthquake waves on standardized recording instruments is called a _____. The number scale for magnitudes is logarithmic rather than arithmetic. Therefore, deflections on a seismograph for a _____ 5 earthquake, for example, are 10 times greater than those for a _____ 4 earthquake, 100 times greater than for a _____ 3 earthquake, and so on.
   a. 1509 Istanbul earthquake
   b. Magnitude12
   c. Undefined
   d. Undefined

10. The point on the Earth's surface that is located directly above the focus of an earthquake is referred to as _____.

Chapter 12. EARTHQUAKES, STRESS, AND FLUIDS

a. AASHTO Soil Classification System
b. Epicenter12
c. Undefined
d. Undefined

11. _____ refers to the change in the shape or volume of a rock that results from stress.
a. 1509 Istanbul earthquake
b. Strain12
c. Undefined
d. Undefined

12. _____ is the part of hydrology that deals with the distribution and movement of groundwater in the soil and rocks of the Earth's crust (commonly in aquifers).
a. Thing
b. Hydrogeology12
c. Undefined
d. Undefined

13. The relationship between distance on a map and the distance on the terrain being represented by that map is a _____.
a. Scale12
b. 1509 Istanbul earthquake
c. Undefined
d. Undefined

14. An _____ is an underground layer of water-bearing permeable rock, or unconsolidated materials (gravel, sand, silt, or clay) from which groundwater can be usefully extracted using a water well.
a. Thing
b. Aquifer12
c. Undefined
d. Undefined

15. _____ refers to the beginning or source area for a stream. Also called the headwaters.
a. 1509 Istanbul earthquake
b. Head12
c. Undefined
d. Undefined

16. One of a series of progressive disturbances that reverberate through the Earth to transmit the energy released from an earthquake is called a _____.
a. 1509 Istanbul earthquake
b. Seismic wave12
c. Undefined
d. Undefined

17. The tendency of a system to vibrate with maximum amplitude when the frequency of the applied force is the same as the vibrating body's natural frequency is calld _____.
a. Resonance12
b. 1509 Istanbul earthquake
c. Undefined
d. Undefined

18. Includes all bodies of water, lakes, rivers, ponds, and so on that are on the surface of the earth, in contrast to groundwater, which lies below the surface is _____.
a. Surface water12
b. Thing
c. Undefined
d. Undefined

19. _____ refers to a place in which water is stored, including the oceans, glaciers and polar ice, groundwater, lakes and rivers, the atmosphere, and the biosphere. A source or place of residence for elements in a chemical cycle or hydrologic cycle.

Chapter 12. EARTHQUAKES, STRESS, AND FLUIDS

    a. 1509 Istanbul earthquake
    b. Reservoir12
    c. Undefined
    d. Undefined

20. _____ refers to a body of water found on the Earth's surface and confined to a narrow topographic depression, down which it flows and transports rock particles, sediment, and dissolved particles. Rivers, creeks, brooks, and runs are all streams.
    a. 1509 Istanbul earthquake
    b. Stream12
    c. Undefined
    d. Undefined

21. _____ refers to a body in which strains are totally recoverable, as in a rubber band.
    a. AASHTO Soil Classification System
    b. Elastic12
    c. Undefined
    d. Undefined

22. The capability of a given substance to allow the passage of a fluid is called _____. _____ depends on the size of and the degree of connection among a substance's pores.
    a. 1509 Istanbul earthquake
    b. Permeability12
    c. Undefined
    d. Undefined

23. _____ refers to a tentative explanation of a given set of data that is expected to remain valid after future observation and experimentation.
    a. Hypothesis12
    b. 1509 Istanbul earthquake
    c. Undefined
    d. Undefined

24. The processes by which crustal forces cause a rock formation to break and slip along a fault are called _____.
    a. 1509 Istanbul earthquake
    b. Faulting12
    c. Undefined
    d. Undefined

25. The percentage of a soil, rock, or sediment's volume that is made up of pores is _____.
    a. 1509 Istanbul earthquake
    b. Porosity12
    c. Undefined
    d. Undefined

26. A fracture dividing a rock into two sections that have visibly moved relative to each other is a _____.
    a. 1509 Istanbul earthquake
    b. Fault12
    c. Undefined
    d. Undefined

27. _____ refers to a basic unit of the geologic time scale that is a subdivision of an era. Periods may be divided into smaller units called epochs.
    a. 1509 Istanbul earthquake
    b. Period12
    c. Undefined
    d. Undefined

28. General term for the processes of folding, faulting, shearing, compression, or extension of rocks as the result of various natural forces is called _____.
    a. Deformation12
    b. 1509 Istanbul earthquake
    c. Undefined
    d. Undefined

Chapter 12. EARTHQUAKES, STRESS, AND FLUIDS

29. The process of determining that two or more geographically distant rocks or rock strata originated in the same time period is referred to as _____.
    a. Correlation12
    b. 1509 Istanbul earthquake
    c. Undefined
    d. Undefined

30. A steep-sided, usually circular depression formed by either explosion or collapse at a volcanic vent is a _____.
    a. Crater12
    b. 1509 Istanbul earthquake
    c. Undefined
    d. Undefined

31. An opening in the Earth's surface through which lava, gases, and hot particles are expelled is a _____. Also called volcanic _____ and volcano.
    a. 1509 Istanbul earthquake
    b. Vent12
    c. Undefined
    d. Undefined

32. Material that is thrown out by a volcano, including pyroclastic material and lava bombs is referred to as _____.
    a. Ejecta12
    b. AASHTO Soil Classification System
    c. Undefined
    d. Undefined

33. Rounded particles coarser than 2 mm in diameter are called _____.
    a. Gravel12
    b. 1509 Istanbul earthquake
    c. Undefined
    d. Undefined

34. _____ in referring to sediment grains, loose, separate, or unattached to one another.
    a. Unconsolidated12
    b. AASHTO Soil Classification System
    c. Undefined
    d. Undefined

35. In mass wasting, the resistance to movement or deformation of material is called _____.
    a. 1509 Istanbul earthquake
    b. Shear strength12
    c. Undefined
    d. Undefined

36. _____ refers to stress that causes two adjacent parts of a body to slide past one another.
    a. Shear12
    b. 1509 Istanbul earthquake
    c. Undefined
    d. Undefined

37. _____ refers to stress due to forces that tend to cause movement or strain parallel to the direction of the forces.
    a. Shear stress12
    b. 1509 Istanbul earthquake
    c. Undefined
    d. Undefined

38. Stress that slices rocks into parallel blocks that slide in opposite directions along their adjacent sides is called _____. _____ may be caused by transform motion.
    a. Shearing stress12
    b. 1509 Istanbul earthquake
    c. Undefined
    d. Undefined

39. The motion of surfaces sliding past one another is called _____.

a. Shearing12
c. Undefined
b. 1509 Istanbul earthquake
d. Undefined

40. The average normal force per unit area that is transmitted directly across grain-to-grain boundaries in a sediment or rock mass is referred to as _____.
   a. Effective stress12
   c. Undefined
   b. AASHTO Soil Classification System
   d. Undefined

41. _____ refers to the solid matter in which a fossil or crystal is embedded.
   a. 1509 Istanbul earthquake
   c. Undefined
   b. Matrix12
   d. Undefined

42. _____ is a term used in geology, engineering and surveying to denote the motion of a surface (usually, the earth's surface) downwards relative to a datum such as sea-level.
   a. Thing
   c. Undefined
   b. Subsidence12
   d. Undefined

43. _____ refers to a vertical conduit through the Earth's crust below a volcano, through which magmatic materials have passed. Commonly filled with volcanic breccia and fragments of older rock.
   a. 1509 Istanbul earthquake
   c. Undefined
   b. Pipe12
   d. Undefined

44. _____ refers to the top few meters of regolith, generally including some organic matter derived from plants.
   a. 1509 Istanbul earthquake
   c. Undefined
   b. Soil12
   d. Undefined

45. Aggregates of minerals or rock fragments are called _____.
   a. Rocks12
   c. Undefined
   b. 1509 Istanbul earthquake
   d. Undefined

46. _____ refers to a naturally formed aggregate of usually inorganic materials from within the Earth.
   a. 1509 Istanbul earthquake
   c. Undefined
   b. Rock12
   d. Undefined

47. A reverse fault marked by a dip of 45° or less is called _____.
   a. 1509 Istanbul earthquake
   c. Undefined
   b. Thrust fault12
   d. Undefined

48. The situation in mass wasting that occurs when material free-falls or bounces down a cliff is called a _____.
   a. Fall12
   c. Undefined
   b. 1509 Istanbul earthquake
   d. Undefined

49. The scientific study of the Earth, its origins and evolution, the materials that make it up, and the processes that act on it is called _____.

Chapter 12. EARTHQUAKES, STRESS, AND FLUIDS

a. Geology12
b. 1509 Istanbul earthquake
c. Undefined
d. Undefined

50. A body of rock identified by lithic characteristics and stratigraphic position and is mappable at the earth's surface or traceable in the subsurface is a _____.
a. 1509 Istanbul earthquake
b. Formation12
c. Undefined
d. Undefined

51. A major branch of a stream system is referred to as a _____.
a. 1509 Istanbul earthquake
b. River12
c. Undefined
d. Undefined

52. The overlying surface of an inclined fault plane is called a _____.
a. 1509 Istanbul earthquake
b. Hanging wall12
c. Undefined
d. Undefined

53. Parallel layers of sedimentary rock are called _____.
a. Strata12
b. 1509 Istanbul earthquake
c. Undefined
d. Undefined

54. Angular chunk of solid rock ejected during an eruption is referred to as a _____.
a. Block12
b. 1509 Istanbul earthquake
c. Undefined
d. Undefined

55. A sedimentary rock formed from the accumulation of carbonate minerals precipitated organically or inorganically is _____.
a. Carbonate rock12
b. 1509 Istanbul earthquake
c. Undefined
d. Undefined

56. One of several minerals containing one central carbon atom with strong covalent bonds to three oxygen atoms and typically having ionic bonds to one or more positive ions is _____.
a. 1509 Istanbul earthquake
b. Carbonate12
c. Undefined
d. Undefined

57. _____ refers to general term referring to the rock underlying other unconsolidated material, i.e. soil.
a. Bedrock12
b. 1509 Istanbul earthquake
c. Undefined
d. Undefined

58. The force of attraction exerted by one body in the universe on another is _____. _____ is directly proportional to the product of the masses of the two attracted bodies. The force of attraction exerted by the Earth on bodies on or near its surface, tending to pull them toward the Earth's center.
a. Gravity12
b. 1509 Istanbul earthquake
c. Undefined
d. Undefined

59. The top of the ocean, where the water meets the atmosphere is called _____.

160 **Chapter 12. EARTHQUAKES, STRESS, AND FLUIDS**

a. 1509 Istanbul earthquake b. Sea level12
c. Undefined d. Undefined

60. A large mass of rock projecting above surrounding terrain is called a _____.
a. 1509 Istanbul earthquake b. Mountain12
c. Undefined d. Undefined

61. The entire area between the tops of the slopes on both sides of a stream is a _____.
a. Valley12 b. 1509 Istanbul earthquake
c. Undefined d. Undefined

62. _____ refers to a bend that develops in an initially horizontal layer of rock, usually caused by plastic deformation. Folds occur most frequently in sedimentary rocks.
a. Fold12 b. 1509 Istanbul earthquake
c. Undefined d. Undefined

63. A feature found in caves that is formed when a stalactite and stalagmite join is referred to as a _____.
a. 1509 Istanbul earthquake b. Column12
c. Undefined d. Undefined

64. _____ refers to a stress due to a force pushing together on a body.
a. 1509 Istanbul earthquake b. Compressive stress12
c. Undefined d. Undefined

65. _____ refers to a timeline based on a stratigraphic succession that provides a chronological record of the history of a region. The entire span of time since the Earth formed.
a. Geologic time12 b. 1509 Istanbul earthquake
c. Undefined d. Undefined

66. The angle formed by the inclined plane of a geological structure and the horizontal plane of the Earth's surface is referred to as a _____.
a. 1509 Istanbul earthquake b. Dip12
c. Undefined d. Undefined

67. The mass movement of a single, intact mass of rock, soil, or unconsolidated material along a weak plane, such as a fault, fracture, or bedding plane is a _____. A _____ may involve as little as a minor displacement of soil or as much as the displacement of an entire mountainside.
a. Slide12 b. 1509 Istanbul earthquake
c. Undefined d. Undefined

68. The stress exerted by the fluids that fill the voids between particles of rock or soil is referred to as _____.
a. 1509 Istanbul earthquake b. Pore pressure12
c. Undefined d. Undefined

69. Usually slow but effective process of weathering and erosion in which rocks are dissolved by water is a _____.

Chapter 12. EARTHQUAKES, STRESS, AND FLUIDS

a. 1509 Istanbul earthquake
b. Solution12
c. Undefined
d. Undefined

70. All processes that adds snow or ice to a glacier or to floating ice or snow cove are referred to as _____.
a. Accumulation12
b. AASHTO Soil Classification System
c. Undefined
d. Undefined

71. Deformation of the earth's crust by natural processes leading to the formation of ocean basins, continents, mountain systems, and other earth features is called _____.
a. Tectonism12
b. 1509 Istanbul earthquake
c. Undefined
d. Undefined

72. _____ refers to the area of dry land that borders on a body of water.
a. 1509 Istanbul earthquake
b. Coast12
c. Undefined
d. Undefined

73. A round or oval depression in the Earth's surface, containing the youngest section of rock in its lowest, central part is a _____.
a. 1509 Istanbul earthquake
b. Basin12
c. Undefined
d. Undefined

74. _____ refers to the upper part of a sedimentary deposit. Its weight causes compaction of the lower part.
a. AASHTO Soil Classification System
b. Overburden12
c. Undefined
d. Undefined

75. A non-crystaline rock that results from very rapid cooling of magma is _____.
a. Glass12
b. 1509 Istanbul earthquake
c. Undefined
d. Undefined

76. A measure of how difficult it is to stretch or break the surface of a liquid is referred to as _____.
a. Surface tension12
b. Event
c. Undefined
d. Undefined

77. Stress that stretches or extends rocks, so that they become thinner vertically and longer laterally is called _____. _____ may be caused by divergence or rifting.
a. 1509 Istanbul earthquake
b. Tension12
c. Undefined
d. Undefined

78. _____ refers to movement in one direction minus the movement in the other.
a. Thing
b. Net movement12
c. Undefined
d. Undefined

79. A section of rock separated from other rock by one or more faults is referred to as _____.
a. Fault block12
b. 1509 Istanbul earthquake
c. Undefined
d. Undefined

Chapter 12. EARTHQUAKES, STRESS, AND FLUIDS

80. A machine for measuring the intensity of earthquakes by recording the seismic waves that they generate is referred to as _____.
   a. 1509 Istanbul earthquake
   b. Seismograph12
   c. Undefined
   d. Undefined

81. _____ refers to an atom or molecule that has gained or lost one or more electrons, thus acquiring an electrical charge.
   a. Ion12
   b. Thing
   c. Undefined
   d. Undefined

82. _____ refers to elongate trenched or crack like valley on the lunar surface.
   a. Rile12
   b. 1509 Istanbul earthquake
   c. Undefined
   d. Undefined

83. The distance that one face of a fault is displaced relative to the other is referred to as a _____.
   a. Slip12
   b. 1509 Istanbul earthquake
   c. Undefined
   d. Undefined

84. A high mountain peak that forms when the walls of three or more cirques intersect is called a _____.
   a. Horn12
   b. 1509 Istanbul earthquake
   c. Undefined
   d. Undefined

85. The periodic, rhythmic rise and fall of the sea surface caused by changes in gravitational forces external to the Earth is referred to as the _____.
   a. Tide12
   b. Thing
   c. Undefined
   d. Undefined

86. _____ is a chemical element in the periodic table that has the symbol Pb and atomic number 82. A soft, heavy, toxic and malleable poor metal, _____ is bluish white when freshly cut but tarnishes to dull gray when exposed to air. _____ is used in building construction, _____-acid batteries, bullets and shot, and is part of solder, pewter, and fusible alloys.
   a. Lead12
   b. Thing
   c. Undefined
   d. Undefined

87. The diagenetic process by which the volume or thickness of sediment is reduced due to pressure from overlying layers of sediment is called _____.
   a. Compaction12
   b. 1509 Istanbul earthquake
   c. Undefined
   d. Undefined

88. _____ occurs when living things move from one biome to another. In most cases organisms migrate to avoid local shortages of food, usually caused by winter. Animals may also migrate to a certain location to breed, as is the case with some fish.
   a. Thing
   b. Migration12
   c. Undefined
   d. Undefined

89. _____ refers to the expansion of a rock's volume caused by stress and deformation.

Chapter 12. EARTHQUAKES, STRESS, AND FLUIDS 163

a. 1509 Istanbul earthquake
b. Dilatancy12
c. Undefined
d. Undefined

90. The tendency of the molecules of a substance to stick together is referred to as _____.
a. Thing
b. Cohesion12
c. Undefined
d. Undefined

91. A permanent strain that entails no rupture is called _____.
a. Plastic deformation12
b. 1509 Istanbul earthquake
c. Undefined
d. Undefined

92. _____ refers to capable of being molded into any form, which is retained.
a. Plastic12
b. 1509 Istanbul earthquake
c. Undefined
d. Undefined

93. Scientists who study earthquake waves and what they tell us about the inside of the Earth are called a _____.
a. Seismologist12
b. 1509 Istanbul earthquake
c. Undefined
d. Undefined

94. _____ refers to a wave that propagates by a side-to-side motion. Shear waves cannot propagate through any fluid, air, water, or the liquid iron in Earth's outer core.
a. Shear wave12
b. 1509 Istanbul earthquake
c. Undefined
d. Undefined

95. _____ refers to the height of floodwaters in feet or meters above an established datum plane.
a. Stage12
b. 1509 Istanbul earthquake
c. Undefined
d. Undefined

96. _____ refers to a crack or break in a rock. To break in random places instead of cleaving.
a. Fracture12
b. 1509 Istanbul earthquake
c. Undefined
d. Undefined

97. Earth's crust that includes both the continents and the continental shelves is the _____.
a. 1509 Istanbul earthquake
b. Continental crust12
c. Undefined
d. Undefined

98. _____ refers to huge slabs of rock that make up the Earth's crust. They can be continental or oceanic.
a. Thing
b. Tectonic plate12
c. Undefined
d. Undefined

99. _____ refers to rigid parts of the Earth's crust and part of the Earth's upper mantle that moves and adjoins each other along zones of seismic activity.
a. Plate12
b. 1509 Istanbul earthquake
c. Undefined
d. Undefined

100. Describing a substance in which the atoms are arranged in a regular, repeating, orderly pattern is called _____.

Chapter 12. EARTHQUAKES, STRESS, AND FLUIDS

a. Crystalline12
b. 1509 Istanbul earthquake
c. Undefined
d. Undefined

101. The innermost layer of the Earth, consisting primarily of pure metals such as iron and nickel is the _____. The _____ is the densest layer of the Earth, and is divided into the outer _____, which is believed to be liquid, and the inner _____, which is believed to be solid.
 a. Core12
 b. 1509 Istanbul earthquake
 c. Undefined
 d. Undefined

102. The extent to which a given substance allows water to flow through it, determined by such factors as sorting and grain size and shape is called _____.
 a. 1509 Istanbul earthquake
 b. Hydraulic conductivity12
 c. Undefined
 d. Undefined

103. A fluid's resistance to flow is called _____. _____ increases as temperatures decreases.
 a. 1509 Istanbul earthquake
 b. Viscosity12
 c. Undefined
 d. Undefined

104. A type of glacial movement that occurs within the glacier, below a depth of approximately 50 meters, in which the ice is not fractured, is referred to as _____.
 a. Plastic flow12
 b. 1509 Istanbul earthquake
 c. Undefined
 d. Undefined

105. The middle layer of the Earth, lying just below the crust and consisting of relatively dense rocks is called the _____. The _____ is divided into two sections, the upper _____ and the lower _____; the lower _____ has greater density than the upper _____.
 a. 1509 Istanbul earthquake
 b. Mantle12
 c. Undefined
 d. Undefined

106. A transition in a rock's mineralogy to a denser, more closely packed crystal structure, signaled by a change in seismic-wave velocity is referred to as the _____.
 a. 1509 Istanbul earthquake
 b. Phase change12
 c. Undefined
 d. Undefined

107. A naturally occurring, usually inorganic, solid consisting of either a single element or a compound, and having a definite chemical composition and a systematic internal arrangement of atoms is referred to as a _____.
 a. Mineral12
 b. 1509 Istanbul earthquake
 c. Undefined
 d. Undefined

108. The horizontal distance between wave crests is a _____.
 a. 1509 Istanbul earthquake
 b. Wavelength12
 c. Undefined
 d. Undefined

109. _____ refers to the upper portion of the mantle extending from the Moho to a depth of 400km.

Chapter 12. EARTHQUAKES, STRESS, AND FLUIDS

a. AASHTO Soil Classification System
b. Upper mantle12
c. Undefined
d. Undefined

110. A ferromagnesian mineral is _____.
a. Olivine12
b. AASHTO Soil Classification System
c. Undefined
d. Undefined

111. _____ refers to a flat thinnish dressed stone.
a. 1509 Istanbul earthquake
b. Slab12
c. Undefined
d. Undefined

112. _____ refers to earth's crust, which is formed at mid-oceanic ridges, typically 5 to 10 kilometers thick with a density of 3.0 grams per centimeter cubed.
a. AASHTO Soil Classification System
b. Oceanic crust12
c. Undefined
d. Undefined

113. The _____ is the solid outermost shell of a rocky planet. On the Earth, the _____ includes the crust and the uppermost layer of the mantle (the upper mantle or lower _____) which is joined to the crust.
a. Lithosphere12
b. Thing
c. Undefined
d. Undefined

114. An igneous rock rich in magnesium that forms soils toxic to many plants is called _____. Soils derived from _____ are toxic to many plants due to their high mineral content, and the flora is generally very distinctive, with specialized, slow-growing species.
a. Serpentine12
b. Thing
c. Undefined
d. Undefined

115. _____ refers to the study of the large-scale processes that collectively deform Earth's crust.
a. Tectonics12
b. 1509 Istanbul earthquake
c. Undefined
d. Undefined

Chapter 13. FLUIDS IN THE OCEANIC CRUST

1. The zone of convergence of two tectonic plates, one of which usually overrides the other is referred to as the _____.
   a. Subduction zone13
   b. 1509 Istanbul earthquake
   c. Undefined
   d. Undefined

2. _____ refers to earth's crust, which is formed at mid-oceanic ridges, typically 5 to 10 kilometers thick with a density of 3.0 grams per centimeter cubed.
   a. AASHTO Soil Classification System
   b. Oceanic crust13
   c. Undefined
   d. Undefined

3. The downward movement of a plate into the mantle that occurs in trenches, which are also known as _____ zones.
   a. Thing
   b. Subduction13
   c. Undefined
   d. Undefined

4. Aggregates of minerals or rock fragments are called _____.
   a. Rocks13
   b. 1509 Istanbul earthquake
   c. Undefined
   d. Undefined

5. A _____ is the outer layer of a planet, part of its lithosphere. Planetary _____ is generally composed of a less dense material than that of its deeper layers. The _____ of the Earth is composed mainly of basalt and granite.
   a. Crust13
   b. Thing
   c. Undefined
   d. Undefined

6. _____ refers to a naturally formed aggregate of usually inorganic materials from within the Earth.
   a. Rock13
   b. 1509 Istanbul earthquake
   c. Undefined
   d. Undefined

7. Ability to do work is referred to as _____. Most evident in glacial systems as radiant _____ from the sun and as latent _____ required to melt ice to water.
   a. AASHTO Soil Classification System
   b. Energy13
   c. Undefined
   d. Undefined

8. The _____ is the solid outermost shell of a rocky planet. On the Earth, the _____ includes the crust and the uppermost layer of the mantle (the upper mantle or lower _____) which is joined to the crust.
   a. Thing
   b. Lithosphere13
   c. Undefined
   d. Undefined

9. _____ refers to rigid parts of the Earth's crust and part of the Earth's upper mantle that moves and adjoins each other along zones of seismic activity.
   a. Plate13
   b. 1509 Istanbul earthquake
   c. Undefined
   d. Undefined

10. A naturally occurring, usually inorganic, solid consisting of either a single element or a compound, and having a definite chemical composition and a systematic internal arrangement of atoms is referred to as a _____.
    a. 1509 Istanbul earthquake
    b. Mineral13
    c. Undefined
    d. Undefined

Chapter 13. FLUIDS IN THE OCEANIC CRUST

11. A chemical _____, often called simply _____, is a chemical substance that cannot be divided or changed into other chemical substances by any ordinary chemical technique. An _____ is a class of substances that contain the same number of protons in all its atoms.
    a. Thing
    b. Element13
    c. Undefined
    d. Undefined

12. _____ is a chemical element in the periodic table that has the symbol C and atomic number 6. An abundant nonmetallic, tetravalent element, _____ has several allotropic forms.
    a. Thing
    b. Carbon13
    c. Undefined
    d. Undefined

13. Rocks formed by solidification of sediments formed and transported at the Earth's surface are referred to as _____.
    a. Sedimentary rocks13
    b. 1509 Istanbul earthquake
    c. Undefined
    d. Undefined

14. _____ is one of the three main rock groups and is formed in three main ways—by the deposition of the weathered remains of other rocks; by the deposition of the results of biogenic activity; and by precipitation from solution.
    a. Sedimentary rock13
    b. Event
    c. Undefined
    d. Undefined

15. _____ refers to the mechanism by which the earth is believed to have formed from a small nucleus by additions of solid bodies, such as meteorites, asteroids, or planetesimals. Also used in plate tectonics to indicate the addition of terranes to a continent.
    a. Accretion13
    b. AASHTO Soil Classification System
    c. Undefined
    d. Undefined

16. _____ is any particulate matter that can be transported by fluid flow and which eventually is deposited as a layer of solid particles on the bed or bottom of a body of water or other liquid.
    a. Thing
    b. Sediment13
    c. Undefined
    d. Undefined

17. _____ is a part of the theory of plate tectonics. _____ is the process by which continental drift occurs. This mechanism, which is a more accurate version of Alfred Wegener's original drift of continents that "plow" through the sea.
    a. Seafloor spreading13
    b. Thing
    c. Undefined
    d. Undefined

18. Describing a mineral that will not react with or convert to a new mineral or substance, given enough time is referred to as _____.
    a. Stable13
    b. 1509 Istanbul earthquake
    c. Undefined
    d. Undefined

19. A round or oval depression in the Earth's surface, containing the youngest section of rock in its lowest, central part is a _____.

Chapter 13. FLUIDS IN THE OCEANIC CRUST

    a. Basin13
    b. 1509 Istanbul earthquake
    c. Undefined
    d. Undefined

20. The middle layer of the Earth, lying just below the crust and consisting of relatively dense rocks is called the _____. The _____ is divided into two sections, the upper _____ and the lower _____; the lower _____ has greater density than the upper _____.
    a. 1509 Istanbul earthquake
    b. Mantle13
    c. Undefined
    d. Undefined

21. Earth's crust that includes both the continents and the continental shelves is the _____.
    a. 1509 Istanbul earthquake
    b. Continental crust13
    c. Undefined
    d. Undefined

22. _____ refers to the zone of transition from a continent to the adjacent ocean basin. It generally includes a continental shelf, continental slope, and continental rise.
    a. Thing
    b. Continental margin13
    c. Undefined
    d. Undefined

23. A _____ compound, mixture, or other such object is one that consists of many different items, which are often not easily sorted or separated, though they are clearly distinct.
    a. Thing
    b. Heterogeneous13
    c. Undefined
    d. Undefined

24. _____ refers both to animals and plants, of having a resemblance in structure, due to descent from a common progenitor with subsequent modification.
    a. Thing
    b. Homogeneous13
    c. Undefined
    d. Undefined

25. A major branch of a stream system is referred to as a _____.
    a. River13
    b. 1509 Istanbul earthquake
    c. Undefined
    d. Undefined

26. The point downstream where a river empties into another stream or water body is called _____.
    a. Mouth13
    b. 1509 Istanbul earthquake
    c. Undefined
    d. Undefined

27. The capability of a given substance to allow the passage of a fluid is called _____. _____ depends on the size of and the degree of connection among a substance's pores.
    a. Permeability13
    b. 1509 Istanbul earthquake
    c. Undefined
    d. Undefined

28. _____ is a common gray to black volcanic rock. It is usually fine-grained due to rapid cooling of lava on the Earth's surface.
    a. Thing
    b. Basalt13
    c. Undefined
    d. Undefined

Chapter 13. FLUIDS IN THE OCEANIC CRUST

29. _____ refers to any of a group of dark, dense, phaneritic, intrusive rocks that are the plutonic equivalent to basalt.
   a. 1509 Istanbul earthquake
   b. Gabbro13
   c. Undefined
   d. Undefined

30. _____ refers to a discordant pluton that is substantially wider than it is thick. Dikes are often steeply inclined or nearly vertical.
   a. Dike13
   b. 1509 Istanbul earthquake
   c. Undefined
   d. Undefined

31. A _____ is formed from magma that cools and solidifies within the earth. Surrounded by pre-existing rock (called country rock), the magma cools slowly, and as a result these rocks are coarse grained.
   a. Thing
   b. Intrusive igneous rock13
   c. Undefined
   d. Undefined

32. Rocks that crystallize from molten material at the surface of the earth or within the earth are called _____.
   a. AASHTO Soil Classification System
   b. Igneous rocks13
   c. Undefined
   d. Undefined

33. A _____ is formed when molten rock (magma) cools and solidifies, with or without crystallization, either below the surface as intrusive (plutonic) rocks or on the surface as extrusive (volcanic) rocks. This magma can be derived from either the Earth's mantle or pre-existing rocks made molten by extreme temperature and pressure changes.
   a. Igneous rock13
   b. Thing
   c. Undefined
   d. Undefined

34. The undifferentiated rocks that underlie the rocks of interest in an area are referred to as _____.
   a. Basement13
   b. 1509 Istanbul earthquake
   c. Undefined
   d. Undefined

35. _____ rocks are formed when molten rock (magma) cools and solidifies, with or without crystallization, either below the surface as intrusive (plutonic) rocks or on the surface as extrusive (volcanic) rocks. This magma can be derived from either the Earth's mantle or pre-existing rocks made molten by extreme temperature and pressure changes.
   a. Thing
   b. Igneous13
   c. Undefined
   d. Undefined

36. A body of rock identified by lithic characteristics and stratigraphic position and is mappable at the earth's surface or traceable in the subsurface is a _____.
   a. 1509 Istanbul earthquake
   b. Formation13
   c. Undefined
   d. Undefined

37. _____ is the part of hydrology that deals with the distribution and movement of groundwater in the soil and rocks of the Earth's crust (commonly in aquifers).
   a. Thing
   b. Hydrogeology13
   c. Undefined
   d. Undefined

38. Cracking or rupturing of a body under stress is referred to as _____.

Chapter 13. FLUIDS IN THE OCEANIC CRUST

a. 1509 Istanbul earthquake
b. Fracturing13
c. Undefined
d. Undefined

39. _____ refers to a crack or break in a rock. To break in random places instead of cleaving.
a. Fracture13
b. 1509 Istanbul earthquake
c. Undefined
d. Undefined

40. The relationship between distance on a map and the distance on the terrain being represented by that map is a _____.
a. 1509 Istanbul earthquake
b. Scale13
c. Undefined
d. Undefined

41. In biology, _____ is the process by which novel traits arise in populations and are passed on from generation to generation. Its action over large stretches of time explains the origin of new species and ultimately the vast diversity of the biological world.
a. Concept
b. Evolution13
c. Undefined
d. Undefined

42. Gradual loss of heat from Earth's interior out into space is called _____.
a. Heat flow13
b. 1509 Istanbul earthquake
c. Undefined
d. Undefined

43. A term used to describe the property of releasing energy or particles from an unstable atom is called _____.
a. Radioactive13
b. Thing
c. Undefined
d. Undefined

44. Silica-deficient igneous rock with a relatively high content of magnesium, iron, and calcium is called _____.
a. 1509 Istanbul earthquake
b. Mafic rock13
c. Undefined
d. Undefined

45. _____ refers to a term used to describe the amount of dark-colored iron and magnesium minerals in an igneous rock.
a. 1509 Istanbul earthquake
b. Mafic13
c. Undefined
d. Undefined

46. _____ refers to the study of the global-scale movements of Earth's crust that have resulted in.
a. Thing
b. Plate tectonics13
c. Undefined
d. Undefined

47. _____ refers to the study of the large-scale processes that collectively deform Earth's crust.
a. Tectonics13
b. 1509 Istanbul earthquake
c. Undefined
d. Undefined

48. Upward movement of deep, nutrient-rich water along coasts is referred to as _____.

Chapter 13. FLUIDS IN THE OCEANIC CRUST

a. Upwelling13
b. Thing
c. Undefined
d. Undefined

49. _____ refers to the upper portion of the mantle extending from the Moho to a depth of 400km.
   a. Upper mantle13
   b. AASHTO Soil Classification System
   c. Undefined
   d. Undefined

50. A distinctive rock sequence found in many mountain ranges on continents is _____.
   a. AASHTO Soil Classification System
   b. Ophiolite13
   c. Undefined
   d. Undefined

51. _____ refers to a timeline based on a stratigraphic succession that provides a chronological record of the history of a region. The entire span of time since the Earth formed.
   a. 1509 Istanbul earthquake
   b. Geologic time13
   c. Undefined
   d. Undefined

52. The spontaneous nuclear disintegration of atoms of certain isotopes is _____.
   a. Radioactivity13
   b. 1509 Istanbul earthquake
   c. Undefined
   d. Undefined

53. The vertical drop in a stream's elevation over a given horizontal distance, expressed as an angle is referred to as a _____.
   a. 1509 Istanbul earthquake
   b. Gradient13
   c. Undefined
   d. Undefined

54. _____ refers to the gradual increase in temperature with depth in the crust. The average is 30°C per kilometer in the upper crust.
   a. 1509 Istanbul earthquake
   b. Geothermal gradient13
   c. Undefined
   d. Undefined

55. _____ is the naturally hot interior of Earth. The heat is maintained by naturally occurring nuclear reactions in Earth's interior.
   a. Thing
   b. Geothermal13
   c. Undefined
   d. Undefined

56. Usually slow but effective process of weathering and erosion in which rocks are dissolved by water is a _____.
   a. Solution13
   b. 1509 Istanbul earthquake
   c. Undefined
   d. Undefined

57. _____ refers to the transfer of heat through matter by molecular activity.
   a. Conduction13
   b. 1509 Istanbul earthquake
   c. Undefined
   d. Undefined

58. _____ refers to a flat thinnish dressed stone.

Chapter 13. FLUIDS IN THE OCEANIC CRUST

    a. 1509 Istanbul earthquake
    b. Slab13
    c. Undefined
    d. Undefined

59. _____ refers to a tentative explanation of a given set of data that is expected to remain valid after future observation and experimentation.
    a. Hypothesis13
    b. 1509 Istanbul earthquake
    c. Undefined
    d. Undefined

60. _____ refers to pertaining to magma.
    a. 1509 Istanbul earthquake
    b. Magmatic13
    c. Undefined
    d. Undefined

61. The movement of surface water into rock or soil through cracks and pore spaces is called _____.
    a. AASHTO Soil Classification System
    b. Infiltration13
    c. Undefined
    d. Undefined

62. The quantity of water in a stream that passes a given point in a period of time is referred to as _____.
    a. 1509 Istanbul earthquake
    b. Discharge13
    c. Undefined
    d. Undefined

63. _____ refers to the addition of new water to an aquifer or to the zone of saturation.
    a. 1509 Istanbul earthquake
    b. Recharge13
    c. Undefined
    d. Undefined

64. A class of silicate minerals containing water in cavities within the crystal structure and formed by metamorphism at very low temperatures and pressures is _____.
    a. Zeolite13
    b. 1509 Istanbul earthquake
    c. Undefined
    d. Undefined

65. An igneous rock rich in magnesium that forms soils toxic to many plants is called _____. Soils derived from _____ are toxic to many plants due to their high mineral content, and the flora is generally very distinctive, with specialized, slow-growing species.
    a. Serpentine13
    b. Thing
    c. Undefined
    d. Undefined

66. One of several rock-forming minerals that contain silicon, oxygen, and usually one or more other common elements is _____.
    a. Silicate13
    b. 1509 Istanbul earthquake
    c. Undefined
    d. Undefined

67. A ferromagnesian mineral is _____.
    a. Olivine13
    b. AASHTO Soil Classification System
    c. Undefined
    d. Undefined

68. _____ is essential to all organisms, except for a few bacteria. It is mostly stably incorporated in the inside of metalloproteins, because in exposed or in free form it causes production of free radicals that are generally toxic to cells.

Chapter 13. FLUIDS IN THE OCEANIC CRUST

    a. Iron13
    c. Undefined
    b. Thing
    d. Undefined

69. _____ is an atmospheric gas comprized of one carbon and two oxygen atoms. A very widely known chemical compound, it is frequently called by its formula CO_2. In its solid state, it is commonly known as dry ice.
    a. Thing
    b. Carbon dioxide13
    c. Undefined
    d. Undefined

70. _____ is the chemical element in the periodic table that has the symbol Mg and atomic number 12 and an atomic mass of 24.31.
    a. Thing
    b. Magnesium13
    c. Undefined
    d. Undefined

71. _____ is the chemical element in the periodic table that has the symbol Na (Natrium in Latin) and atomic number 11. _____ is a soft, waxy, silvery reactive metal belonging to the alkali metals that is abundant in natural compounds (especially halite). It is highly reactive.
    a. Thing
    b. Sodium13
    c. Undefined
    d. Undefined

72. An unusually large deposit of sulfide minerals is called a _____.
    a. Massive sulfide deposit13
    b. 1509 Istanbul earthquake
    c. Undefined
    d. Undefined

73. One of the minerals that is abundant in the hot water that seeps through hydrothermal vents is _____.
    a. Thing
    b. Sulfide13
    c. Undefined
    d. Undefined

74. An igneous pluton that is not tabular in shape is _____.
    a. 1509 Istanbul earthquake
    b. Massive13
    c. Undefined
    d. Undefined

75. An opening in the Earth's surface through which lava, gases, and hot particles are expelled is a _____. Also called volcanic _____ and volcano.
    a. 1509 Istanbul earthquake
    b. Vent13
    c. Undefined
    d. Undefined

76. _____ refers to any condensed water falling from the atmosphere to the surface of the earth. Common types include rain, snow, sleet, and hail.
    a. Precipitation13
    b. 1509 Istanbul earthquake
    c. Undefined
    d. Undefined

77. A _____ is a type of hydrothermal vent found on the ocean floor. Generally hundreds of meters wide, they are formed when superheated water from below the Earth's crust comes through the ocean floor.
    a. Black smoker13
    b. Thing
    c. Undefined
    d. Undefined

Chapter 13. FLUIDS IN THE OCEANIC CRUST

78. A spring in which the water is 6-9°C warmer than the mean annual air temperature of its locality is called _____.
   a. 1509 Istanbul earthquake
   b. Hot spring13
   c. Undefined
   d. Undefined

79. _____ refer to elongated fractures or cracks on the slopes of a volcano. Fissure eruptions typically produce liquid flows, but pyroclastics may also be ejected.
   a. 1509 Istanbul earthquake
   b. Fissures13
   c. Undefined
   d. Undefined

80. A crack in rock along which there is a distinct separation is the _____.
   a. 1509 Istanbul earthquake
   b. Fissure13
   c. Undefined
   d. Undefined

81. _____ is the chemical element in the periodic table that has the symbol S and atomic number 16. It is an abundant, tasteless, odorless, multivalent non-metal. _____, in its native form, is a yellow crystaline solid. In nature, it can be found as the pure element or as sulfide and sulfate minerals.
   a. Sulfur13
   b. Thing
   c. Undefined
   d. Undefined

82. The time between winter and summer is _____.
   a. Spring13
   b. 1509 Istanbul earthquake
   c. Undefined
   d. Undefined

83. A _____ is a fissure in a planet's surface from which geothermally heated water issues. Hydrothermal vents are commonly found in places that are also volcanically active, where hot magma is relatively near the planet's surface.
   a. Thing
   b. Hydrothermal vent13
   c. Undefined
   d. Undefined

84. _____ refers to drop out of a saturated solution as crystals. The crystals that drop out of a saturated solution.
   a. 1509 Istanbul earthquake
   b. Precipitate13
   c. Undefined
   d. Undefined

85. _____ refers to a chemical combination of silicon and oxygen.
   a. Silica13
   b. 1509 Istanbul earthquake
   c. Undefined
   d. Undefined

86. The subterranean cavity containing the gas-rich liquid magma, which feeds a volcano, is a _____.
   a. Magma chamber13
   b. 1509 Istanbul earthquake
   c. Undefined
   d. Undefined

87. Molten rock that forms naturally within the Earth is _____. _____ may be either a liquid or a fluid mixture of liquid, crystals, and dissolved gases.
   a. 1509 Istanbul earthquake
   b. Magma13
   c. Undefined
   d. Undefined

Chapter 13. FLUIDS IN THE OCEANIC CRUST

88. _____ refers to the ratio of the size of a compartment to the flux through it, expressed in units of time; thus, the average time spent by energy or a substance in the compartment.
   a. Thing
   b. Residence time13
   c. Undefined
   d. Undefined

89. _____ is the transfer of heat by currents within a fluid. It may arise from temperature differences either within the fluid or between the fluid and its boundary, other sources of density variations (such as variable salinity), or from the application of an external motive force.
   a. Convection13
   b. Event
   c. Undefined
   d. Undefined

90. _____ refers to the smallest possible unit of a substance that has the properties of that substance.
   a. Molecule13
   b. 1509 Istanbul earthquake
   c. Undefined
   d. Undefined

91. The circulation of water through hot volcanic rocks and magmas, producing hot springs and geysers on the surface is called _____.
   a. 1509 Istanbul earthquake
   b. Hydrothermal activity13
   c. Undefined
   d. Undefined

92. _____ refers to a descriptive term applied to igneous rocks that are transitional between basic and acidic with silica between 54% and 65%.
   a. Intermediate13
   b. AASHTO Soil Classification System
   c. Undefined
   d. Undefined

93. An _____ is a volcanic event that is distinguished by its duration or style.
   a. Episode13
   b. AASHTO Soil Classification System
   c. Undefined
   d. Undefined

94. The _____ is a derived unit defined as the work done or energy required, to exert a force of one newton for a distance of one metre, so the same quantity may be referred to as a newton metre or newton-metre with the symbol N·m.
   a. Joule13
   b. Thing
   c. Undefined
   d. Undefined

95. A form of mechanical weathering in which cold causes a mineral's crystal structure to contract is called _____.
   a. 1509 Istanbul earthquake
   b. Thermal contraction13
   c. Undefined
   d. Undefined

96. Gaseous components of magma dissolved in the melt are called _____. _____ will readily vaporize at surface pressures.
   a. 1509 Istanbul earthquake
   b. Volatiles13
   c. Undefined
   d. Undefined

97. The force acting on a rock or another solid to deform it, measured in kilograms per square centimeter or pounds per square inch is _____.

Chapter 13. FLUIDS IN THE OCEANIC CRUST

a. Stress13
b. 1509 Istanbul earthquake
c. Undefined
d. Undefined

98. The _____ is the lowest layer in an ocean, existing below the thermocline. The _____ is not well mixed, consists of horizontal layers of equal density, and is often as cold as -1 to 4 degrees Celsius. Ninety percent of the total volume of Earth's oceans is found in the _____.
a. Thing
b. Deep ocean13
c. Undefined
d. Undefined

99. A _____ is a landscape form or region that receives little precipitation - less than 250 mm (10 in) per year. It is a biome characterized by organisms adapted to sparse rainfall and rapid evaporation.
a. Desert13
b. Thing
c. Undefined
d. Undefined

100. The _____ refers to those areas of oceans to which little or no light penetrates.
a. Thing
b. Deep sea13
c. Undefined
d. Undefined

101. _____ refers to an atom or molecule that has gained or lost one or more electrons, thus acquiring an electrical charge.
a. Ion13
b. Thing
c. Undefined
d. Undefined

102. _____ is the biological conversion of 1-carbon molecules (usually carbon dioxide or methane) and nutrients into organic matter using the oxidation of inorganic molecules (e.g. hydrogen gas, hydrogen sulfide) or methane as a source of energy
a. Chemosynthesis13
b. Thing
c. Undefined
d. Undefined

103. _____ refers to a sequence of food transfers from one species to another within an ecosystem.
a. Food chain13
b. Thing
c. Undefined
d. Undefined

104. Group of organisms of the same species occupying a certain area and sharing a common gene pool is referred to as _____.
a. Population13
b. Thing
c. Undefined
d. Undefined

105. Of either earth or stone pebbles, generally covering a burial chamber or deposit is called _____.
a. 1509 Istanbul earthquake
b. Mound13
c. Undefined
d. Undefined

106. _____ refers to the set of physical features, such as mountains, valleys, and the shapes of landforms, that characterizes a given landscape.

Chapter 13. FLUIDS IN THE OCEANIC CRUST

a. Topography13
b. 1509 Istanbul earthquake
c. Undefined
d. Undefined

107. The process of determining that two or more geographically distant rocks or rock strata originated in the same time period is referred to as _____.
a. Correlation13
b. 1509 Istanbul earthquake
c. Undefined
d. Undefined

108. _____ refers to the process by which solid, liquid, and gaseous materials are ejected into the earth's atmosphere and onto the earth's surface by volcanic activity. Eruptions range from the quiet overflow of liquid rock to the tremendously violent expulsion of pyroclastics.
a. Eruption13
b. AASHTO Soil Classification System
c. Undefined
d. Undefined

109. General term for the processes of folding, faulting, shearing, compression, or extension of rocks as the result of various natural forces is called _____.
a. 1509 Istanbul earthquake
b. Deformation13
c. Undefined
d. Undefined

110. The solid structure created when lava, gases, and hot particles escape to the Earth's surface through vents is called a _____. Volcanoes are usually conical. A _____ is 'active' when it is erupting or has erupted recently. Volcanoes that have not erupted recently but are considered likely to erupt in the future are said to be 'dormant.' A _____ that has not erupted for a long time and is not expected to erupt in the future is 'extinct'.
a. Volcano13
b. 1509 Istanbul earthquake
c. Undefined
d. Undefined

111. A fracture dividing a rock into two sections that have visibly moved relative to each other is a _____.
a. Fault13
b. 1509 Istanbul earthquake
c. Undefined
d. Undefined

112. A movement within the Earth's crust or mantle, caused by the sudden rupture or repositioning of underground rocks as they release stress is an _____.
a. AASHTO Soil Classification System
b. Earthquake13
c. Undefined
d. Undefined

113. _____ refers to the change in the shape or volume of a rock that results from stress.
a. 1509 Istanbul earthquake
b. Strain13
c. Undefined
d. Undefined

114. _____ is a chemical element in the periodic table that has the symbol Pb and atomic number 82. A soft, heavy, toxic and malleable poor metal, _____ is bluish white when freshly cut but tarnishes to dull gray when exposed to air. _____ is used in building construction, _____-acid batteries, bullets and shot, and is part of solder, pewter, and fusible alloys.
a. Lead13
b. Thing
c. Undefined
d. Undefined

Chapter 13. FLUIDS IN THE OCEANIC CRUST

115. The processes by which crustal forces cause a rock formation to break and slip along a fault are called _____.
    a. 1509 Istanbul earthquake
    b. Faulting13
    c. Undefined
    d. Undefined

116. All processes that adds snow or ice to a glacier or to floating ice or snow cove are referred to as _____.
    a. AASHTO Soil Classification System
    b. Accumulation13
    c. Undefined
    d. Undefined

117. _____ refers to a chain of volcanic islands generally located a few hundred kilometers from a trench where there is active subduction of one oceanic plate beneath another.
    a. Volcanic island arc13
    b. 1509 Istanbul earthquake
    c. Undefined
    d. Undefined

118. Sediment made up of fine-grained clay and the skeletons of microscopic organisms that settle slowly down through the ocean water is referred to as _____.
    a. Pelagic sediment13
    b. 1509 Istanbul earthquake
    c. Undefined
    d. Undefined

119. Seafloor sediments derived from terrestrial weathering and erosion is _____.
    a. Terrigenous sediment13
    b. 1509 Istanbul earthquake
    c. Undefined
    d. Undefined

120. A type of biogenous sediment that consists mostly of the silica shell and skeletons of marine organism is referred to as _____.
    a. Siliceous ooze13
    b. Thing
    c. Undefined
    d. Undefined

121. One of several minerals containing one central carbon atom with strong covalent bonds to three oxygen atoms and typically having ionic bonds to one or more positive ions is _____.
    a. Carbonate13
    b. 1509 Istanbul earthquake
    c. Undefined
    d. Undefined

122. _____ is the displacement of solids (soil, mud, rock, and other particles) by the agents of wind, water, ice, movement in response to gravity, or living organisms.
    a. Thing
    b. Erosion13
    c. Undefined
    d. Undefined

123. A reverse fault marked by a dip of 45° or less is called _____.
    a. Thrust fault13
    b. 1509 Istanbul earthquake
    c. Undefined
    d. Undefined

124. Stress that reduces the volume or length of a rock, as that produced by the convergence of plate margins is called _____.
    a. 1509 Istanbul earthquake
    b. Compression13
    c. Undefined
    d. Undefined

Chapter 13. FLUIDS IN THE OCEANIC CRUST

125. 1 _____ is the amount of electric charge carried by a current of 1 ampere flowing for 1 second.
a. Thing
b. Coulomb13
c. Undefined
d. Undefined

126. _____ refers to the top few meters of regolith, generally including some organic matter derived from plants.
a. Soil13
b. 1509 Istanbul earthquake
c. Undefined
d. Undefined

127. Distinct crystals of ice are called _____. Commonly accumulates with a density of 50 - 200 kg·m, although wind-abraded and packed _____ may have a higher initial density.
a. 1509 Istanbul earthquake
b. Snow13
c. Undefined
d. Undefined

128. _____ refers to stress due to forces that tend to cause movement or strain parallel to the direction of the forces.
a. 1509 Istanbul earthquake
b. Shear stress13
c. Undefined
d. Undefined

129. _____ refers to stress that causes two adjacent parts of a body to slide past one another.
a. 1509 Istanbul earthquake
b. Shear13
c. Undefined
d. Undefined

130. A mass of sediment and oceanic lithosphere that is transferred from a subducting plate to the less dense, overriding plate with which it converges is an _____.
a. AASHTO Soil Classification System
b. Accretionary wedge13
c. Undefined
d. Undefined

131. The stress exerted by the fluids that fill the voids between particles of rock or soil is referred to as _____.
a. Pore pressure13
b. 1509 Istanbul earthquake
c. Undefined
d. Undefined

132. The distance that one face of a fault is displaced relative to the other is referred to as a _____.
a. 1509 Istanbul earthquake
b. Slip13
c. Undefined
d. Undefined

133. _____ refers to bodies of rock or magma that ascends within Earth's interior because they are less dense than the surrounding rock.
a. 1509 Istanbul earthquake
b. Diapir13
c. Undefined
d. Undefined

134. _____ refers to capable of being molded into any form, which is retained.
a. Plastic13
b. 1509 Istanbul earthquake
c. Undefined
d. Undefined

135. Parallel layers of sedimentary rock are called _____.

Chapter 13. FLUIDS IN THE OCEANIC CRUST

a. 1509 Istanbul earthquake
b. Strata13
c. Undefined
d. Undefined

136. _____ refers to a round or oval bulge on the Earth's surface, containing the oldest section of rock in its raised, central part.
a. 1509 Istanbul earthquake
b. Dome13
c. Undefined
d. Undefined

137. A region of considerable extent where the combination of deposition and subsidence has formed thick accumulations of sediment and sedimentary rock is called _____.
a. 1509 Istanbul earthquake
b. Sedimentary basin13
c. Undefined
d. Undefined

138. The average normal force per unit area that is transmitted directly across grain-to-grain boundaries in a sediment or rock mass is referred to as _____.
a. AASHTO Soil Classification System
b. Effective stress13
c. Undefined
d. Undefined

139. Metamorphism in which buried sedimentary rocks are altered by the progressive increase in pressure exerted by overlying sediments and sedimentary rocks and by the increase in heat associated with increased depth of burial in the Earth is a _____.
a. Low-grade metamorphism13
b. 1509 Istanbul earthquake
c. Undefined
d. Undefined

140. The process by which conditions within the Earth, below the zone of diagenesis, alter the mineral content, chemical composition, and structure of solid rock without melting it is called _____. Igneous, sedimentary, and metamorphic rocks may all undergo _____.
a. 1509 Istanbul earthquake
b. Metamorphism13
c. Undefined
d. Undefined

141. The diagenetic process by which the volume or thickness of sediment is reduced due to pressure from overlying layers of sediment is called _____.
a. 1509 Istanbul earthquake
b. Compaction13
c. Undefined
d. Undefined

142. The study of rock strata, especially of their distribution, deposition, and age is called _____.
a. Stratigraphic13
b. 1509 Istanbul earthquake
c. Undefined
d. Undefined

143. The percentage of a soil, rock, or sediment's volume that is made up of pores is _____.
a. Porosity13
b. 1509 Istanbul earthquake
c. Undefined
d. Undefined

144. _____ refers to a passage followed by magma in a volcano.

Chapter 13. FLUIDS IN THE OCEANIC CRUST

    a. Conduit13
    b. 1509 Istanbul earthquake
    c. Undefined
    d. Undefined

145. _____ is a term used for ionic compounds composed of positively charged cations and negatively charged anions, so that the product is neutral and without a net charge.
    a. Salt13
    b. Thing
    c. Undefined
    d. Undefined

146. _____ refer to hydrous aluminum silicates that have a layered atomic structure. They are very fine grained and become plastic when wet. Most belong to one of three clay groups: kaolinite, illite, and smectite.
    a. Clay minerals13
    b. 1509 Istanbul earthquake
    c. Undefined
    d. Undefined

147. A hydrous aluminum-silicate that occurs as a platy grain of microscopic size with a sheet silicate structure is _____.
    a. Clay mineral13
    b. 1509 Istanbul earthquake
    c. Undefined
    d. Undefined

148. Describing a substance in which the atoms are arranged in a regular, repeating, orderly pattern is called _____.
    a. Crystalline13
    b. 1509 Istanbul earthquake
    c. Undefined
    d. Undefined

149. The innermost layer of the Earth, consisting primarily of pure metals such as iron and nickel is the _____. The _____ is the densest layer of the Earth, and is divided into the outer _____, which is believed to be liquid, and the inner _____, which is believed to be solid.
    a. Core13
    b. 1509 Istanbul earthquake
    c. Undefined
    d. Undefined

150. A numerical expression of the amount of energy released by an earthquake, determined by measuring earthquake waves on standardized recording instruments is called a _____. The number scale for magnitudes is logarithmic rather than arithmetic. Therefore, deflections on a seismograph for a _____ 5 earthquake, for example, are 10 times greater than those for a _____ 4 earthquake, 100 times greater than for a _____ 3 earthquake, and so on.
    a. 1509 Istanbul earthquake
    b. Magnitude13
    c. Undefined
    d. Undefined

151. The liquid portion of magma excluding the solid crystals is called _____.
    a. Melt13
    b. 1509 Istanbul earthquake
    c. Undefined
    d. Undefined

152. _____ refers to a block of rock that lies between two faults and has moved downward to form a depression between the two adjacent fault blocks.
    a. Graben13
    b. 1509 Istanbul earthquake
    c. Undefined
    d. Undefined

153. The entire area between the tops of the slopes on both sides of a stream is a _____.

Chapter 13. FLUIDS IN THE OCEANIC CRUST

    a. 1509 Istanbul earthquake
    b. Valley13
    c. Undefined
    d. Undefined

154. A block of rock that lies between two faults and has moved upward relative to the two adjacent fault blocks is referred to as a _____.
    a. Horst13
    b. 1509 Istanbul earthquake
    c. Undefined
    d. Undefined

155. Mineral with the formula SiO is referred to as _____.
    a. Quartz13
    b. 1509 Istanbul earthquake
    c. Undefined
    d. Undefined

156. An extrusive igneous rock is referred to as _____.
    a. 1509 Istanbul earthquake
    b. Volcanic rock13
    c. Undefined
    d. Undefined

157. _____ refers to term pertaining to a highly basic, as opposed to acidic, subtance.
    a. AASHTO Soil Classification System
    b. Alkaline13
    c. Undefined
    d. Undefined

158. _____ is a chemical element in the periodic table that has the symbol Ti and atomic number 22. It is a light, strong, lustrous, corrosion-resistant (including resistance to sea water and chlorine) transition metal with a white-silvery-metallic color. _____ is used in strong light-weight alloys (most notably with iron and aluminium) and its most common compound, _____ dioxide, is used in white pigments.
    a. Titanium13
    b. Thing
    c. Undefined
    d. Undefined

159. _____ is a chemical element in the periodic table that has the symbol Rb and atomic number 37. Rb is a soft, silvery-white metallic element of the alkali metal group. Rb-87, a naturally occurring isotope, is (slightly) radioactive. _____ is highly reactive, with properties similar to other elements in group 1, like igniting spontaneously in air.
    a. Thing
    b. Rubidium13
    c. Undefined
    d. Undefined

160. _____ is a chemical element in the periodic table that has the symbol Nb and atomic number 41. A rare, soft, gray, ductile transition metal, _____ is found in niobite and used in alloys. The most notable alloys are used to make special steels and strong welded joints.
    a. Niobium13
    b. Thing
    c. Undefined
    d. Undefined

161. _____ refers to a positively charged atom; an atom with fewer electrons than protons.
    a. 1509 Istanbul earthquake
    b. Cation13
    c. Undefined
    d. Undefined

162. _____ is a chemical element in the periodic table that has the symbol Ba and atomic number 56. A soft silvery metallic element, _____ is an alkaline earth metal and melts at a very high temperature. Its oxide is historically known as baryta but is never found in nature in its pure form due to its reactivity with air.

Chapter 13. FLUIDS IN THE OCEANIC CRUST

    a. Thing
    b. Barium13
    c. Undefined
    d. Undefined

163. The _____ is an eon prior to the first abundant complex life on Earth. The _____ Eon extended from 2500 Ma to 542 Ma (million years ago).
    a. Proterozoic13
    b. Thing
    c. Undefined
    d. Undefined

164. An _____ is composed of several eras, which in turn are composed of periods, which are composed of epochs. One definition of an _____ puts it as "a unit of geologic time equal to one billion years", although it is rarely used in this manner.
    a. Concept
    b. Eon13
    c. Undefined
    d. Undefined

165. _____ refers to igneous plutonic rock, less felsic than granite, typically light in color; rough plutonic equivalent of dacite.
    a. Granodiorite13
    b. 1509 Istanbul earthquake
    c. Undefined
    d. Undefined

166. The scientific study of the Earth, its origins and evolution, the materials that make it up, and the processes that act on it is called _____.
    a. 1509 Istanbul earthquake
    b. Geology13
    c. Undefined
    d. Undefined

167. Earth's _____ is a layer of gases surrounding the planet Earth and retained by the Earth's gravity. It contains roughly 78% nitrogen and 21% oxygen, with trace amounts of other gases.
    a. Thing
    b. Atmosphere13
    c. Undefined
    d. Undefined

168. _____ in physical geography, describes the collective mass of water found on, under, and over the surface of a planet.
    a. Hydrosphere13
    b. Thing
    c. Undefined
    d. Undefined

169. The _____ is that part of a planet's outer shell — including air, land, surface rocks and water — within which life occurs, and which biotic processes in turn alter or transform.
    a. Thing
    b. Biosphere13
    c. Undefined
    d. Undefined

170. The release of gases and water vapor from molten rocks, leading to the formation of the earth's atmosphere and oceans is _____.
    a. Outgassing13
    b. AASHTO Soil Classification System
    c. Undefined
    d. Undefined

171. An elongated depression in the seafloor produced by bending of oceanic crust during subduction is a _____.

Chapter 13. FLUIDS IN THE OCEANIC CRUST

a. 1509 Istanbul earthquake
b. Trench13
c. Undefined
d. Undefined

172. _____ refers to an object which circles the sun in a non-circular orbit. Commonly made up of a large mass of rock debris and ice.
a. 1509 Istanbul earthquake
b. Comet13
c. Undefined
d. Undefined

173. _____ refers to water molecules in the gaseous state. Also is one state of the water cycle.
a. Water vapor13
b. Thing
c. Undefined
d. Undefined

174. _____ is a physical or chemical phenomenon or a process in which atoms, molecules, or ions enter some bulk phase - gas, liquid or solid material. In nutrition, amino acids are broken down through digestion, which begins in the stomach.
a. Absorption13
b. Thing
c. Undefined
d. Undefined

175. _____ refers to water in the gaseous state.
a. Vapor13
b. 1509 Istanbul earthquake
c. Undefined
d. Undefined

176. A body of water that can be identified by its temperature and salinity is _____.
a. Thing
b. Water mass13
c. Undefined
d. Undefined

177. The branch of geology that studies the physics of the Earth, using the physical principles underlying such phenomena as seismic waves, heat flow, gravity, and magnetism to investigate planetary properties is called _____.
a. Geophysics13
b. 1509 Istanbul earthquake
c. Undefined
d. Undefined

Chapter 14. FLUIDS AND ORE DEPOSITS

1. The same as a mineral reserve except that it refers only to a metal-bearing deposit is referred to as _____.
   a. Ore deposit14
   b. AASHTO Soil Classification System
   c. Undefined
   d. Undefined

2. A naturally occurring, usually inorganic, solid consisting of either a single element or a compound, and having a definite chemical composition and a systematic internal arrangement of atoms is referred to as a _____.
   a. Mineral14
   b. 1509 Istanbul earthquake
   c. Undefined
   d. Undefined

3. A _____ is the outer layer of a planet, part of its lithosphere. Planetary _____ is generally composed of a less dense material than that of its deeper layers. The _____ of the Earth is composed mainly of basalt and granite.
   a. Crust14
   b. Thing
   c. Undefined
   d. Undefined

4. A mineral deposit that can be mined for a profit is called _____.
   a. AASHTO Soil Classification System
   b. Ore14
   c. Undefined
   d. Undefined

5. _____ refers to a descriptive term applied to igneous rocks that are transitional between basic and acidic with silica between 54% and 65%.
   a. AASHTO Soil Classification System
   b. Intermediate14
   c. Undefined
   d. Undefined

6. The process by which exposure to atmospheric agents, such as air or moisture, causes rocks and minerals to break down is called _____. This process takes place at or near the Earth's surface. _____ entails little or no movement of the material that it loosens from the rocks and minerals.
   a. Weathering14
   b. 1509 Istanbul earthquake
   c. Undefined
   d. Undefined

7. Aluminium is the chemical element in the periodic table that has the symbol Al and atomic number 13. It is a silvery and ductile member of the poor metal group of chemical elements. Aluminium is found primarily as the ore bauxite and is remarkable for its resistance to corrosion (due to the phenomenon of passivation) and its light weight. Aluminium is used in many industries to make millions of different products and is very important to the world economy.
   a. Thing
   b. Aluminum14
   c. Undefined
   d. Undefined

8. Low latitude areas characterized by high temperatures and high precipitation are referred to as _____. At high elevations, however, _____ mountains may be both cold and relatively dry.
   a. 1509 Istanbul earthquake
   b. Tropical14
   c. Undefined
   d. Undefined

9. A chemical _____, often called simply _____, is a chemical substance that cannot be divided or changed into other chemical substances by any ordinary chemical technique. An _____ is a class of substances that contain the same number of protons in all its atoms.
   a. Element14
   b. Thing
   c. Undefined
   d. Undefined

Chapter 14. FLUIDS AND ORE DEPOSITS

10. _____ refers to the principal ore of aluminum.
    a. 1509 Istanbul earthquake
    b. Bauxite14
    c. Undefined
    d. Undefined

11. The scientific study of the Earth, its origins and evolution, the materials that make it up, and the processes that act on it is called _____.
    a. Geology14
    b. 1509 Istanbul earthquake
    c. Undefined
    d. Undefined

12. _____ refers to a timeline based on a stratigraphic succession that provides a chronological record of the history of a region. The entire span of time since the Earth formed.
    a. 1509 Istanbul earthquake
    b. Geologic time14
    c. Undefined
    d. Undefined

13. _____ refers to the process of emplacement of magma in pre-existing rock. Also, the term refers to igneous rock mass so formed within the surrounding rock.
    a. Intrusion14
    b. AASHTO Soil Classification System
    c. Undefined
    d. Undefined

14. _____ refers to pertaining to magma.
    a. Magmatic14
    b. 1509 Istanbul earthquake
    c. Undefined
    d. Undefined

15. Parallel layers of sedimentary rock are called _____.
    a. 1509 Istanbul earthquake
    b. Strata14
    c. Undefined
    d. Undefined

16. _____ refers to any condensed water falling from the atmosphere to the surface of the earth. Common types include rain, snow, sleet, and hail.
    a. 1509 Istanbul earthquake
    b. Precipitation14
    c. Undefined
    d. Undefined

17. A form of chemical weathering in which water molecules, sometimes in combination with acid or another compound in the environment, attract and remove oppositely charged ions or ion groups from a mineral or rock is a _____.
    a. Dissolution14
    b. 1509 Istanbul earthquake
    c. Undefined
    d. Undefined

18. The vertical drop in a stream's elevation over a given horizontal distance, expressed as an angle is referred to as a _____.
    a. Gradient14
    b. 1509 Istanbul earthquake
    c. Undefined
    d. Undefined

19. Ability to do work is referred to as _____. Most evident in glacial systems as radiant _____ from the sun and as latent _____ required to melt ice to water.

Chapter 14. FLUIDS AND ORE DEPOSITS

a. AASHTO Soil Classification System
b. Energy14
c. Undefined
d. Undefined

20. _____ refers to the beginning or source area for a stream. Also called the headwaters.
a. Head14
b. 1509 Istanbul earthquake
c. Undefined
d. Undefined

21. The capability of a given substance to allow the passage of a fluid is called _____. _____ depends on the size of and the degree of connection among a substance's pores.
a. 1509 Istanbul earthquake
b. Permeability14
c. Undefined
d. Undefined

22. Any accumulation of material, by mechanical settling from water or air, chemical precipitation, evaporation from solution, etc is referred to as _____.
a. Deposition14
b. 1509 Istanbul earthquake
c. Undefined
d. Undefined

23. _____ refers to the solid matter in which a fossil or crystal is embedded.
a. Matrix14
b. 1509 Istanbul earthquake
c. Undefined
d. Undefined

24. The entire area between the tops of the slopes on both sides of a stream is a _____.
a. 1509 Istanbul earthquake
b. Valley14
c. Undefined
d. Undefined

25. _____ is a chemical element in the periodic table that has the symbol Pb and atomic number 82. A soft, heavy, toxic and malleable poor metal, _____ is bluish white when freshly cut but tarnishes to dull gray when exposed to air. _____ is used in building construction, _____-acid batteries, bullets and shot, and is part of solder, pewter, and fusible alloys.
a. Thing
b. Lead14
c. Undefined
d. Undefined

26. _____ refers to a naturally formed aggregate of usually inorganic materials from within the Earth.
a. 1509 Istanbul earthquake
b. Rock14
c. Undefined
d. Undefined

27. The study of rock strata, especially of their distribution, deposition, and age is called _____.
a. 1509 Istanbul earthquake
b. Stratigraphic14
c. Undefined
d. Undefined

28. An unusually large deposit of sulfide minerals is called a _____.
a. Massive sulfide deposit14
b. 1509 Istanbul earthquake
c. Undefined
d. Undefined

29. An extrusive igneous rock is referred to as _____.

Chapter 14. FLUIDS AND ORE DEPOSITS

a. Volcanic rock14
b. 1509 Istanbul earthquake
c. Undefined
d. Undefined

30. One of the minerals that is abundant in the hot water that seeps through hydrothermal vents is _____.
a. Thing
b. Sulfide14
c. Undefined
d. Undefined

31. An igneous pluton that is not tabular in shape is _____.
a. 1509 Istanbul earthquake
b. Massive14
c. Undefined
d. Undefined

32. Aggregates of minerals or rock fragments are called _____.
a. Rocks14
b. 1509 Istanbul earthquake
c. Undefined
d. Undefined

33. A fracture dividing a rock into two sections that have visibly moved relative to each other is a _____.
a. Fault14
b. 1509 Istanbul earthquake
c. Undefined
d. Undefined

34. A mineral deposit consisting of a zone of veins in consolidated rock, as opposed to a placer deposit is called _____.
a. Lode14
b. 1509 Istanbul earthquake
c. Undefined
d. Undefined

35. _____ is the part of hydrology that deals with the distribution and movement of groundwater in the soil and rocks of the Earth's crust (commonly in aquifers).
a. Thing
b. Hydrogeology14
c. Undefined
d. Undefined

36. _____ is a chemical element with the symbol Ag. A soft white lustrous transition metal, it has the highest electrical and thermal conductivity of any metal and occurs in minerals and in free form.
a. Thing
b. Silver14
c. Undefined
d. Undefined

37. _____ is a chemical element in the periodic table that has the symbol Au and atomic number 79. A soft, shiny, yellow, dense, malleable, ductile (trivalent and univalent) transition metal, _____ does not react with most chemicals but is attacked by chlorine, fluorine and aqua regia.
a. Gold14
b. Thing
c. Undefined
d. Undefined

38. Upward movement of deep, nutrient-rich water along coasts is referred to as _____.
a. Thing
b. Upwelling14
c. Undefined
d. Undefined

39. An _____ is a form of an element whose nuclei have the same atomic number - the number of protons in the nucleus - but different mass numbers because they contain different numbers of neutrons.

Chapter 14. FLUIDS AND ORE DEPOSITS

a. Thing
b. Isotope14
c. Undefined
d. Undefined

40. _____ is a chemical element in the periodic table. It has the symbol O and atomic number 8. _____ is the second most common element on Earth, composing around 46% of the mass of Earth's crust and 28% of the mass of Earth as a whole, and is the third most common element in the universe.
   a. Thing
   b. Oxygen14
   c. Undefined
   d. Undefined

41. The relationship between distance on a map and the distance on the terrain being represented by that map is a _____.
   a. 1509 Istanbul earthquake
   b. Scale14
   c. Undefined
   d. Undefined

42. The part of an ore, usually metallic, that is economically desirable is called _____.
   a. AASHTO Soil Classification System
   b. Ore mineral14
   c. Undefined
   d. Undefined

43. _____ rocks are formed when molten rock (magma) cools and solidifies, with or without crystallization, either below the surface as intrusive (plutonic) rocks or on the surface as extrusive (volcanic) rocks. This magma can be derived from either the Earth's mantle or pre-existing rocks made molten by extreme temperature and pressure changes.
   a. Igneous14
   b. Thing
   c. Undefined
   d. Undefined

44. _____ refers to a massive discordant pluton with a surface area greater than 100 square kilometers, typically having a depth of about 30 kilometers. Batholiths are generally found in elongated mountain ranges after the country rock above them has eroded.
   a. 1509 Istanbul earthquake
   b. Batholith14
   c. Undefined
   d. Undefined

45. Describing a substance in which the atoms are arranged in a regular, repeating, orderly pattern is called _____.
   a. Crystalline14
   b. 1509 Istanbul earthquake
   c. Undefined
   d. Undefined

46. A numerical expression of the amount of energy released by an earthquake, determined by measuring earthquake waves on standardized recording instruments is called a _____. The number scale for magnitudes is logarithmic rather than arithmetic. Therefore, deflections on a seismograph for a _____ 5 earthquake, for example, are 10 times greater than those for a _____ 4 earthquake, 100 times greater than for a _____ 3 earthquake, and so on.
   a. Magnitude14
   b. 1509 Istanbul earthquake
   c. Undefined
   d. Undefined

47. The innermost layer of the Earth, consisting primarily of pure metals such as iron and nickel is the _____. The _____ is the densest layer of the Earth, and is divided into the outer _____, which is believed to be liquid, and the inner _____, which is believed to be solid.

Chapter 14. FLUIDS AND ORE DEPOSITS

    a. Core14
    c. Undefined
    b. 1509 Istanbul earthquake
    d. Undefined

48. _____ refers both to animals and plants, of having a resemblance in structure, due to descent from a common progenitor with subsequent modification.
    a. Thing
    b. Homogeneous14
    c. Undefined
    d. Undefined

49. _____ refer to varieties of the same element that have different mass numbers; their nuclei contain the same number of protons but different numbers of neutrons.
    a. AASHTO Soil Classification System
    b. Isotopes14
    c. Undefined
    d. Undefined

50. A sheetlike deposit of minerals precipitated in fractures or joints that are foreign to the host rock is called a _____.
    a. Vein14
    b. 1509 Istanbul earthquake
    c. Undefined
    d. Undefined

51. The precipitation of condensed water from clouds as rain, snow, sleet, or hail is _____.
    a. Meteoric water14
    b. 1509 Istanbul earthquake
    c. Undefined
    d. Undefined

52. _____ refers to a compositional group of igneous rocks, indicating that the rock contains at least 25 percent dark silicate minerals. The other dominant mineral is plagioclase feldspar.
    a. AASHTO Soil Classification System
    b. Intermediate composition14
    c. Undefined
    d. Undefined

53. Earth's crust that includes both the continents and the continental shelves is the _____.
    a. Continental crust14
    b. 1509 Istanbul earthquake
    c. Undefined
    d. Undefined

54. _____ is the transfer of heat by currents within a fluid. It may arise from temperature differences either within the fluid or between the fluid and its boundary, other sources of density variations (such as variable salinity), or from the application of an external motive force.
    a. Convection14
    b. Event
    c. Undefined
    d. Undefined

55. _____ refers to the study of the large-scale processes that collectively deform Earth's crust.
    a. 1509 Istanbul earthquake
    b. Tectonics14
    c. Undefined
    d. Undefined

56. _____ is a chemical reaction in which two molecules or moieties react and become covalently bonded to one another by the concurrent loss of a small molecule, often water, methanol, or a type of hydrogen halide such as HCl..
    a. Thing
    b. Dehydration reaction14
    c. Undefined
    d. Undefined

Chapter 14. FLUIDS AND ORE DEPOSITS

57. _____ is a process in biology by which an individual physically develops after birth or hatching, and involves significant change in form as well as growth and differentiation.
    a. Metamorphosis14
    b. Thing
    c. Undefined
    d. Undefined

58. Includes all bodies of water, lakes, rivers, ponds, and so on that are on the surface of the earth, in contrast to groundwater, which lies below the surface is _____.
    a. Thing
    b. Surface water14
    c. Undefined
    d. Undefined

59. _____ refer to elongated fractures or cracks on the slopes of a volcano. Fissure eruptions typically produce liquid flows, but pyroclastics may also be ejected.
    a. Fissures14
    b. 1509 Istanbul earthquake
    c. Undefined
    d. Undefined

60. A crack in rock along which there is a distinct separation is the _____.
    a. Fissure14
    b. 1509 Istanbul earthquake
    c. Undefined
    d. Undefined

61. Water stored beneath the surface in open pore spaces and fractures in rock is called _____.
    a. 1509 Istanbul earthquake
    b. Groundwater14
    c. Undefined
    d. Undefined

62. Preexisting rocks that have been altered by heat, pressure, or chemically active fluids are _____.
    a. 1509 Istanbul earthquake
    b. Metamorphic rocks14
    c. Undefined
    d. Undefined

63. _____ is the result of the transformation of a pre-existing rock type, the protolith, in a process called metamorphism, which means "change in form". The protolith is subjected to heat (greater than 150 degrees Celsius) and extreme pressure causing profound physical and/or chemical change.
    a. Thing
    b. Metamorphic rock14
    c. Undefined
    d. Undefined

64. _____ refers to the process of water seeping down through cracks and pores in soil or rock.
    a. Thing
    b. Percolation14
    c. Undefined
    d. Undefined

65. _____ refers to the term from the Greek 'meta' and 'morph', commonly occurs to rocks which are subjected to increased heat and/or pressure. Also applies to the conversion of snow into glacial ice.
    a. 1509 Istanbul earthquake
    b. Metamorphic14
    c. Undefined
    d. Undefined

66. A mineral or fuel deposit, known or not yet discovered, that may be or become available for human exploitation is called a _____.

Chapter 14. FLUIDS AND ORE DEPOSITS

a. Resource14
b. 1509 Istanbul earthquake
c. Undefined
d. Undefined

67. _____ refers to the top few meters of regolith, generally including some organic matter derived from plants.
a. 1509 Istanbul earthquake
b. Soil14
c. Undefined
d. Undefined

68. _____ occurs when living things move from one biome to another. In most cases organisms migrate to avoid local shortages of food, usually caused by winter. Animals may also migrate to a certain location to breed, as is the case with some fish.
a. Thing
b. Migration14
c. Undefined
d. Undefined

69. _____ refers to a place where an organism lives; an environmental situation in which an organism lives.
a. Thing
b. Habitat14
c. Undefined
d. Undefined

70. Any place where bedrock is visible on the surface of the Earth is referred to as _____.
a. AASHTO Soil Classification System
b. Outcrop14
c. Undefined
d. Undefined

71. The hypothesis that Earth developed gradually through natural processes, similar to those at work today, that occur over long periods of time is referred to as _____.
a. Uniformitarianism14
b. Thing
c. Undefined
d. Undefined

72. Rocks that crystallize from molten material at the surface of the earth or within the earth are called _____.
a. Igneous rocks14
b. AASHTO Soil Classification System
c. Undefined
d. Undefined

73. A _____ is formed when molten rock (magma) cools and solidifies, with or without crystallization, either below the surface as intrusive (plutonic) rocks or on the surface as extrusive (volcanic) rocks. This magma can be derived from either the Earth's mantle or pre-existing rocks made molten by extreme temperature and pressure changes.
a. Thing
b. Igneous rock14
c. Undefined
d. Undefined

74. A large mass of rock projecting above surrounding terrain is called a _____.
a. 1509 Istanbul earthquake
b. Mountain14
c. Undefined
d. Undefined

75. A pink-colored, felsic, plutonic rock that contains potassium and usually sodium feldspars, and has quartz content of about 10% is _____. _____ is commonly found on continents but virtually absent from the ocean basins.
a. 1509 Istanbul earthquake
b. Granite14
c. Undefined
d. Undefined

Chapter 14. FLUIDS AND ORE DEPOSITS

76. A coarse-grained, strongly foliated metamorphic rock that develops from phyllite and splits easily into flat, parallel slabs is _____.
    a. Schist14
    b. 1509 Istanbul earthquake
    c. Undefined
    d. Undefined

77. _____ is a sedimentary rock composed largely of the mineral calcite (calcium carbonate: $CaCO_3$). _____ often contains variable amounts of silica in the form of chert or flint, as well as varying amounts of clay, silt and sand as disseminations, nodules, or layers within the rock.
    a. Thing
    b. Limestone14
    c. Undefined
    d. Undefined

78. Zone of contact metamorphism adjacent to a pluton is called the _____.
    a. Aureole14
    b. AASHTO Soil Classification System
    c. Undefined
    d. Undefined

79. A _____ refers to a portion of a larger molecule, a specific monomer of a polysaccharide, protein or nucleic acid.
    a. Thing
    b. Residue14
    c. Undefined
    d. Undefined

80. _____ refers to the water that lies beneath the ground surface, filling the cracks, crevices, and pore space of rocks.
    a. 1509 Istanbul earthquake
    b. Ground water14
    c. Undefined
    d. Undefined

81. _____ refers to two parallel rows of standing stones or a grand ceremonial way bordered by ditches and banks of earth leading to a ceremonial centre such as at Stonehenge.
    a. Avenue14
    b. AASHTO Soil Classification System
    c. Undefined
    d. Undefined

82. _____ is a term used in geology, engineering and surveying to denote the motion of a surface (usually, the earth's surface) downwards relative to a datum such as sea-level.
    a. Subsidence14
    b. Thing
    c. Undefined
    d. Undefined

83. A piece of one rock unit contained within another is called _____. Inclusions are used in relative dating. The rock mass adjacent to the one containing the _____ must have been there first in order to provide the fragment.
    a. Inclusion14
    b. AASHTO Soil Classification System
    c. Undefined
    d. Undefined

84. _____ is a solid in which the constituent atoms, molecules, or ions are packed in a regularly ordered, repeating pattern extending in all three spatial dimensions.
    a. Thing
    b. Crystal14
    c. Undefined
    d. Undefined

85. A hole or opening, as at the bed of a glacier is a _____. When the rate of deformation into a space behind an obstacle is less the rate of movement past the obstacle, a _____ will form.

Chapter 14. FLUIDS AND ORE DEPOSITS

    a. 1509 Istanbul earthquake   b. Cavity14
    c. Undefined   d. Undefined

86. _____ refers to the total amount of salts dissolved in seawater. It is generally expressed in parts per thousand.
    a. Salinity14   b. Thing
    c. Undefined   d. Undefined

87. _____ refers to drop out of a saturated solution as crystals. The crystals that drop out of a saturated solution.
    a. 1509 Istanbul earthquake   b. Precipitate14
    c. Undefined   d. Undefined

88. General term for the processes of folding, faulting, shearing, compression, or extension of rocks as the result of various natural forces is called _____.
    a. Deformation14   b. 1509 Istanbul earthquake
    c. Undefined   d. Undefined

89. A body of rock identified by lithic characteristics and stratigraphic position and is mappable at the earth's surface or traceable in the subsurface is a _____.
    a. Formation14   b. 1509 Istanbul earthquake
    c. Undefined   d. Undefined

90. _____ refers to pyroclastic material derived directly from magma reaching the surface.
    a. Juvenile14   b. 1509 Istanbul earthquake
    c. Undefined   d. Undefined

91. Molten rock that forms naturally within the Earth is _____. _____ may be either a liquid or a fluid mixture of liquid, crystals, and dissolved gases.
    a. 1509 Istanbul earthquake   b. Magma14
    c. Undefined   d. Undefined

92. To dissolve from a rock is called _____.
    a. 1509 Istanbul earthquake   b. Leach14
    c. Undefined   d. Undefined

93. _____ is the chemical element in the periodic table that has the symbol S and atomic number 16. It is an abundant, tasteless, odorless, multivalent non-metal. _____, in its native form, is a yellow crystaline solid. In nature, it can be found as the pure element or as sulfide and sulfate minerals.
    a. Thing   b. Sulfur14
    c. Undefined   d. Undefined

94. _____ refers to an atom or molecule that has gained or lost one or more electrons, thus acquiring an electrical charge.
    a. Ion14   b. Thing
    c. Undefined   d. Undefined

95. Usually slow but effective process of weathering and erosion in which rocks are dissolved by water is a _____.

Chapter 14. FLUIDS AND ORE DEPOSITS

    a. Solution14
    c. Undefined
    b. 1509 Istanbul earthquake
    d. Undefined

96. A solution at equilibrium that cannot hold any more solute is said to be saturated. The equilibrium of a solution is mainly dependent on temperature. The maximum equilibrium amount of solute which can normally dissolve per amount of solvent is the _____ of that solute in that solvent.
    a. Thing
    c. Undefined
    b. Solubility14
    d. Undefined

97. The vertical column of seawater that extends from the surface to the bottom is called _____.
    a. Water column14
    c. Undefined
    b. Thing
    d. Undefined

98. A feature found in caves that is formed when a stalactite and stalagmite join is referred to as a _____.
    a. Column14
    c. Undefined
    b. 1509 Istanbul earthquake
    d. Undefined

99. _____ refers to a process leading to chemical changes in matter; involves the making and/or breaking of chemical bonds.
    a. Thing
    c. Undefined
    b. Chemical reaction14
    d. Undefined

100. A single proton with a charge of + 1. The dissociation of a water molecule leads to the generation of a hydroxide ion and a _____. The _____ is hydrated in aqueous solutions and is usually written as H_3O^+.
    a. Hydrogen ion14
    c. Undefined
    b. Thing
    d. Undefined

101. _____ is a chemical element in the periodic table that has the symbol H and atomic number 1. At standard temperature and pressure it is a colorless, odorless, nonmetallic, univalent, tasteless, highly flammable diatomic gas.
    a. Thing
    c. Undefined
    b. Hydrogen14
    d. Undefined

102. _____ refers to the loss of electrons from a substance involved in a redox reaction; always accompanies reduction.
    a. Oxidation14
    c. Undefined
    b. Thing
    d. Undefined

103. _____ refers to rigid parts of the Earth's crust and part of the Earth's upper mantle that moves and adjoins each other along zones of seismic activity.
    a. Plate14
    c. Undefined
    b. 1509 Istanbul earthquake
    d. Undefined

104. _____ refers to an iron deposit consisting essentially of iron oxides and chert occurring in prominent layers or bands of brown or red and black.

Chapter 14. FLUIDS AND ORE DEPOSITS

a. Banded-iron formation14
b. 1509 Istanbul earthquake
c. Undefined
d. Undefined

105. The _____ is an informal name for the eons of the geologic timescale that came before the current Phanerozoic eon. It spans from the formation of Earth around 4500 Ma (million years ago) to the evolution of abundant macroscopic hard-shelled fossils, which marked the beginning of the Cambrian.
a. Thing
b. Precambrian14
c. Undefined
d. Undefined

106. The _____ Eon is the period of geologic time during which abundant animal life has existed. It covers roughly 545 million years and goes back to the time when diverse hard-shelled animals first appeared.
a. Thing
b. Phanerozoic14
c. Undefined
d. Undefined

107. _____ is essential to all organisms, except for a few bacteria. It is mostly stably incorporated in the inside of metalloproteins, because in exposed or in free form it causes production of free radicals that are generally toxic to cells.
a. Iron14
b. Thing
c. Undefined
d. Undefined

108. The _____ is a major division of the geologic timescale that extends from the end of the Devonian period, about 359.2 Ma (million years ago), to the beginning of the Permian period, about 299.0 Ma (ICS 2004).
a. Thing
b. Carboniferous14
c. Undefined
d. Undefined

109. Earth's _____ is a layer of gases surrounding the planet Earth and retained by the Earth's gravity. It contains roughly 78% nitrogen and 21% oxygen, with trace amounts of other gases.
a. Atmosphere14
b. Thing
c. Undefined
d. Undefined

110. A member of a group of easily combustible, organic sedimentary rocks composed mostly of plant remains and containing a high proportion of carbon is called _____.
a. Coal14
b. 1509 Istanbul earthquake
c. Undefined
d. Undefined

111. _____ refers to iron in which the atoms have lost two of the electrons they have in metallic form. Found in silicate minerals such as pyroxene.
a. 1509 Istanbul earthquake
b. Ferrous iron14
c. Undefined
d. Undefined

112. _____ refers to a place in which water is stored, including the oceans, glaciers and polar ice, groundwater, lakes and rivers, the atmosphere, and the biosphere. A source or place of residence for elements in a chemical cycle or hydrologic cycle.
a. 1509 Istanbul earthquake
b. Reservoir14
c. Undefined
d. Undefined

Chapter 14. FLUIDS AND ORE DEPOSITS

113. In biology, _____ is the process by which novel traits arise in populations and are passed on from generation to generation. Its action over large stretches of time explains the origin of new species and ultimately the vast diversity of the biological world.
    a. Evolution14
    b. Concept
    c. Undefined
    d. Undefined

114. _____ refers to a basic unit of the geologic time scale that is a subdivision of an era. Periods may be divided into smaller units called epochs.
    a. Period14
    b. 1509 Istanbul earthquake
    c. Undefined
    d. Undefined

115. _____ refers to a tentative explanation of a given set of data that is expected to remain valid after future observation and experimentation.
    a. Hypothesis14
    b. 1509 Istanbul earthquake
    c. Undefined
    d. Undefined

116. _____ is the name given to the supercontinent that existed during the Paleozoic and Mesozoic eras, before the process of plate tectonics separated each of the component continents into their current configuration.
    a. Pangea14
    b. Thing
    c. Undefined
    d. Undefined

117. _____ refers to a round or oval bulge on the Earth's surface, containing the oldest section of rock in its raised, central part.
    a. 1509 Istanbul earthquake
    b. Dome14
    c. Undefined
    d. Undefined

118. _____ refers to a general term applied to all mineral material transported by a glacier and deposited directly by or from the ice, or by running water emanating from the glacier. Generally applies to Pleistocene glacial deposits.
    a. Drift14
    b. 1509 Istanbul earthquake
    c. Undefined
    d. Undefined

119. A chemical compound composed only of the elements carbon and hydrogen is called _____.
    a. Thing
    b. Hydrocarbon14
    c. Undefined
    d. Undefined

120. The middle layer of the Earth, lying just below the crust and consisting of relatively dense rocks is called the _____. The _____ is divided into two sections, the upper _____ and the lower _____; the lower _____ has greater density than the upper _____.
    a. Mantle14
    b. 1509 Istanbul earthquake
    c. Undefined
    d. Undefined

121. _____ refers to any of a group of naturally occurring substances made up of hydrocarbons. These substances may be gaseous, liquid, or semi-solid.
    a. Petroleum14
    b. 1509 Istanbul earthquake
    c. Undefined
    d. Undefined

Chapter 14. FLUIDS AND ORE DEPOSITS

122. The undifferentiated rocks that underlie the rocks of interest in an area are referred to as _____.
    a. Basement14
    b. 1509 Istanbul earthquake
    c. Undefined
    d. Undefined

123. One of several minerals containing one central carbon atom with strong covalent bonds to three oxygen atoms and typically having ionic bonds to one or more positive ions is _____.
    a. 1509 Istanbul earthquake
    b. Carbonate14
    c. Undefined
    d. Undefined

124. _____ is a chemical element in the periodic table that has the symbol C and atomic number 6. An abundant nonmetallic, tetravalent element, _____ has several allotropic forms.
    a. Carbon14
    b. Thing
    c. Undefined
    d. Undefined

125. _____ is a chemical element; it is a colorless, odorless, tasteless, non-toxic, and nearly inert monatomic that heads the noble gas series in the periodic table. Its atomic number is 2 and its boiling and melting points are the lowest among the elements. It exists only as a gas except in extreme conditions.
    a. Thing
    b. Helium14
    c. Undefined
    d. Undefined

126. _____ is one of the three main rock groups and is formed in three main ways—by the deposition of the weathered remains of other rocks; by the deposition of the results of biogenic activity; and by precipitation from solution.
    a. Event
    b. Sedimentary rock14
    c. Undefined
    d. Undefined

127. _____ refers to the reduction of the body of a formerly living organism into simpler forms of matter.
    a. Thing
    b. Decomposition14
    c. Undefined
    d. Undefined

128. A gaseous mixture of naturally occurring hydrocarbons is _____.
    a. 1509 Istanbul earthquake
    b. Natural gas14
    c. Undefined
    d. Undefined

129. Describing a mineral that will not react with or convert to a new mineral or substance, given enough time is referred to as _____.
    a. 1509 Istanbul earthquake
    b. Stable14
    c. Undefined
    d. Undefined

130. _____ is the naturally hot interior of Earth. The heat is maintained by naturally occurring nuclear reactions in Earth's interior.
    a. Geothermal14
    b. Thing
    c. Undefined
    d. Undefined

131. A distinctive rock sequence found in many mountain ranges on continents is _____.

Chapter 14. FLUIDS AND ORE DEPOSITS

a. Ophiolite14
b. AASHTO Soil Classification System
c. Undefined
d. Undefined

132. _____ in referring to sedinent grains, loose, separate, or unattached to one another.
a. AASHTO Soil Classification System
b. Unconsolidated14
c. Undefined
d. Undefined

133. _____ is any particulate matter that can be transported by fluid flow and which eventually is deposited as a layer of solid particles on the bed or bottom of a body of water or other liquid.
a. Thing
b. Sediment14
c. Undefined
d. Undefined

134. Gravity is called the _____.
a. 1509 Istanbul earthquake
b. Driving force14
c. Undefined
d. Undefined

135. _____ refers to a vertical conduit through the Earth's crust below a volcano, through which magmatic materials have passed. Commonly filled with volcanic breccia and fragments of older rock.
a. Pipe14
b. 1509 Istanbul earthquake
c. Undefined
d. Undefined

136. An igneous rock composed primarily of the iron-magnesium silicate olivine and having a silica content of less than 40% is _____.
a. 1509 Istanbul earthquake
b. Peridotite14
c. Undefined
d. Undefined

137. The decrease in temperature with increasing elevation caused by the expansion of air in the lower atmospheric pressure is referred to as _____.
a. Adiabatic cooling14
b. Thing
c. Undefined
d. Undefined

138. A liquid mixture of naturally occurring hydrocarbons is referred to as _____.
a. 1509 Istanbul earthquake
b. Crude oil14
c. Undefined
d. Undefined

139. _____ refers to the upper portion of the mantle extending from the Moho to a depth of 400km.
a. Upper mantle14
b. AASHTO Soil Classification System
c. Undefined
d. Undefined

140. _____ refers to a clastic rock composed of particles that range in diameter from 1/16 millimeter to 2 millimeters in diameter. Sandstones make up about 25% of all sedimentary rocks.
a. 1509 Istanbul earthquake
b. Sandstone14
c. Undefined
d. Undefined

141. A round or oval depression in the Earth's surface, containing the youngest section of rock in its lowest, central part is a _____.

Chapter 14. FLUIDS AND ORE DEPOSITS

a. 1509 Istanbul earthquake
b. Basin14
c. Undefined
d. Undefined

142. The angle formed by the inclined plane of a geological structure and the horizontal plane of the Earth's surface is referred to as a _____.
a. 1509 Istanbul earthquake
b. Dip14
c. Undefined
d. Undefined

143. Inorganic chemical sediment that precipitates when the salty water in which it had dissolved evaporates is called _____.
a. Evaporite14
b. AASHTO Soil Classification System
c. Undefined
d. Undefined

144. Substance that is dissolved in a solvent, forming a solution is referred to as a _____.
a. Solute14
b. Thing
c. Undefined
d. Undefined

145. _____ refers to the set of physical features, such as mountains, valleys, and the shapes of landforms, that characterizes a given landscape.
a. 1509 Istanbul earthquake
b. Topography14
c. Undefined
d. Undefined

146. A sedimentary rock formed from the accumulation of carbonate minerals precipitated organically or inorganically is _____.
a. 1509 Istanbul earthquake
b. Carbonate rock14
c. Undefined
d. Undefined

147. A high mountain peak that forms when the walls of three or more cirques intersect is called a _____.
a. Horn14
b. 1509 Istanbul earthquake
c. Undefined
d. Undefined

148. Dominantly unsorted and unstratified drift, generally unconsolidated deposited directly by and underneath a glacier without subsequent reworking by meltwater, and consisting of a hetergeneous mixture of clay, silt, sand, gravel, stones, and boulders is called _____.
a. 1509 Istanbul earthquake
b. Till14
c. Undefined
d. Undefined

ANSWER KEY

Chapter 1

1. a	2. b	3. a	4. b	5. a	6. a	7. a	8. a	9. a	10. b
11. a	12. b	13. a	14. a	15. b	16. b	17. a	18. a	19. b	20. b
21. b	22. a	23. b	24. b	25. a	26. b	27. b	28. a	29. a	30. b
31. a	32. b	33. b	34. b	35. b	36. a	37. b	38. a	39. b	40. b
41. a	42. a	43. b	44. a	45. a	46. a	47. b	48. a	49. b	50. b
51. b	52. b	53. b	54. a	55. b	56. b	57. a	58. b	59. a	60. b
61. b	62. b	63. b	64. b	65. a	66. a	67. a	68. b	69. b	70. b
71. b	72. a	73. a	74. b	75. a	76. a	77. a	78. a	79. b	80. b
81. a	82. b	83. a	84. b	85. a	86. a	87. b	88. a	89. a	90. b
91. b	92. b	93. a	94. a	95. a	96. a	97. a	98. b	99. b	100. a
101. a	102. b	103. b	104. b	105. b	106. a	107. a	108. b	109. a	110. b
111. a	112. b	113. b	114. b	115. b	116. a	117. b	118. b	119. b	120. b
121. b	122. b	123. a	124. a	125. b	126. a	127. b	128. a	129. b	130. a
131. a	132. b	133. b	134. a	135. b	136. a	137. a	138. b	139. b	140. b
141. b	142. a	143. a	144. a	145. b	146. b	147. b	148. b	149. b	150. b

Chapter 2

1. b	2. b	3. b	4. b	5. b	6. b	7. b	8. b	9. b	10. b
11. b	12. a	13. b	14. a	15. a	16. b	17. b	18. a	19. a	20. a
21. b	22. a	23. b	24. a	25. a	26. b	27. b	28. b	29. a	30. a
31. a	32. b	33. b	34. b	35. b	36. a	37. b	38. b	39. a	40. a
41. b	42. a	43. a	44. a	45. a	46. b	47. a	48. a	49. a	50. b
51. b	52. a	53. a	54. a	55. a	56. a	57. a	58. a		

Chapter 3

1. b	2. a	3. b	4. a	5. b	6. b	7. b	8. a	9. b	10. a
11. b	12. b	13. b	14. b	15. a	16. a	17. b	18. b	19. b	20. b
21. a	22. a	23. a	24. a	25. b	26. b	27. b	28. a	29. b	30. a
31. b	32. b	33. b	34. b	35. a	36. b	37. b	38. b	39. a	40. a
41. b	42. a	43. a	44. b	45. b	46. a	47. a	48. b	49. b	50. b
51. b	52. b	53. b	54. b	55. b	56. b	57. a	58. a	59. a	60. b
61. b	62. a	63. b	64. a	65. a	66. b	67. a	68. a	69. a	70. a
71. a	72. a	73. a	74. b	75. a	76. b	77. b	78. a	79. b	80. a
81. a	82. a								

Chapter 4

1. b	2. b	3. b	4. b	5. b	6. b	7. a	8. b	9. b	10. a
11. b	12. a	13. a	14. b	15. b	16. a	17. a	18. a	19. a	20. a
21. b	22. a	23. b	24. a	25. a	26. b	27. b	28. b	29. a	30. a
31. b	32. a	33. a	34. a	35. b	36. b	37. a	38. a	39. a	40. a
41. b	42. b	43. b	44. a	45. a	46. a	47. b	48. b	49. a	50. a
51. a	52. a	53. b	54. b	55. a	56. a	57. a	58. b	59. a	60. a
61. a	62. a	63. b	64. a	65. b	66. a	67. a	68. a	69. a	70. a
71. b	72. a	73. b	74. b	75. b	76. a	77. a	78. b	79. b	80. a
81. b	82. b	83. b	84. a	85. b	86. b	87. a	88. a	89. b	90. b
91. a	92. a	93. a	94. a	95. a	96. a	97. b	98. b	99. a	100. b
101. b	102. a	103. a	104. b	105. a	106. b	107. a	108. a	109. b	110. b
111. a	112. a	113. b	114. a	115. b	116. a	117. b	118. a	119. a	120. b
121. b	122. a	123. a	124. b	125. b					

Chapter 5

1. a	2. a	3. a	4. a	5. b	6. a	7. a	8. a	9. a	10. b
11. a	12. b	13. b	14. b	15. b	16. a	17. b	18. b	19. a	20. a
21. a	22. b	23. a	24. a	25. a	26. a	27. b	28. b	29. a	30. a
31. a	32. a	33. a	34. b	35. a	36. a	37. a	38. a	39. a	40. b
41. b	42. b	43. a	44. b	45. a	46. b				

Chapter 6

1. a	2. b	3. b	4. b	5. b	6. a	7. a	8. a	9. a	10. a
11. b	12. b	13. b	14. a	15. a	16. a	17. b	18. a	19. b	20. b
21. b	22. a	23. a	24. a	25. a	26. a	27. b	28. a	29. b	30. b
31. b	32. b	33. b	34. a	35. b	36. b	37. a	38. b	39. a	40. a
41. a	42. b	43. b	44. b	45. b	46. b	47. b	48. a	49. b	50. a
51. b	52. a	53. b	54. a	55. a	56. b	57. b	58. b	59. a	60. a
61. a	62. a	63. b	64. a	65. a	66. b	67. a	68. b	69. a	70. b
71. a	72. a	73. a	74. b	75. a	76. a	77. a	78. a	79. b	80. b
81. b	82. a	83. b	84. b	85. a	86. a	87. b	88. b	89. b	90. b
91. a	92. a	93. a	94. b	95. b	96. a	97. b	98. a	99. b	100. b
101. b	102. a	103. a	104. b	105. a	106. a	107. b	108. a	109. a	110. a
111. b	112. b	113. b	114. a	115. b	116. b	117. b	118. b	119. b	120. b
121. b	122. b	123. a	124. a	125. a	126. b				

ANSWER KEY

Chapter 7

1. b	2. a	3. b	4. b	5. a	6. b	7. b	8. a	9. a	10. a
11. b	12. a	13. b	14. a	15. a	16. a	17. a	18. a	19. b	20. a
21. b	22. b	23. a	24. a	25. a	26. b	27. b	28. a	29. a	30. a
31. a	32. b	33. b	34. b	35. b	36. b	37. b	38. b	39. b	40. b
41. a	42. b	43. a	44. a	45. b	46. b	47. a	48. a	49. a	50. b
51. b	52. b	53. a	54. a	55. b	56. a	57. a	58. a	59. b	60. b
61. b	62. a	63. b	64. b	65. a	66. a	67. b	68. b	69. b	70. a
71. a	72. b	73. a	74. a	75. a	76. a	77. b	78. a	79. a	80. a
81. a	82. a	83. b	84. a	85. b	86. b	87. a	88. a	89. a	90. b
91. b	92. b	93. b	94. b	95. b	96. b	97. a	98. a	99. b	100. b
101. b	102. a	103. a	104. a						

Chapter 8

1. a	2. b	3. a	4. a	5. b	6. b	7. b	8. b	9. b	10. b
11. b	12. a	13. b	14. a	15. b	16. b	17. a	18. a	19. b	20. b
21. a	22. a	23. b	24. b	25. a	26. a	27. b	28. b	29. b	30. a
31. a	32. a	33. b	34. b	35. a	36. b	37. a	38. b	39. a	40. a
41. b	42. b	43. a	44. b	45. b	46. b	47. b	48. b	49. a	50. b
51. a	52. b	53. a	54. a	55. a	56. b	57. a	58. b	59. b	60. a

Chapter 9

1. b	2. a	3. b	4. a	5. b	6. b	7. b	8. b	9. a	10. b
11. b	12. b	13. a	14. a	15. b	16. a	17. a	18. a	19. a	20. b
21. b	22. b	23. a	24. b	25. b	26. b	27. a	28. a	29. a	30. b
31. a	32. a	33. a	34. b	35. a	36. b	37. a	38. a	39. a	40. b
41. b	42. a	43. b	44. a	45. a	46. b	47. a	48. b	49. b	50. a
51. a	52. b	53. b	54. a	55. b	56. b	57. b	58. b	59. a	60. b
61. a	62. a	63. b	64. b	65. a	66. b	67. b	68. a	69. a	70. a
71. b	72. a	73. a	74. a	75. b	76. a	77. a	78. a	79. a	80. b
81. b	82. b	83. a	84. a	85. b	86. a	87. b	88. b	89. a	90. a
91. b	92. b	93. a	94. b	95. a	96. a	97. b	98. a	99. a	100. a
101. b	102. a	103. a	104. b	105. b	106. b	107. b	108. a	109. a	110. a
111. b	112. a	113. b	114. b	115. b	116. b	117. b	118. b	119. a	120. b
121. a	122. a	123. b	124. b	125. b	126. b	127. b	128. a	129. b	130. b
131. a	132. a	133. a	134. b	135. b	136. b	137. a	138. a	139. a	140. a
141. b	142. b	143. a	144. b	145. a	146. b	147. b	148. b	149. a	150. a
151. a	152. a	153. a	154. b	155. a	156. b	157. a	158. a	159. a	160. b
161. a	162. a	163. b	164. a	165. a	166. a	167. b	168. b	169. a	170. b
171. b	172. b	173. a	174. b	175. b	176. b	177. b	178. a	179. a	180. b
181. a	182. b	183. b	184. b	185. a	186. a	187. b	188. b	189. b	190. b
191. a	192. a	193. b	194. b	195. b	196. b	197. b	198. a	199. b	200. a
201. b	202. b	203. b	204. a	205. a	206. b	207. a	208. a	209. a	210. b
211. b	212. b	213. b	214. b	215. a	216. a	217. b	218. b	219. b	220. b
221. a	222. a	223. a	224. a	225. b	226. a	227. b	228. b	229. a	230. a
231. b	232. b	233. a	234. b	235. a	236. a	237. b	238. a	239. b	240. a
241. b	242. a	243. b	244. a	245. b	246. a	247. a	248. a	249. b	250. a
251. a	252. b	253. b	254. a	255. b	256. b	257. a	258. b	259. b	260. a
261. b	262. a	263. a							

Chapter 10

1. b	2. a	3. b	4. a	5. a	6. b	7. b	8. b	9. b	10. a
11. a	12. b	13. a	14. b	15. b	16. b	17. b	18. b	19. a	20. b
21. b	22. a	23. b	24. a	25. b	26. a	27. a	28. b	29. b	30. b
31. b	32. a	33. b	34. b	35. b	36. a	37. b	38. b	39. a	40. a
41. a	42. a	43. b	44. a	45. b	46. a	47. b	48. a	49. b	50. a
51. b	52. b	53. b	54. b	55. a	56. b	57. b	58. a	59. b	60. b
61. b	62. a	63. b	64. a	65. b	66. a	67. a	68. a	69. a	70. b
71. b	72. b	73. a	74. a	75. a	76. b	77. b	78. a	79. b	80. b
81. a	82. b	83. a	84. a	85. b	86. b	87. b	88. a	89. b	90. b
91. b									

ANSWER KEY

Chapter 11

1. b	2. b	3. a	4. a	5. b	6. a	7. b	8. a	9. a	10. b
11. b	12. a	13. b	14. a	15. a	16. a	17. a	18. b	19. b	20. a
21. a	22. a	23. b	24. a	25. a	26. a	27. b	28. b	29. a	30. b
31. b	32. b	33. a	34. a	35. b	36. b	37. a	38. b	39. a	40. a
41. a	42. a	43. a	44. a	45. b	46. a	47. a	48. a	49. b	50. b
51. a	52. a	53. a	54. b	55. b	56. a	57. b	58. a	59. a	60. a
61. b	62. a	63. a	64. a	65. a	66. b	67. a	68. a	69. b	70. a
71. b	72. a	73. a	74. b	75. a	76. b	77. a	78. a	79. a	80. b
81. b	82. b	83. a	84. a	85. a	86. a	87. b	88. a	89. b	90. b
91. a	92. a	93. a	94. b	95. b	96. b	97. b	98. b	99. b	100. a
101. a	102. b	103. a	104. a	105. b	106. b	107. a	108. a	109. a	

Chapter 12

1. a	2. a	3. a	4. a	5. a	6. a	7. a	8. b	9. b	10. b
11. b	12. b	13. a	14. b	15. b	16. b	17. a	18. a	19. b	20. b
21. b	22. b	23. a	24. b	25. b	26. b	27. b	28. a	29. a	30. a
31. b	32. a	33. a	34. a	35. b	36. a	37. a	38. a	39. a	40. a
41. b	42. b	43. b	44. b	45. a	46. b	47. b	48. a	49. a	50. b
51. b	52. b	53. a	54. a	55. a	56. b	57. a	58. a	59. b	60. b
61. a	62. a	63. b	64. b	65. a	66. b	67. a	68. b	69. b	70. a
71. a	72. b	73. b	74. b	75. a	76. a	77. b	78. b	79. a	80. b
81. a	82. a	83. a	84. a	85. a	86. a	87. a	88. b	89. b	90. b
91. a	92. a	93. a	94. a	95. a	96. a	97. b	98. b	99. a	100. a
101. a	102. b	103. b	104. a	105. b	106. b	107. a	108. b	109. b	110. a
111. b	112. b	113. a	114. a	115. a					

Chapter 13

1. a	2. b	3. b	4. a	5. a	6. a	7. b	8. b	9. a	10. b
11. b	12. b	13. a	14. a	15. a	16. b	17. a	18. a	19. a	20. b
21. b	22. b	23. b	24. b	25. a	26. a	27. a	28. b	29. b	30. a
31. b	32. b	33. a	34. a	35. b	36. b	37. b	38. b	39. a	40. b
41. b	42. a	43. a	44. b	45. b	46. b	47. a	48. a	49. a	50. b
51. b	52. a	53. b	54. b	55. b	56. a	57. a	58. b	59. a	60. b
61. b	62. b	63. b	64. a	65. a	66. a	67. a	68. a	69. b	70. b
71. b	72. a	73. b	74. b	75. b	76. a	77. a	78. b	79. b	80. b
81. a	82. a	83. b	84. b	85. a	86. a	87. b	88. b	89. a	90. a
91. b	92. a	93. a	94. a	95. b	96. b	97. a	98. b	99. a	100. b
101. a	102. a	103. a	104. a	105. b	106. a	107. a	108. a	109. b	110. a
111. a	112. b	113. b	114. a	115. b	116. b	117. a	118. a	119. a	120. a
121. a	122. b	123. a	124. b	125. b	126. a	127. b	128. b	129. b	130. b
131. a	132. b	133. b	134. a	135. b	136. b	137. b	138. b	139. a	140. b
141. b	142. a	143. a	144. a	145. a	146. a	147. a	148. a	149. a	150. b
151. a	152. a	153. b	154. a	155. a	156. b	157. b	158. a	159. b	160. a
161. b	162. b	163. a	164. b	165. a	166. b	167. b	168. a	169. b	170. a
171. b	172. b	173. a	174. a	175. a	176. b	177. a			

Chapter 14

1. a	2. a	3. a	4. b	5. b	6. a	7. b	8. b	9. a	10. b
11. a	12. b	13. a	14. a	15. b	16. b	17. a	18. a	19. b	20. a
21. b	22. a	23. a	24. b	25. b	26. b	27. b	28. a	29. a	30. b
31. b	32. a	33. a	34. a	35. b	36. b	37. a	38. b	39. b	40. b
41. b	42. b	43. a	44. b	45. a	46. a	47. a	48. b	49. b	50. a
51. a	52. b	53. a	54. a	55. b	56. b	57. a	58. b	59. a	60. a
61. b	62. b	63. b	64. b	65. b	66. a	67. b	68. b	69. b	70. b
71. a	72. a	73. b	74. b	75. b	76. a	77. b	78. a	79. b	80. b
81. a	82. a	83. a	84. b	85. b	86. a	87. b	88. a	89. a	90. a
91. b	92. b	93. b	94. a	95. a	96. b	97. a	98. a	99. b	100. a
101. b	102. a	103. a	104. a	105. b	106. b	107. a	108. b	109. a	110. a
111. b	112. b	113. a	114. a	115. a	116. a	117. b	118. a	119. b	120. a
121. a	122. a	123. b	124. a	125. b	126. b	127. b	128. b	129. b	130. a
131. a	132. b	133. b	134. b	135. a	136. b	137. a	138. b	139. a	140. b
141. b	142. b	143. a	144. a	145. b	146. b	147. a	148. b		

www.ingramcontent.com/pod-product-compliance
Lightning Source LLC
Chambersburg PA
CBHW081352230426
43667CB00017B/2805